D1594320

In Our Own Voices, Redux

In Our Own Voices, Redux

The Faces of Librarianship Today

Edited by
Teresa Y. Neely and Jorge R. López-McKnight

ROWMAN & LITTLEFIELD
Lanham • Boulder • New York • London

FEB 1 5 2019

Published by Rowman & Littlefield
An imprint of The Rowman & Littlefield Publishing Group, Inc.
4501 Forbes Boulevard, Suite 200, Lanham, Maryland 20706
www.rowman.com

Unit A, Whitacre Mews, 26-34 Stannary Street, London SE11 4AB

British Library Cataloguing in Publication Information Available

Library of Congress Cataloging-in-Publication Data Available

ISBN 9781538115367 (cloth : alk. paper) | ISBN 9781538115374 (pbk : alk. paper) | ISBN 9781538115381 (ebook)

♾ ™ The paper used in this publication meets the minimum requirements of American National Standard for Information Sciences Permanence of Paper for Printed Library Materials, ANSI/NISO Z39.48-1992.

Printed in the United States of America

Hand-lettered illustrations on part pages by Joanna Chen Cham.

For those we've lost on our journey from there to here, the ones we know about, and the ones we haven't yet learned about: Doris Hargrett Clack, E. J. Josey, Claude Mac Neely Sr., Lucinda Mac Neely Smarr, Patricia Sutton Hedgepeth, James Frazier Neely, Claudette Mac Neely McManus, James Junior Thompson, Carl Lee Thompson, Michael Anthony Thompson, Richard Dale Brown, Reverend Mallothi Brown, Esmie Louise Morales Brown, Henry T. Burwell, Edward Elder, Ethel Effie Asher Elder, Maybellene Evans, Richard O. Hollis, Hanny Mansfelt Hollis, Dovough S. White, Liduvina Rivera, Blanche Monk Williams, Barbara Jean Greenley Page, Gloria Berta-Cruz López, Lewis McKnight, and Mattie Lee Thomson Neely.

—Teresa Y. Neely

For my family. Always.

Gloria Berta-Cruz López and Lewis McKnight—it is nice to see your names together. In December of 1981, Catholic Social Services called and you picked up the telephone. My life changed forever because of that, and I miss you every day.

Rafaela, Jaime, and Sasha, I love you all deeply.

Tiffany, mi amor, mi reina, the earth shifted and became a much more beautiful place when I met you. I am eternally grateful for your love, strength, and light.

—Jorge R. López-McKnight

Contents

List of Figures

Foreword

This book succeeds *In Our Own Voices: The Changing Face of Librarianship*, written by Neely and Abif in 1996 (see appendix A). Like the first book, it includes the work of librarians who represent different racial/ethnic groups. Some of the contributors are the same as those who, twenty years ago, were embarking on their careers in the library and information science profession. New contributors from the same racial/ethnic groups are writing for the first time about their experiences as librarians of color.

In each of their voices, the contributors give readers a good sense of who they are—racially or ethnically—by sharing personal stories; experiences as librarians encountering prejudice, bigotry, and intolerance (albeit often subtle); positive experiences that made them feel whole, worthwhile, and appreciated as colleagues in their work environments; and their successes as professionals despite all the overt and subtle prejudice.

Today that subtleness has a term—*microaggression*. Although it was coined in the 1970s, it surfaced much later after the first *In Our Own Voices* book. In the case of the contributors, microaggression was present when offhanded remarks, dismissals, and/or insults were made to each of them. Examples of that are remarks like "You don't talk like an Indian" (Monica Dorame, Diné contributor); remarks pointing out differences and questioning one's work ethic, clothes, and colors worn (Jimena Bretón, Mexicana contributor); and remarks like being an "angry black woman" (Evangela Oates, African American contributor).

Even today when our profession (both practitioners and LIS educators) claims to be enlightened in dealing with diversity and inclusivity, I was not so surprised by the negative treatment of some contributors starting in childhood and continuing during their professional careers. However, I was deeply saddened that there hasn't been significant progress in twenty years in advancing (not just lip service) diversity and inclusiveness. As contributor Deborah R. Hollis wrote, "The *language* we use to describe marginalized groups and misconduct in the workplace has changed, as has the discussion, yet the actions speak louder than the words." Indeed, the terms have changed, but the lack of action hasn't.

These contributors are all survivors and successes despite all the trials, tribulations, obstacles, and oppression they have faced. One of the reasons for this relates to a recurring theme mentioned by most of them: the importance of having informal mentors and/or someone who appreciated their diversity and who took them under their wings to help them be successful. Some of the contributors are "passing the gift" of mentoring to other librarians of color now.

Who should read this book? The following types of individuals in our profession:

- Those who think that diversity and inclusion are not necessary in their libraries—that is, that the professional/social/emotional conditions of their minority colleagues in their libraries are fine.
- Those who would emphatically and adamantly deny that they might have even a "tinge" of racism but have no concept of what *institutional* racism is.
- Those who may not have a clue what it is like to work in an environment where they are the only person representing their "group."
- Those who are library administrators and managers who need to comprehend the effect that their noninclusive environments have on the hiring, retention, and well-being of minority librarians.
- New library professionals, both those who represent any one minority group and those who do not.

Finally, this book has wonderful tips to help minority professionals look for and avoid pitfalls and to show them how to recover when they experience them. The contributors also provide insights for library administrators to consider during situations such as the following:

- determining the makeup of search committees
- providing on-boarding of new racial/ethnic librarians
- completing or reviewing evaluations
- conducting meetings with all librarians

I congratulate all the contributors for their willingness to reopen wounds and, in doing so, reopen their vulnerability. By sharing their voices, they are helping our profession *ultimately* serve our multiracial/ethnic/cultural population in this country, no matter the library type. The bottom line is that this book gives readers a good sense of what it might be like wearing the shoes of any one of a number of different voices. Hopefully, it will also serve as a much-needed call to action.

Camila A. Alire
dean emeritus, Colorado State University and University of New Mexico
2009–2010 president of the American Library Association

Acknowledgments

We would like to thank the Collective—the OGs who contributed in 1996, those who returned twenty years later to speak their truth, and those who bring new voices to this circle. We see you. We hear you. We love you. There were voices that intended to be part of this volume but were unable to participate fully, and there were those who struggled with personal loss but persevered. We salute them and are grateful for their voices and their presence in this profession and in this universe. We would like to acknowledge and thank Dr. Camila Alire for agreeing to participate in this project and Joanna Chen Cham for her beautiful and expressive artwork.

—Teresa and Jorge

I would like to acknowledge my Minnesota family. Though this project started before we all came together in Minneapolis in the summer of 2016, meeting you all changed me in ways that I am still understanding. I see all of you in these words, and I hear all of you in these voices. I carried you all with me, and you all carried me.

Lori Townsend, I appreciated your patience, understanding, and support throughout this entire experience. It was needed.

Teresa, thank you for *In Our Own Voices* 1996; I'm glad it, and you, found me. Much respect and love for going down this path again, together, twenty years later. It took courage to both look back and look forward, and you never blinked. You sat in your office, focused your eyes on me, and asked, "What are you fighting for deep down in your soul?" It is this, and it is us. You made dreams come true.

—Jorge

I would like to acknowledge Jorge for reminding me that *In Our Own Voices* 1996 still existed and remained relevant. You followed where I led. You supported me when I faltered. You trusted me when I didn't trust myself. Thank you.

Khafre K. Abif, your presence and input and contribution were missed. The journey was not the same without you.

I would be remiss here if I did not acknowledge Dr. E. J. Josey (1924–2009). He believed we could do this in 1996 when no one else did. More than 30 percent of the contributors to the 1996 book received their library degrees from the University of Pittsburgh, and most of us were personally recruited by him. He was here, and his work and life mattered tremendously.

—Teresa

Introduction

The Struggle Renewed

In June 2016, Jorge showed up to a meeting with a strangely familiar-looking green book tucked under his arm. When queried about said book, he reluctantly revealed a copy of *In Our Own Voices: The Changing Face of Librarianship* (*IOOV* 1996).[1] In his research for his chapter in *Topographies of Whiteness: Mapping Whiteness in Library and Information Science* (López-McKnight 2017), he was introduced to Isabel Espinal's 2001 publication on Whiteness, which cited Deborah Hollis's *IOOV* 1996 chapter. His research, grounded in critical race theory, led him to explore other chapters in *IOOV* 1996 (see appendix A), and here we are.

Later that week, I began searching for original contributors to *IOOV* 1996, affectionately named the OGs[2] by Jorge. I was successful in locating contact information for more than half and queried them about their interest in potentially contributing to another volume on the twentieth anniversary of the book's publication. Receiving mostly positive interest, I then sent an inquiry to the library science editor at Rowman & Littlefield. His enthusiastically positive response less than twelve hours later set us on the path to what has become *In Our Own Voices, Redux: The Faces of Librarianship Today.*

BY INVITATION ONLY

Abif and Neely had to beat the bushes and beg people to write for the *IOOV* 1996. Jorge finds my stories of us preparing flyers to hand out at conferences humorous, but back then, it was the only way we knew how to reach those who might possibly agree to tell their stories. By comparison, this time around, selecting contributors in addition to the OGs was way too easy. We found ourselves in a position where we could pick who we wanted to participate, and as a result, we were able to select a highly diverse group, much more so than in 1996. Unfortunately, we were unable to retain all the OGs we contacted who initially agreed to contribute a chapter to *In Our Own Voices, Redux*. Throughout this eighteen-month-long odyssey, we felt, and still feel, their absence. *In Our Own Voices, Redux* would not have been possible without their original voices. We are hopeful that their experiences and voices are being heard by those who need to hear them most.

After convincing Jorge to be my copilot for this project, we looked to his contemporaries, as well as my mentees, and other colleagues new(ish) to the profession to fill the slots left by original contributors we could not locate, or who did not wish to revisit their original contributions. Thirty-one library and information science professionals contributed twenty-nine chapters, including the preface and introduction, to *In Our Own Voices, Redux*.

We have assembled a group that represents a beautiful spectrum of race and ethnicity, geographic origins, gender identities, sexuality, and academic and professional backgrounds. We have contributors with undergraduate degrees from all disciplines, representing academic and public libraries, a library school, a state department of education, a historical society, and a vendor—as well as the U.S. Department of State. Fifteen OGs are continuing their stories from 1996 alongside sixteen newcomers.

We are smart, funny, and articulate—if I may appropriate the one term White people can muster to describe all parts of us—particularly a well-educated us. We are well read and well spoken. We are beautiful, and we write beautifully. We are male, female, woman, cismale, cisfemale, cisgender, nonbinary, and gender fluid. We are queer, heterosexual, bisexual, straight, and *macha caliente*.

Among chapter contributors, we have earned thirty master's degrees accredited by the American Library Association, and one master's of public administration, from the lone non-credentialed library and information professional with nearly twenty-five years' experience in our midst. Twelve of us have completed a second master's degree. Six of us have completed doctoral degrees, two within the last ten years, and there are three currently in progress. All totaled, we represent more than four hundred years of post-MLS experience, and nearly one hundred years of postdoctoral experience. We are widely traveled, fluent in varying levels of multiple languages including Spanish, Portuguese, Italian, French, Vietnamese, Latin, German, Zuni, Navajo, Mandarin, Turkish, and English. This means we all have had to watch what we say, who we say it to, and how we say it in order to get to this point in our professional and academic lives.

At times, we have been too Black, too Mexican, and too White; or not Black, White, or Mexican enough. However, we represent the spectrum of skin tones. We are ambiguous, mixed race, miscellaneous, extra, and possibly white, just to keep you guessing. We are Asian American, Chinese American, Taiwanese American, and Vietnamese American. We are African American, Black, Blackish, and Black American. We are Brown, Coharie, Indigenous, Diné, Shoshone-Paiute, and Zuni. We are Latinx, Chicano/a, Mexican, Mexican American, Mexicana, and Tejana.

We are warrior women and men, forging a path in White and other spaces where paths should have already been blazed by 2017 CE. We are hungry, thirsty, and angry. And you are most likely not ready for us. But we are ready for you.

(RE)INTRODUCING THE OGS — JORGE

Deborah R. Hollis, Malore I. Brown, Dexter R. Evans, Teresa Y. Neely, Mark D. Winston, José A. Aguiñaga, Monica García Brooks, Sheree D. White, Kimberly Black, Lisa Burwell, Mee-Len Hom, Tanya Elder, Ngoc-Mỹ Guidarelli, Lisa Pillow, and Zora J. Sampson. You all came back to speak; to wake us up. And I hope we are, finally, awake and ready to listen.

I was thinking about librarians of color, thinking about those who have left, and asking these questions: Shouldn't we be learning from the folks who have left the profession? Wouldn't that benefit new and existing librarians of color if we knew why folks left?

It wasn't that I was asking the wrong questions, because we should probably think about those, too, but maybe more importantly, we should be asking the ones who are still here, why they've stayed, what has sustained them, what has kept them going. Because if we're going to get anywhere, if we're going to make any sort of movement, we must learn from them. We must center their voices, bodies, and experiences. They have been teaching us all along; I'm not convinced we have been willing to learn. The OGs deserve to be held up; we must celebrate their will to stare down this profession and not be afraid. I hope that embracing the truths they are sharing with us in these pages just might get us a little bit closer to change.

Simplistically, and a bit naively, I thought the OGs' contributions this time around would be in direct conversation with their 1996 chapters (see appendix A). I thought that they would remember, tracing their path from that point to now, contending with a previous version of their self, of their particular librarianship, and of our profession. They would tell us, and we would listen to that wisdom being passed along, so that we could understand, so that we would know how to, now, move. They did do that, and they did more. They shared their hearts, pain, observations, and beauty. They looked back, looked forward, and all around; if we understand their stories to be true, then we can ask ourselves and our profession different sets of questions that will require different approaches.

To the OGs: Your stories, then and now, are required reading. Your voices mattered in 1996, your voices mattered in 2016, and your voices continue to matter.

INTRODUCING THE NEWCOMERS AND THE MIX TAPE—TERESA

Sarah R. Kostelecky, Lori Townsend, Jennifer Brown, Rachel E. Winston, Joanna Chen Cham, Evangela Q. Oates, Silvia Lin Hanick, Nicholae Cline, Jorge R. López-McKnight, Madelyn Shackelford Washington, Leni Matthews, Irlanda Estelí Jacinto, Monica Etsitty Dorame, Jimena Bretón, and Sofia Leung.

As we began to receive chapters, we noticed similar themes, experiences, and triumphs throughout, which led to a rethinking of how we wanted to present them for reading. Jorge wanted to "lay down tracks for a mix tape": to create a collection meant to tell the reader a story. He wanted to hear which song the chapters were singing/performing. This structure allows for a natural flow between and among chapters to engage in conversation with each other. A symphony of sorts. This soundtrack did not lend itself to division by library type, like *IOOV* 1996, by age or type of librarian, by race or gender. The chapters played songs/stories about our truths, our trauma; our persistence; our magic; our strength; our weaknesses; our warrior spirit within, in the face of—and despite—the system; and our homecoming. We have assembled them here for your listening pleasure.

Back in the Day

Back in the Day starts in 1996 and ends in 2016. This twenty-year span acknowledges our struggle and accomplishments and provides a historical context for the overall chapters to come. We have language now to describe what was written about in *IOOV* 1996, but throughout, these stories reveal little has changed in the profession. There is nothing new here; nothing groundbreaking or earth shattering. The profession is still White, female (Schonfeld and Sweeney 2017), and hostile. And it's not changing. OG Deborah has been firing shots, "shooting off her mouth since 96" (St. Lifer and Nelson 1997) and is still at it. In her chapter, she poses difficult questions for difficult times, simultaneously challenging us, as well as showing us the path that we might dare to take that could possibly lead to progress. Her original chapter sparked the flame for *In Our Own Voices, Redux*, and that says something.

They Have Magic

In *They Have Magic*, these contributors are magical dreamers who created their own path and then lit the way with their bright light, standing tall; they are role models for all of us to aspire to. OG Dr. Brown's library path has been anything but conventional: from public libraries to library school educator; from a library not-for-profit association to the Sesame Workshop at the Electric Company; from the National Endowment for the Humanities to the U.S. Department of State. Her intersectional analysis on race, gender, and age in the various positions she has held is powerful and awakening. Of course, you can't stop brilliance; she decided enough is enough and reclaimed her life and her body. She will be reading this in Bogotá, Colombia, next year, living well and laughing the hardest.

Native American librarians make up less than 1 percent of librarians in the United States. In most studies of library demographics, the numbers are far too low to be recorded or reported. This book has four Native American contributors (13 percent). That number is magical in and of itself. Because they are so underrepresented and under/dis-counted, it literally does not matter what they have to say. We should always be listening. Sarah and Lori challenge our perceptions of what a "Native American librarian" looks like, where she works, and what she does; they let us listen in on their conversation as they share their stories exploring the intersections of their work and home lives.

OG Dexter is still running (Evans 1996), moving, making connections, and inspiring others. He's still motivating others, and he is still in service to our community of learners. The only one in our Collective to make the transition from academic libraries to library vendorship, his contribution—a three-way telephone interview—focused on the influence of his mother and sister, mentoring, community, passing along knowledge and wisdom to folks coming up, and ensuring his legacy is intact and in place while he's still here.

Jennifer and Rachel are unicorns, in every sense of the word. The paths they have forged are unlike anything we've seen in this profession. Jennifer's journey takes her clear across the country from her beginnings in Los Angeles to science librarianship in New York. Along the way, she surrenders herself to impostor syndrome and abandons her desire to write; later in the midst and wake of a devastating loss, she reclaimed herself with her art and by finding her people and feeding her passions. Rachel is the first Black diaspora archivist at the University of Texas, Austin (UT) in the Nettie Lee Benson Latin American Collection, a position she applied for when she was employed in the UT Department of Black Studies curating *their* art collection and developing archival projects. She is one of a number of archivists represented in *In Our Own Voices, Redux*.

Strength

The women in this section sacrificed a lot to get to where they are. Although at times, Teresa, Joanna, and Silvia have not felt very strong or anchored, Evangela reminds us that strength is relative. Her battles in her first professional position were minimized because of the sisterhood and Black Girl Magic. Mentoring is a huge part of the success of contributors and the advice given in this book. Evangela's story, while her own, echoes the truths of many Black women in librarianship and other professions (Croom 2017) and reminds us that the intersection of racism and gender continues to haunt Black women.

Silvia and Joanna are both children of immigrants. They have both experienced and overcome rampant overt racism, and sexism, in the workplace. Silvia's strength was revealed when she stopped actively covering it up and began living her truth on her terms. She, too, fell victim to imposter syndrome, but she shares deeply personal stories about herself and her family on her journey to uncovering her own self. Joanna speaks to all of us, letting us know that "we are not alone," even as underrepresented people of color in our profession, as she shares her own journey of what it means to be an Asian American. She leads us through her experiences growing up in a Los Angeles suburb, attending UC Berkeley, and being one of a handful of Asian Americans in archives, museums, and libraries.

OG Teresa writes about being the only one, still, two decades plus later; and makes peace with sacrificing the convenience of living near family, and having a family of her own; not living near Black people; and the mental, emotional, and physical toll White spaces, hostile environments, and microaggressions have taken on her mind, body, and spirit. Loss, personal and family, is present throughout her chapter, and she unpacks White privilege for us to get an up close, intimate look at her intersectional life. Take notes. She's thrived in this profession on her own terms.

Leading by Reflection

Two seasoned OGs, Mark and José, write about their journeys through the ranks, and in both of their chapters they reflect on their careers and their desire to lead. Both have held positions of leadership in public and academic libraries. José takes us with him and his family as he assumes different library positions in Arizona and California and achieves his educational dream. These directions and experiences influence his understanding of the profession and, perhaps more important, himself. Mark, with access to information as a guiding principle to his leadership, the importance of diversity shaping his vision, and having the willingness to be a learner throughout his professional journey, shares with us the importance of moving forward and achieving goals. Their willingness to learn and lead and take us along on the journey from east to west, north to south is dizzying and insightful, if you can read between the lines.

Family

In the only chapter in this section, Nicholae, Jorge, and Madelyn write about finding community, family, each other, and themselves among the White spaces of the library school in Bloomington, Indiana. They "had to find each other." There was no other option. Their chapter, like Sarah and Lori's, and Dexter and the coeditors', is a conversation, how they met, survived, and thrived. They had indeed been invited to the party (library school at Indiana University), but they had *not* been asked to dance (Myers 2017b).

Disrupting the System

Dr. Brooks, Dr. Black, and Ms. White put everything on the line for the communities in their charge. They are doing the work. Dr. Brooks takes a deep, hard, critical look at West Virginia, the state she has called home her entire personal and professional life. As the economic, social, and political struggles impact the state on all levels, her love for the region, her community, and her profession remain strong; she stays committed to the struggle, thriving in desperate times that include a declining coal economy, skyrocketing unemployment, heroin overdoses and a growing opioid/drug epidemic, and a more visible hate culture.

Dr. Black, in three acts, shines light on the educational budget crisis in Illinois and its impact on her, communities of color, and the profession. She describes crossroads, then and now. From finishing her PhD, and becoming a library school professor, to working on Chicago's Southside, she shows us beauty, power, and struggle. Her critical analysis of our profession, of our library schools is clear and strong and right.

Ms. White wrote something that made Jorge take off his glasses—"if I'm going to give up my soul then I might as well do so for my community." Working at a youth detention center, she provides library instruction to Black and Brown boys who would otherwise be in school in grades eight through twelve. Her chapter investigates the school-to-prison pipeline and the impact it has had, and continues to have, on youth of color around literacy and education. The three choices she teaches her students they have when they find themselves in structures that are not to their liking are the same choices librarians of color face in our profession.

They Persisted

The women in *They Persisted* could have fit in any number of the other sections, but we think they should be here. Not because they all have similar stories, but because they persisted, in different ways. With the exception of OG Lisa B., they are all new to the Collective. One of two retirees, Lisa B. reflects on how her love for librarianship from a young age became a source of frustration and actual physical pain. Her story goes from happy to horrible when she is encouraged to take a leadership position that she wasn't ready for and did not really want. She went from a thriving branch to a struggling one in her hometown of Chicago, with disastrous results. All led to a significant decline in her health, and she simultaneously was dealing with her father's declining health. She offers excellent advice; library love is starting to come back, and she's starting to feel better.

Madelyn's journey among the "Sons and Daughters of Mechanics and Farmers in the Crossroads of America" is unique in that she is the privileged one. She shares entries from her home, travel, and work journals to frame her experiences teaching a first-year experience seminar in Columbus, Indiana, the home of our current vice president. Leni, a Chicago native, diagnoses and dissects her journey from teaching to her first professional academic librarian position. Her plan to attend the top school in the country, coupled with years of teaching in the Chicago Public School system, did not give her the leg up she thought she would have. Two hundred plus applications later, and after rotating through Kübler-Ross's five stages of grief (2016) she is employed at a library in Texas, and she has hard learned tips and advice for anyone who finds themselves in that particular predicament.

In 2016, Irlanda applied for a position at the University of New Mexico. Teresa was blown away by her presentation. She had no PowerPoint or other visual aids, and she seemed to have no notes. She was incredible. Teresa knew immediately that we would never hire her; but she also knew that Irlanda had to write for this book. The only child of Mexican immigrants, she, too, is the first and only faculty member of color at the University of Wyoming's American Heritage Center. Her journey as a super token is told by way of systems. Cleverly, she uses critical race theory and Voorhees's (2008) identity traits to share her experiences within the "systems" in Tucson, Arizona; Albuquerque, New Mexico; and Laramie, Wyoming.

Warrior Women

The revolution will be wearing *faldas* and *chals*. The women in *Warrior Women* have been through it. Repeatedly. Monica D. survived a near death experience at the age of three, Indian boarding school at the age of eight, and cancer at the age of fifty-one. She endured racist teachers in three states at three universities and finally earned her undergraduate degree eleven years after she started. She begins a PhD program in 2018. She's a Diné warrior woman, and she persisted. Similarly, it took Jimena nine years to earn her undergraduate degree. She is currently enrolled in a PhD program. Her evolution as a revolutionary on a mission of social justice who finds her voice and purpose is revealed through her experiences with racism, sexism, privilege, education, and enlightenment. Both Monica and Jimena come from a long line of strong Diné (Monica D.) and Mexicana (Jimena) women.

OG Mee-Len's struggle is real and all too common. In an environment where lip service is paid to diversity recruitment, she has seen the numbers of faculty of color in her library decline. She has been told by an administrator, out loud, in a faculty meeting, "Statistically, you don't exist." She is here to tell you that we do exist and that there is still hope for a brighter tomorrow, even if she is not there to see it. Not mentored, not supported, not treated equally, disrespected, discounted, ostracized, and labeled a troublemaker, she still manages, somehow, to keep hope. She's a soldier; and when she retires, the profession, and CUNY, will feel the void.

OG Tanya's dilemma is like no other. As an adult, she's had to confront her Blackness and her Whiteness and reconcile long-held family secrets. Tanya's chapter is deeply intimate and honest. She did what a lot of us cannot or are not willing to do. She looked back at her life and her family's life, and she contended with the stories she was told and the stories she told herself that have shaped who (and what) she is, and how she is seen by others. The path toward understanding oneself in this world can be a lifelong journey, and she takes us along for the ride.

Bringing Us Home

OGs Ngoc-Mỹ and Mee-Len are at the same institution and in the same positions they were in when they wrote in 1996. The name "Mỹ" means beautiful, or American in Vietnamese, and Ngoc-Mỹ was destined to end up here. Her story chronicles her journey from refugee (in France) to citizen (in the United States). Ngoc-Mỹ has continued to push diversity and inclusion efforts in multiple areas of her life—as a cataloger, a linguist, and a teacher—within her academic and library community in Virginia and in the Vietnamese community. She expands the definition of what it means to be Asian in this country, and having witnessed, firsthand, propaganda during the Vietnam conflict, she cautions us, in her chapter, to be very careful in these troubling times because she has seen it all before.

OG Lisa P.'s story is a perfect counterpoint to Debbie's shots fired at the beginning of this book. Debbie throws Molotov cocktails, and Lisa P. campaigns against land mines. They both ask similar questions but in different ways; both keep it real. Lisa P. is still here, challenging us to think differently about the retention of librarians of color and to create healthy, sustainable work environments. She also offers us tips on how to remain in this profession, with our sanity intact, amid issues and actions of race, marginalization, inclusion, and diversity.

Zora is back. She was the only Native American voice in *IOOV* 1996. Her early submission of her chapter made this Collective *real*. Her storytelling and lyrical prose about her family, community, and career are moving and beautiful and alive, and like many of the OGs, she asks hard questions that we all must contend with.

Sofia literally brings us home. Her letter to new and existing librarians, library workers, and library students of color is sobering, honest, and hard hitting. She writes the letter she wished she had received when she was beginning in this profession. She reminds us how important are the people we surround ourselves with for support as well as the importance of professional development and self-motivation. And finally, she reminds us that mental health awareness and care is absolutely necessary, and that a mental health issue is a medical condition caused by stressful, hostile workplaces.

"SAME SHIT, DIFFERENT CENTURY"

In 1997, two researchers at *Library Journal*, a White male and a Black female, "[s]purred by the collective portrayal of librarianship as professionally limiting to minorities that emerges from" *IOOV* 1996, conducted telephone surveys and numerous interviews to "explore the depiction [for] themselves" (St. Lifer and Nelson 1997). After rereading the article, Teresa shared it with the Collective mostly for the cover photo of Neely and Abif but also for the study findings. Responses from four hundred librarians via the telephone survey, "100 from each major race represented in the field—white, black, Latino, and Asian" (note the absence of Native American librarians) resulted in one of the contributors to *In Our Own Voices, Redux* to say, "*dying* over the pie charts where white people don't think it's easier for white people to be white." Deborah R. Hollis was less diplomatic: "Same shit, different century." Indeed, across the board, white librarians' responses were in opposition to those from librarians of color. Sixty percent of white librarians disagreed that "white librarians have better career opportunities than librarians from other racial groups"; 84 percent agreed that "awareness of racism in the library profession improved"; and 61 percent reported "racism in the library profession was less prevalent compared with other professions." The his-, her-, the their-stories represented in *In Our Own Voices, Redux* provide stark, unequivocal evidence that counteract each of the points in the previous sentence, and so much more.

Sometimes, however, we do not feel smart, or pretty, or seen, or understood. We have endured criticism and micro- and macroaggressions from White people and from people who look like us. We have used everything in our respective arsenals including our gender, race, and skin color to get those bootstraps up high enough to be considered somewhat (un)equal enough. We are first-generation college graduates, first in our family college attendees, native U.S. citizens, naturalized U.S. citizens, and first- and second-generation immigrants. We represent the best our families, villages, and communities had to offer to this profession and to the world.

We have been verbally, emotionally, and spiritually flayed to our cores in predominantly White spaces that were not built for us, but where we have fought, sacrificed, and neglected ourselves, our families, and our friends to pursue and attain success. We are not going anywhere; although, at times, persisting was the thing we wanted to do the least. We have worked too hard and struggled too long to give it all up because you made us cry, or questioned our commitment, or doubted our abilities, literacy, or competency. Some of the OGs have retired, and some are contemplating it. Library and information science is definitely not rocket science, but more than a couple of us have left or are currently seriously considering leaving the profession. The struggle is more real than you can imagine. Most of us work in environments where the core of the organization is completely clueless that every meeting of the faculty, team, committee, task force, or group is systemically toxic and hostile.

In the words of the famous poet, activist, and hip-hop recording artist Clifford Joseph "T.I." Harris Jr. in the poetry set to music "We Will Not," which appears on his tenth studio album, *Us or Else: Letter to the System* (2016):

> No, we will not be run amuck, led astray or bamboozled. The buck will be stopping today.

NOTES

1. In 1996, Teresa Y. Neely and Khafre K. Abif edited *In Our Own Voices: The Changing Face of Librarianship*. On the twentieth anniversary of that book, *In Our Own Voices, Redux: The Faces of Librarianship Today* includes contributions from many of the authors from the 1996 volume along with some new contributors, the majority of whom refer to the 1996 volume in their chapters. To that end, *IOOV* 1996 will be used in place of a traditional author date citation throughout this volume to refer to the 1996 book.

2. OGs (original gangstas) are the individuals from back in the day. They were at the beginning of what was created—a group, a club, a gang, a crew. Here, in this specific context, it refers to the original contributors to *IOOV* 1996.

Part One

Back in the Day

Chapter One

Still Ambiguous after All These Years

Reflections on Diversity in Academic Libraries

Deborah R. Hollis

In 1995 two intrepid librarians, Teresa Y. Neely and Khafre K. Abif, asked early-career librarians from underrepresented groups to write about the changing face of a predominantly White and female profession. Professor Emeritus E. J. Josey, from the School of Library and Information Science at the University of Pittsburgh, authored the preface of *IOOV* 1996 and described the work as "a collective gesture by a total of 26 new generation of minority librarians comprised of 14 African American women, 5 African American men, 3 Asian American women, an American Indian woman, 2 Chicanos—1 woman and 1 man, and a Latin American woman, in honor of their having a shared similar and unique experience in transition from library school to work in a library and information environment . . . to contemplate that they are experiencing some of the same problems and difficulties that minority professionals have confronted for the last fifty years" (Josey 1996, xi).

Around the same time in the profession, Carla Hayden became the 1995 recipient of *Library Journal*'s Librarian of the Year Award, possibly foreshadowing that in twenty years she would be tapped by the future president, Barack Obama, to become the Librarian of Congress (*Wikipedia*, "Carla Hayden"). In 1996, a relatively unknown Barack Hussein Obama was elected to the Illinois state senate. Colin Powell and Condoleezza Rice were known to the public through their respective terms as secretary of state in the George W. Bush administration (*Wikipedia*, "List of Secretaries of State"). Things seemed bright to this Afro-Asian librarian and the future held promise. The United States Census Bureau was preparing to support a multiracial category for the 2000 census when *IOOV* 1996 was published; however, at that time I identified as African American. That was the dominant culture's accepted norm—the "one drop rule" held that one black parent designated the racial classification of a biracial child (Davis 1991). It was a social construct that my Dutch Indonesian mother would forever be annoyed with, but so it was in the United States of America. Historically, one drop—meaning one parent or relative within a number of generations—does a Negro make; however, for Native Americans, identity and the politics of "blood quantum" work in the opposite direction. To be recognized as a member of a tribe or nation by the U.S. federal government, and therefore qualify for housing, education, financial aid, or certain other benefits, a person must prove the percentage of Native American ancestry in their family line (Association on American Indian Affairs 2006). One drop does not a Native American make.

As a child, my female role models were my mother and strong women my father admired such as Barbara Jordan (*Wikipedia*, "Barbara Jordan"), a Texas state legislator and congresswoman, and Shirley Chisholm (*Wikipedia*, "Shirley Chisholm"), an elected representative to Congress from New York's 12th Congressional District. They were prominent African American women at the national level who defied stereotypes. I was proud of my mother, a naturalized U.S. citizen, who explained to fellow citizens who had not heard of Indonesia where the country was located and why her first language was Dutch (it was a former colony of the Netherlands, and she came to the United States as a Dutch citizen). The U.S. Census was also a challenge for my mother to complete since the options under the Asian category did not fit her family history. My use of the word *ambiguous* in this chapter's title is a play on words—I took aim at the lack of a diverse library workforce and acknowledged that often the general public incorrectly guesses my racial background because I do not fit American stereotypes for people of color.

Initially, when invited to contribute to this volume on the twentieth anniversary of *IOOV* 1996, I was reminded of a review published in the April 15, 1996, issue of *Library Journal*. Terry Shoptaugh, then a history professor and university archivist at Minnesota State University–Moorhead, wrote, in my opinion, a condescending review of the work. The reader could almost hear the sigh that came off the page as Mr. Shoptaugh stated, "This volume is the result of a laudable idea" and concluded with, "Overall, the book is weak and its contributors too new to the profession to offer much insight into our troubled times. . . . It would be interesting to wait 25 years and then ask some of these young men and women to rewrite their reminiscences" (Shoptaugh 1996).

Nothing new here; just move along, gentle reader. These new professionals, and their views, are too green to be taken seriously, and additionally, their personal experiences with workplace racism cannot teach us anything we do not already know. Did that observation alone not make apparent the need for a publication that documented the tortured, awkward reality of the absence of diversity across the library and archive landscape? I interpreted his remarks as recognition of the lack of change in these work environments, yet somehow by reporting bad behavior, marginalization, mistreatment, or neglect, we, the authors, were not telling him anything new. It appeared that Shoptaugh had not read nor considered Professor Josey's preface that noted how *IOOV* 1996 traced the continued struggle, and these authors confirmed that diversity, equal opportunity, or affirmative action—as it was known in the last century—remained as elusive in 1996 as it had been to the generations of minority librarians before us in 1946. I remember noting Shoptaugh's use of the phrase *"troubled times"* and thinking, "What does that mean, and how, exactly, does he define *troubled times*?" It was 1996: William Jefferson Clinton was president of the United States, as the country was headed into the Whitewater saga, and Theodore Kaczynski, the face of terrorism aka "the Unabomber"—a White male loner—had been arrested (*Wikipedia*, "1996 in the United States"). I was a government documents librarian with not a thought about special collections and archives, an arena I would enter after achieving promotion and tenure in 2000. Little did I realize that the demographics of the rare book and archive administrative field were predominantly male and White. I would learn in due time.

I wondered why our voices were not "new insights" pointing "toward change." *IOOV* 1996 was deemed "weak" and contained "very little that cannot be found in other works" (Shoptaugh 1996). Likewise, I found Shoptaugh's review to be weak and lacking substantive feedback. Although he acknowledged something significant—"troubled times"—without explanation, the tone was dismissive. A thoughtful analysis of why these young authors' hopes and fears and reported workplace experiences—bias, open rudeness, racism, passive neglect, microaggression, and lack of inclusion or mentorship—would have been constructive. To a reader of Shoptaugh's review, it appeared that *IOOV* 1996 was a compilation of complaints he had heard before. Were the *IOOV* 1996 authors responsible for the workplace culture that we had entered? Was that not an indictment on the lack of progress? What, exactly, would Shoptaugh have defined as new and informative? Who was responsible for the fact that a new generation of librarians reported the same bad behavior and hostile or neglectful work environments as those who entered the profession after World War II? I did not make time to contact him with my questions and instead moved on. The goal of attaining promotion and tenure beckoned. It was, after all, a brief thumbs-down *Library Journal* book review. Time passed, and in 2017, I have the opportunity to reflect on my experiences. Shoptaugh's review floated back into memory, and a Google search listed him as retired and a published author of local history.

The majority of *IOOV* 1996 authors remain in the profession and come together in this new volume to reflect on our career paths. My cohort and I share similar experiences with socially awkward, naive, or racially biased colleagues, and some of us continue to have problematic, outrageous, or outlandish experiences, still. Twenty years on, added to the mix, is a new generation of underrepresented librarians, passionate and as excited as my cohort and I were, entering the library and information science profession in which the demographics of the profession in the last century—White and female—have not significantly changed. To be fair, *IOOV* 1996 authors and I can relay uplifting stories of White allies who did not, and do not, stand by silently when they observe bias, intimidation, or harassment. Yet, twenty years later, for some librarians of color, was being passed over for a leadership position about race, age, or politics? Could it be all these? As some of us found out, the answer is yes, yes, and yes. The chapters in this volume trace the ups and downs of careers, the community we developed among ourselves, the joyous highs and the lowest low moments, and the observations that a diverse library workforce remains an elusive goal.

Shoptaugh wrote from a position of privilege. Was Shoptaugh dismissive because he knew that changing an organization's culture is akin to Sisyphus, the mythological Greek destined to roll that boulder up the hill for all eternity? Is that where we, the *IOOV* 1996 authors, lacked insight, and perhaps were naive—or in Shoptaugh's mind, egotistical—because we wrote from the perspective of new hires in entry-level positions? Perhaps he considered that transformational change requires leadership, and from where he sat, he could not identify library leaders able, or willing, to hold their staff accountable for acts of implicit bias or blatantly bad behavior, or poor supervisory and communication skills. Did Shoptaugh understand that supervisors must exercise accountability and act responsibly to document misconduct and uncivil behavior? Did he reason away incivility by thinking that an uncivil coworker was really a nice person and did not intend for a crass statement to be hurtful to a colleague who was not a member of the dominant culture? Did he sincerely believe that all administrators evaluate personnel in a fair and equitable manner and do not retaliate against those who question or challenge decisions in the spirit of transparent debate? Perhaps he could not propose specific solutions because he understood that change, in a predominantly White profession's organizational culture, would take a generation, hence the suggestion to check back in twenty-five years once he and his cohort retired. Did he realize that he was not a transformational leader and perhaps he recognized the enormity of the challenge to the profession? Was Shoptaugh that self-aware and prescient? I think not; however, I needed to consider the possibility. Would knowing Shoptaugh's backstory impact the way in which I read and interpreted his review? Would my reaction differ if he was a person of color, married to a person of color, or the parent of a person of color? Context matters—or does it?

My experiences and observations over twenty years in a profession that prides itself on being socially aware, combined with national events (the 2016 U.S. presidential campaign rhetoric, police shootings of Black children and adults, media-fueled Islamophobia and fear of the "other," etc.), informed and shaped this chapter. The history of minorities in libraries is straightforward. The first wave of underrepresented people was challenged with gaining access to libraries and archives—experiences ranging from being allowed to check out books from a public library, to admission in a bachelor's or master's library science program, to being hired on staff and promoted. Sheila Delacroix,[1] E. J. Josey,[2] Mary Penny Key,[3] Emily Mobley,[4] Mildred Nilon,[5] James F. Williams II,[6] and in the archive world, Brenda Banks[7] and Harold Pinkett[8] were just a few of many role models to my *IOOV* 1996 cohort and me, the majority of whom experienced middle management and leadership roles in the mid-to-late twentieth century.

After *IOOV* 1996 was published, my 1999 article "Affirmative Action or Increased Competition: A Look at Women and Minority Library Deans" was published in the *Journal of Library Administration*. Building on Barbara Moran's 1985 *Library Trends* article, "The Impact of Affirmative Action on Academic Libraries," I analyzed twelve years of demographic data for eighty-six academic libraries by region in search of academic library leadership that reflected a diverse nation. What I found was that the pipeline contained White women who, as middle managers, were ready to advance into leadership positions. Affirmative action initiatives may be a contributing factor to a greater degree in promoting White women while increasing competition for top positions between female and male librarians of color (Hollis 1999).

It bears repeating that the history of academic libraries is one in which librarians and staff have been predominantly white and female. Library literature has covered the demographics of the profession over the decades, and popular magazines like *Library Journal* provide periodic census reports about the profession's population and salaries. The Association of Research Libraries (ARL) analyzes employment trends on a regular basis, and *In the Library with a Lead Pipe*, an open-access, peer-reviewed journal, entered the scene in 2008 to bring a new generation of voices to the discussion of diversity and inclusion. Because open access sites, social media, and blogs allow for real time discussion of library and information science demographics, I will not use this space for a formal literature review of library employment statistics. My *IOOV* 1996 chapter provided baseline statistics, and, to date, the needle has not moved in a substantive direction (Hollis 1996). To the profession's credit, lesbian, gay, bisexual, transgender, and questioning (LGBTQ) colleagues are not in the shadows as they once were, and it may be argued that librarians who identify as members of these communities maneuver in the profession with only slightly greater ease, depending foremost on one's geographic location. This development makes me proud of my country, and yet, I am not so naive to think that LGBTQ librarians do not experience workplace intimidation or bigotry, be it any type of work environment or discipline. Inclusiveness is embraced despite the segment of society that is currently hard at work to roll back social progress. A racially and ethnically diverse workforce, on the other hand, remains elusive. Research that analyzes whether LGBTQ people of color are advancing in the ranks of library leadership is the next necessary step.

Within the library and archive profession, what does the decision-making authority look like? What are the demographics? We know the answer. In the twentieth century, White men dominated library leadership positions, and White women since then have secured top administrative and middle management positions in school, public, college, and university libraries (Najmabadi 2017). The demographics in archive administration are similar. Where does this leave men and women of color? Administrators decide library and archive budgets, which shape collections, archival holdings, and services. Ultimately, a collective cultural memory continues to be curated by members of the dominant culture. The adage that history is written and preserved by the winners remains true, and diversifying the workforce and historical record has been a process with minor progress.

ARL is leading efforts to recruit a diverse workforce, as is the Society of American Archivists (SAA). I have witnessed a slow awakening in the latter profession and acknowledgment that society benefits from an inclusive workforce. Dennis Meissner spoke of this in his 2016 SAA presidential address (Meissner 2017), a welcomed counterbalance to Shoptaugh's review that seemed to admonish *IOOV* 1996 authors for not bringing a new conversation to the metaphorical table. Have we come a long way? Expanded access to libraries stemming from the civil rights movement of the 1960s was but one positive outcome, when women and minorities demanded equal access to education and employment opportunities. Fast forward, and the profession continues to develop a pipeline of underrepresented candidates for an array of administrative library positions. While this pipeline of interested candidates awaits, transformation within the discipline is impacting this profession and applying new market force pressures. White men and women—some young and some older—attracted to the information technology (IT) aspect of libraries, archives, and museums enter the profession with skills from the IT realm. Position descriptions and skill sets are evolving, as they should, to respond to the changing information landscape, and the hiring in one's own image continues. This explains why the needle has moved only slightly in librarianship. Or does it?

So, what has changed in twenty years? Currently, a new presidential drama is underway, and the face of terrorism is portrayed as Brown or Black or Muslim rather than a White lone wolf. The jaded answer to the question of library workplace diversity, using a musical metaphor, is that people of color continue to be the back-up singers; but now, instead of the White boy bands, we are backing up the White girl bands. Is it cruel and unprofessional to say that? How do I feel about the lack of progress since the publication of *IOOV* 1996? Frustrated and resentful. Professor Josey noted, "In spite of the displays of meanness and the vulgarity of racism and prejudice, all of the essayists stand out as a shining beacon of magnificent clarity with faith in freedom and in justice for all time to come" (Josey 1996, xi). I certainly felt that way at the time; however, I do not anymore. Should I abandon hope? Is the idea of a diverse workforce futile or Sisyphean? I understand that, when it comes to leadership positions, it is an issue of power and politics. A new generation of White women has entered the profession, energized to assume leadership positions, and this generation sincerely believes that it is committed to a diverse workforce. It is a transitional time in library leadership, and yet White female library administrators do not manage in a way that supports diversity or inclusivity. The hiring process is where an organization's commitment is proven. Is it the region of the country? Further research is necessary to track whether an increase in diverse hires has occurred in the last twenty years. Additional questions include whether the number of underrepresented groups has increased in tenure-track librarian hires. Twenty years ago, I would have signed on to conduct this analysis, but now, attending any library conference is a barometer to gauge change in the profession. Underrepresented people continue to be present at academic library conferences in small numbers. The farther one searches in library leadership positions across the United States, the fewer administrators of color one finds. Is this a backlash to the election of the country's first African American president? Or, is it no backlash at all? Instead, it is the normal course of events when it comes to power and authority in any professional arena. Within academic libraries, the gender shift in administrative leaders is best summed up in the vernacular as switching out White men for White women. Thus far, White women appear to use the same managerial methods that White men were criticized for using—making decisions without discussion or transparency—but now these types of approaches are seen as indicators of strength, resolve, and vision. Perhaps Shoptaugh was right without realizing that what he predicted was truly "nothing new here." From my vantage point, the profession's tepid response to the recruitment and retention of a diverse workforce continues to be ambiguous and unremarkable.

The question remaining is this: Is the idea of a representative workforce achievable in the world of libraries and archives? Did we, the *IOOV* 1996 authors, believe that our experiences would differ from our elders? Yes, we did. In the same way that our elders were hopeful that after serving in World War II and surviving such a catastrophic event, people of color would return home and receive respect and equal opportunity in education and employment. The *IOOV* 1996 authors thought we were the change we sought. What do we do, or better yet, what can we do? All eyes are on this generation of academic library leaders. Will the shiny distraction of all things IT related and digital be the excuse to not push for an aggressive effort of diverse hires? New mentorship programs are now offered that promote the development of IT skills and experience for underrepresented and marginalized groups. It seems that this particular development in the field provides the business justification for continuing to hire in one's own image. What we can do is mentor the next generation of librarians and archivists. It is what our elders did for us. The fundamental vision of workplace diversity remains the same, yet we now have tools, such as social media, to communicate and strategize in an attempt to hold administrators accountable for their ambiguous response. The next generation of underrepresented librarians can work with my cohort to develop a shared strategy across geographic locations aimed at helping the community at large remain strong and connected.

In the end, what has changed since the publication of *IOOV* 1996 is that the rhetoric is new, and we realize that words matter. *Affirmative action* and *"equal opportunity"* morphed into the language of *diversity, equity, inclusivity,* and *organizational fit.* Another example of change is that the U.S. federal government finally acknowledged that citizens may self-identify as biracial or multiracial. According to the U.S. Census Bureau, I can self-identify and be recognized as no longer solely the race of my father and can acknowledge my mother's existence and contribution to making me who I am. Thus, the government has evolved with a less ambiguous response to the social construction of race, but it involved a process that took over two hundred years. However, in the library and archive profession, there is not much to show for the past twenty years, other than an increase in published analytical hand wringing that documents little progress. No doubt, this chapter will be seen as a plaintive wail, no different from the first I penned, and yet, I beg to differ. The *language* we use to describe marginalized groups and misconduct in the workplace has changed, as has the discussion, yet the actions speak louder than the words.

NOTES

1. Sheila Delacroix, PhD, was dean of the Lupton Library at the University of Tennessee, Chattanooga, from 1995 until 2003. Steve Cox, *History of the Library at the University of Tennessee, Chattanooga*, http://www.tnla.org/?384.
2. E. J. Josey, PhD, was a librarian and activist (*Wikipedia*, "E. J. Josey").
3. Mary Penny Key was a librarian at the Ohio State University Libraries and head of the Agricultural Library until her retirement in 1998. See https://library.osu.edu/about/osul-committees/diversity-and-inclusion/Mary-P-Key-Diversity-Residency-Program/.
4. Emily Mobley was dean of libraries at Purdue University from 1989 until 2004. http://www.purdue.edu/uns/html3month/030617.Mobley.libraries.html.

5. Nancy Mildred Nilon was the first African American librarian hired at the University of Colorado Boulder Libraries and retired as the assistant director for public services in 1986.

6. James F. Williams II served as dean of libraries at the University of Colorado Boulder from 1988 until 2017.

7. Brenda Banks was an archivist, leader, and member of the Society of American Archivists. See https://en.wikipedia.org/wiki/Brenda_Banks.

8. Harold Pinkett was the first African American archivist at the National Archives and Records Administration. See https://www.historians.org/publications-and-directories/perspectives-on-history/november-2001/in-memoriam-harold-t-pinkett.

Part Two

They Have Magic

THEY HAVE magic

Chapter Two

Malore the Explorer

Becoming Global with a Library Touch

Malore I. Brown

It really doesn't seem like twenty years have passed by since I wrote the chapter "I Fell into Librarianship and Fell in Love" (Brown 1996) for *IOOV* 1996. That young PhD student was eager to save and collect multicultural books for children in public libraries. Although I did not intentionally plan on being a librarian, and since the two public library jobs at the Milwaukee Public Library and the Chicago Public Library I initially mentioned in the book chapter twenty years ago (Brown 1996, 362–67), I have not been a traditional librarian. Being a stalwart advocate of library services no matter my career choice; libraries have always played an integral part of my being.

When last I left off at the end of my chapter I had short-term goals of becoming a professor and teaching children's and young adult (YA) literature in addition to collection development in a school of library and information science. My long-term goals were lofty, including playing a significant administrative role in a public library system in an urban setting. As with most master plans, my plan was adjusted along the way. As a professor of children's and young adult literature and collection development, I taught at two major library schools, my alma mater, the University of Wisconsin–Milwaukee, School of Library and Information Science, and Rutgers University, School of Communication, Library and Information Science. During the five years that I worked as an assistant professor, I had the opportunity to focus on my research topic, multicultural children's book selection. I also noticed that a variety of multicultural children's and YA books were being published. The 1990s and early 2000s were a booming time for multicultural children's books.[1]

Looking back twenty years, there are numerous things that I would tell my young librarian of color self. I would tell her, first, that the most important characteristics people will remember about you are what you know, how you treat people, and what type of impact you make in their lives. Use this opportunity to do the best that you can do. I am proud to say that I educated many of the Milwaukee public librarians during a certain era. Often I would walk into a neighborhood library or the Central Library on Wisconsin Avenue, and I would hear, "Hi Dr. Brown," or "Hello, Malore." My dad once asked how I knew so many library staff since it had been several years since I worked for the library. I told him that I taught most of them in their master's degree of library and information science program. Having my former students working at nearby institutions was also a benefit to my current classes; they were readily available guest speakers and provided opportunities for field trips to libraries, which enhanced the real-world learning experience.

The second piece of advice I would offer to my young librarian of color self is to learn to say "no." You don't have to say yes to every request to give a lecture or presentation, serve on a committee, or chair a committee because you are the only Black female in the department at your institution. The onus is not on you! You do not carry the whole race on your back. Yes, it is an honor to serve, but when you look around the room and you are the only woman or the only person of color in the boardroom and you are exhausted because of your heavy workload, multiple committees, professional service demands, and student advising, don't pretend you are Wonder Woman and can do it all. Just say no! Don't let your priorities or research and publishing suffer so that you can be an illustration for an institution. It's not worth it; it gets tiring, and if you don't get tenure, the institution will replace you. I know that this advice is curt and distilled; however, these were my cumulative observations.

The tests and trials of race, gender, and youth in a leadership role is often daunting. I recall one end-of-semester evaluation when I was a brand new assistant professor. Students filled out a multiple-choice evaluation in class and were also given the opportunity to write their assessment of the course. When the dean called me into his office weeks later, he handed me the aggregate score of my evaluations and the sheets of colored paper on which the graduate students had written their thoughts on the class. The last paper he handed me was a pink onion skin stationery; it was a typed (not printed on a printer, but typed on a typewriter), two-page, scathing "'evaluation" of my performance. I started reading, and tears involuntarily ran down my cheeks. This is important, because crying doesn't come easy to me. The first line read, "Dr. Brown dresses nicely and that's the only good thing I can say about her." After that sentence, the rest was an outright attack on my character, my being, and my soul. Of course, this was personal, and it hurt. After all the hard work and preparation I put into my classes, I could not imagine the gall of someone to be so mean spirited. The dean saw the "evaluation" for what it was, and I was totally confused as to why a graduate student would write such a malice-filled diatribe and what their objective was in doing so. "This is jealousy," said the dean. He explained to me that he was not sure if the tirade was race, gender, or age based; whatever it was, it was apparent that this student did not like being taught by me. This assessment could not be classified as an act of microaggression because it was blatant and premeditated. Moving forward, I learned that there would be a few more "pink-onion-skin-stationery-typing" individuals who would cross my path during my career. Fortunately for me, my resilience was stalwart and resolute.

In 2001, while I was working at Rutgers University as a visiting assistant professor, I was invited to apply for a position at the American Library Association (ALA). My intentions of staying in the academic arena were firm; however, at least three individuals and two mentors suggested I apply for the ALA position. Not only did the job description pique my interest but, at that time, I had been a member of the Association for Library Service to Children (ALSC) for almost ten years. When I received the call from ALA inviting me for an interview in Chicago for the ALSC executive director position, I was delighted. No matter what the search committee decided, I still had two faculty jobs I could go back to. When I was offered the job, it was a tough decision to make, but, eventually, I decided to leave academic life and enter association management.[2] I thought that I could always go back to teaching and research. In my mind, serving my profession in a management staff position at the ALA would have more impact and reach in the field of librarianship. The board and executive committee members of ALSC who hired me stated that I was their top candidate because I understood the inner workings of children's librarianship, had an understanding of the organization, and was abreast with the latest trends and research in children's services. Their deciding factor was they were looking for innovative ways of moving the association forward. I was excited and eager to get started to revitalize the association. When meeting with members at my first ALSC reception as executive director, I asked what fulfilled their professional needs with their membership in ALSC. I followed up my question by asking about changes they would like implemented in the organization. Many of the younger members wanted to participate on committees and see term limits put on individuals serving on the executive board or on awards committees. The members also indicated that being asked their thoughts was a great step because they had not been asked before. One of the first initiatives I undertook was getting committee nomination forms circulated and placed prominently online allowing all members to serve on committees. The idea that many young members of ALSC believed that there existed an "old girls network" and the same people rotated on and off the executive board and the premium award committees was very disheartening. During my four-year tenure as executive director of ALSC, I established myself as a nonprofit executive and learned the inner workings of association management. Having held memberships in ALA and ALSC, I understood the underlying mission behind the associations; however, managing and working with a board of directors, executive committee, thousands of members, and external stakeholders required administration expertise that I skillfully acquired. Whether it was attending the American Society of Association Executives (ASAE) conferences, workshops, and meetings; reading the latest books like *Good to Great* (Collins 2001) and *First Break All the Rules* (Buckingham and Coffman 1999); or receiving a certificate in nonprofit management, I threw myself into learning mode to be the best nonprofit executive that I could be. I was also fortunate to have an exceptional team in the staff of ALSC. We worked tirelessly for the association to thrive and succeed. I owe a lot of my success in the job to their dedication to our association's mission and support of their executive director. To date, twelve years after I separated from this job, I am still friends with this extraordinary group of people.

I found that being a nonprofit executive of color in my thirties was just as challenging, if not more, than being a university professor in my twenties. Once again, race, gender, and age played a part in many of the challenges that came my way. I experienced many victories and a few disappointments in my career; yet still, I persevered. I didn't have a name for it, or maybe it was that I didn't know the name or what to call it or how to describe what I was going through. Today we would call that microaggression. For a while, I thought I was paranoid, reading too much into scenarios. On the other hand, after a conference call, when my assistant mentioned to me that she worked for other executive directors and they were never treated the way that I was treated or spoken to on the call or in person, I knew it wasn't me. I was not imagining the statements, actions, or suggestions that were instances of indirect, subtle, or unintentional discrimination. It was not my naïveté, youth, or innocence that caused me to dismiss the microaggressions; I just did not have a name for it, and I could not believe that adult professional individuals would be so vicious. I don't want to dwell on the negative because I had triumphs and highs in this position that I still think fondly of today. My team and I brought many projects to the organization. We worked with external partners such as National Aeronautics and Space Administration (NASA), Apple, the National Endowment for Humanities, Sesame Workshop, and many more. Our ALSC book awards grew in number and recognition; under my leadership, we institutionalized the *El día de los niños/El día de los libros* (Children's Day/Book Day), commonly known as the Día! Initiative, with author Pat Mora. This is formally observed annually on April 30, when libraries and schools hold celebrations throughout the spring. "Día is a nationally recognized initiative that emphasizes the importance of literacy for all children from all backgrounds. It is a daily commitment to linking children and their families to diverse books, languages and cultures" (Association for Library Service to Children 2017).

I am also proud of the creative ways in which I engaged my staff. One cold November afternoon in Chicago, right before our regularly scheduled weekly staff meeting, I sent the ALSC staff an e-mail and told them to get their coats because our staff meeting was going to be held offsite. I hailed two taxis, and we were on our way to our "meeting." When the taxis arrived at the movie theater nearest our office, the staff seemed perplexed. I purchased tickets for everyone and told them we were about to embark on a learning experience. You see, in 2001, the first Harry Potter movie, *Harry Potter and the Sorcerer's Stone* (2001), an adaptation of J. K. Rowling's first novel of the popular children's series, by the same name, was released. The phone at ALSC was "ringing off the hook" with renewed interest in banning the book in schools and libraries, and people were boycotting the movie because the book was "too dark and promoted witchcraft." At the time, I was fielding most of the calls or referring callers to ALA's Office of Intellectual Freedom. My assistant and I were the only two ALSC staff who read any of the Harry Potter books. In lieu of requiring the team to read the book, I decided to take them all to the matinee showing of the movie to have a better understanding of why our telephones were ringing nonstop regarding a movie about an English boy with a scar on his forehead and a wand. After the movie, the ALSC staff had a lengthy discussion. I channeled my previous position as a university professor of collection development and explained why the association did not condone banning books. We were all "on the same page," and this instance of professional development became an ALSC staff meeting tradition whenever a Harry Potter movie was released.

The ALSC office often received calls about the book award seals that were affixed to books immediately after the awards were announced at the ALA Youth Media Awards press conference every January. In the same creative vein of the Harry Potter movies, I decided that the ALSC team needed to see how and where these award seals were made. After all, we were buying and selling award seals, and none of us, not even our longest serving staff of over twenty years, knew how the seals were made. I contacted the manufacturer, whom I'd met several times in person in the ALSC office, and asked him if the ALSC staff could have a field trip to see the seal production in person at their suburban Chicago plant. We were all amazed at the precision and meticulousness that went into the production of seals for ALSC awards.

My mother has always said, "self-praise is no recommendation"; however, I am proud of the innovative ways in which I enriched the working relationship with the ALSC staff by making the work that we did more relevant and putting it in context in a framework that was relatable. The ALSC team worked hard and enjoyed the work we did. After four years at

ALA, I decided that it was time to move on. I was literally burned out. My whole world revolved around my job, and there was no work/life balance. I went to my primary care physician in April 2005 because I thought I had a cold. It turned out I had developed allergies; however, upon more probing, my doctor told me that I was stressed out. I responded by saying, "No, it's just that my job keeps me very busy." And then she asked me something that shook me to the core: "If a bus hits you when you cross Michigan Avenue, who takes your next meeting?" I responded, "I look both ways before I cross the street, what are you talking about?" She asked again. I told her that my deputy or my boss would take the meeting, or it would be rescheduled. Her response, "A bus just hit you. Go home, rest, and think about having a healthier work and life balance. If you don't, you won't live to see forty years old." Ummm, excuse me? I thought I had a cold? Where did this all come from? After contemplating this discussion with my physician, I decided that living past forty years old was on my list of things to do.

The ALA Annual Conference in 2005 was my last conference as the executive director of ALSC. I packed up my things, put them in storage, and decided to get my life back through traveling the world. No, I wasn't trying to "find" myself. I realized that from the day I graduated high school at age sixteen, to the then present as a consummate overachiever, I had been pushing myself nonstop academically and professionally. My body finally pushed back, and I listened. And behold, "Malore the Explorer" was born. Travel had always been my vice, so it was no surprise to friends and family that I was going to travel. However, many an eyebrow was raised at me quitting my "good" job. Reclaiming my life was one of the best things that I did for myself and my career. I was financially sound. I had no debt, and I had a sizable amount of savings. My travels occurred well before the book *Eat, Pray, Love* was published. While traveling to different countries, I visited a variety of libraries for the fun of it the way librarians always seem to seek out a library on vacation. I planned on taking a six-month hiatus before going back on the job market. After six months, I sensed that I needed a little more time. During one of my literary vacations, I attended the Guadalajara Book Fair in 2006. At the largest book fair in Mexico, I met someone at a reception sponsored by the ALA, and when I inquired what his job was, he responded "Information Resource Officer." "What's that?" I replied. This was the first time that I had been introduced to the possibility of working in a library-type outreach environment overseas with the U.S. government. This gentleman told me that there were no vacancies at the time, but that maybe in two or three years there should be openings due to retirement. We exchanged business cards and decided we would keep in touch. At this time, I was already trying my hand at being an independent education and library consultant. After a year of consulting, I decided that I needed a "real" job. As luck would have it, I landed a position with Sesame Workshop, the nonprofit educational organization behind Sesame Street and other productions that make a meaningful difference in the lives of children worldwide. As the project director (assistant vice president) of *The Electric Company*, I spearheaded overall operational responsibility for the relaunch of *The Electric Company*. I was able to combine my expertise in children's literacy and experience as an educator and project manager into this new role. The goal of *The (New) Electric Company* was to strengthen children's literacy skills by engaging them in compelling activities across multiple media platforms (television, outreach, and broadband). Once again, I stretched out a little far afield from librarianship, yet still held on to the core of literacy and my passion for outreach. Unfortunately, due to the economic downturn the Sesame Workshop job only lasted a year; however, the experience I garnered while there was invaluable.

Remember the gentleman I met at the Guadalajara Book Fair a few years prior? Well, he was true to his word. I received an e-mail from him stating there were vacancies due to retirements. The e-mail also stated that the U.S. Department of State had posted an opening for an Information Resource Officer online, and if I was still interested, I should take a look. I looked, applied, made it through several rounds of evaluations, and landed a job. I thought that working for ALA was the highlight of my career, and then I could not imagine a position comparable to the one I had with Sesame Workshop. Now, here I was embarking on a new adventure that encompassed all my skills and passion rolled into one. I would be conducting outreach, giving presentations about the United States to foreign audiences, developing innovating programs in public engagement in library-like spaces, and using my foreign language abilities and management and budgeting experience while living and traveling worldwide. "Malore the Explorer" had come full circle. Who knew that the once children's and outreach librarian turned university professor and nonprofit executive would end up as a U.S. federal government employee with a global reach and library touch? Never in my wildest dreams could I have imagined that PhD student ending up here twenty years later. It was not an easy journey. I learned a lot about myself, my work ethic, human nature, and resolve. I grew in every employment opportunity I sought out and challenged myself at every interval. After one of my very challenging positions, a library director of color whom I respected greatly saw me at an ALA conference and commented how proud she was of me. She uttered the statement, "Living well is the best revenge."[3]

As I write this chapter, I am sitting in Accra, Ghana, where I have lived and worked for the past twenty months. I am contemplating my next assignment in a different region of the world, promulgating international information programs through public and cultural diplomacy of the United States through the development and delivery of policy-oriented programming in American spaces and conducting training on a wide variety of platforms, e-resources, and digital and analytics tools. That global reach is there, and although the traditional "library" has been distilled, the essence of literacy, outreach, and programming still exists. I eagerly anticipate my next posting in Bogotá, Colombia, as I serve my country and engage Colombian civil society and others through effective public diplomacy platforms that advance foreign policy goals.

NOTES

1. The Cooperative Children's Book Center, out of the School of Education at the University of Wisconsin–Madison, complies yearly statistics on the number of multicultural children's books. See http://ccbc.education.wisc.edu/books/pcstats.asp.

2. To my knowledge, I was the only African American woman with a PhD who was executive director of ALSC.

3. The quote is attributed to the English poet George Herbert (1593–1633).

Chapter Three

The Less Than One Percent

Native Librarians in Conversation

Sarah R. Kostelecky and Lori Townsend

What's your first thought when hearing the phrase "Native American librarian"? If you form any image, it is likely of a reservation library with one woman librarian working hard for little pay to provide services to her community, supporting cultural revitalization efforts. While this image is a reality in many tribal communities and is critically important, this is not the only reality for Native American librarians. Indigenous people work in all types of libraries but represent less than 1 percent of academic librarians (Morris 2017).

As mixed-race/Native women academic librarians, we offer our stories in conversation, exploring the intersectionality encountered in our jobs, communities, and experiences navigating identity within the dominant culture. After five years as colleagues and friends, we have gotten to know and trust each other by sharing the funny, frustrating, happy, and hurtful experiences in our lives. Here we hope to offer support to other mixed-race librarians crossing boundaries.

WHO WE ARE: SARAH AND LORI

SK. I'm from Zuni Pueblo in New Mexico, the largest pueblo with over 8,000 tribal members (Bureau of Indian Affairs 2017). The pueblo is on our reservation land; our ancestral land and village life revolves around the traditional religious calendar. Zuni—like the other pueblos—have been studied since first contact by outsiders who dissect our lives and share information about our culture that is often misinterpreted.

My mother is Zuni, and my father is White. My paternal grandmother was English; my paternal grandfather was from Nebraska via the former Czechoslovakia (his father immigrated), which is where my last name originates. My mother's parents both were Zuni and grew up in the village, as did their six children, including my mother.

LT. I was born in California and I'm Shoshone-Paiute from Duck Valley in Nevada and Northern Paiute out of Fort Bidwell in California. Both of my parents are Shoshone-Paiute and were born in Owyhee (my family's shorthand for the reservation). My mom grew up in Owyhee. My dad grew up in Southern California, near Sherman Indian High School (Sherman), where both of his parents worked.

Until a few years ago, I had never thought of myself as "mixed race," even though I'm light skinned. Recently I finally stopped to think about why. In short, both sides of my family are Native. My mom is half White, but we don't know who her White father was. So I haven't had the common mixed-race experience of parents of different races.

SK. I was regularly questioned about my racial identity, and since Indians generally talk about ethnicity in percentages—I assume because of blood quantum[1]—I always identified as half Zuni, half White. It was unusual to not be full Zuni, and classmates teased me about my language pronunciation so I stopped speaking my language. I am working on relearning it, and I regret my choice to let others judge my authenticity. Today, more kids in the village are mixed, and I have hope things are changing; it's less unusual to be a mixed Native person.

I was a nerd and recognized it, and it saved me from pressure to do drugs or alcohol, which were easily accessible. In sixth grade, kids were smoking weed (which was readily available), but being the nerd, they didn't ask me to join in. Also, I had no interest in drinking or smoking because my dad is a recovering alcoholic and my paternal grandmother died of lung cancer.

In that instance, it was beneficial to be different, but other times, it was a negative to stand out. I couldn't articulate it then, but now realize I wanted to get good grades so my different-ness would be positive and might distract classmates from teasing me about my mixed-ness.

I always liked reading (my parents are also readers), and we had a variety of books, magazines, and newspapers around the house, which I later recognized was not the norm in the village generally.

LT. I always had books around as a kid, too, because my parents liked to encourage my reading habit. Like you, recovering alcoholics in my family meant I chose to be a teetotaler in high school, thus upping the nerd quotient exponentially. I was also good at school, though growing up largely in California meant I was generally surrounded by a multiethnic mix of other nerdy kids.

IDENTITY WITHIN ACADEMIC LIBRARIES

Before we share our experiences in academic libraries, we thank Karin Griffin (2013) for sharing her story in "Pursuing Tenure and Promotion in the Academy: A Librarian's Cautionary Tale." We both read it, and her experiences navigating racism, sexism, and classism resonated with us.

SK. I have professional experience at a public library, tribal college library, and an academic library. My identity as a Native woman varied in prominence in each organization.

My first librarian position was in Albuquerque's public library system as a children's librarian. I knew two other Native employees; my identity rarely factored into my role in the library.

After working there for almost four years, I applied for and was hired as library director at the Institute of American Indian Arts (IAIA), an arts-focused tribal college. There my identity as a Zuni woman was integral to my role, and I felt added value to the organization.

At IAIA, many students also identified as mixed with multiple tribal affiliations and non-Native backgrounds and noted them all. It was invigorating to be part of an organization with a culture of acceptance, a space with freedom to share stories that didn't fit the mythical "Native American experience."

LT. One of my earlier library jobs was as the librarian at Sherman. At the time, my mom also worked there, as did several cousins. The legacy of Indian boarding schools is terrible, yet Sherman endures because the mission has shifted and many of the current staff are Native.

Native identity was also a part of my professional identity at Sherman. Tribal affiliations often formed the basis of the various cliques, though the usual high school groups also came into play—like athletes and nerds. Though I feel like the "rez" experience is seen as the more authentic experience because it means you grow up inside your tribal community, at Sherman, I also felt like my urban background was just seen as a part of the larger diversity of Native experiences.

Since leaving Sherman, my Native identity has not been a part of my professional identity. In fact, as a result of talking with you, I realized I wasn't listing my tribal affiliations because I didn't want non-Indians to think I was trying to get some advantage from being Native. Sooo . . . I'm now including that information everywhere—I'm proud to be Shoshone-Paiute.

SK. That's great! For me, the benefits to working in a Native organization became outweighed by barriers to professional achievement. There the hurdles came from gender and age, rather than ethnicity. I decided to find a path to a position at the University of New Mexico, thinking it would provide opportunities for growth and advancement while staying in New Mexico near family and my tribal community.

Getting here wasn't easy: I applied twice, and the second time I was offered a faculty position. Throughout the process, my identity as a Native woman played a large part in how colleagues viewed me and, ultimately, options for promotion within the organization.

During the interview, I was told about a change: after receiving unexpected funding, two people would be hired for the position of an Access Services Librarian. And instead of solely being in Access Services, both hires would have duties in the Indigenous Nations Library Program (INLP).[2] When offered this option, I felt conflicted. I had experience working with Native students, so the split time probably seemed a natural fit, despite noting throughout the interview process that I wanted a new challenge. I accepted the arrangement and with the other hire (a White male colleague who I had worked with at the public library) we shared hours in INLP. But it was an unequal split: I officially spent twenty hours there and he worked for ten, and my office was physically located in INLP while his office was in Access Services.

LT. From my outsider's perspective, it looked like they shoved the Native person in the Native program, even though they hired her to do something else. I actually know all of the people involved in this process, and I like all of them as individuals. I don't think they are racists, but it was still a problem. This happened at our institution, and it was racist.

SK. This situation was created by well-intentioned people I like, too, but is an example of how structural racism can be invisible within an organization. I was glad to be hired but have felt uncomfortable about what happened.

Looking back, there weren't the same opportunities for advancement because of the initial hiring decision. Rather than being in the busy Access Services department (the official job), I was in a geographically separate location, tucked away in a physically separate space.

Also, if there had been a separate hiring process specifically for INLP, maybe someone else would have been a better fit. I did a good job and supported students despite how I ended up in the position almost inadvertently.

Finding the term "cultural taxation"[3] while doing research helped me name what happened. And hearing your perspective about the situation was helpful because you validated this wasn't just in my head.

LT. It was during this time that we started chatting and getting to know each other. I remember telling you that I was frustrated watching this happen. Your work in INLP wasn't as visible in the library as work in Access Services. But you being you, you succeeded anyway.

AUTHENTICITY AND CHECKLISTS

LT. Patricia Hill Collins (Hill Collins 2009) writes about "controlling images," which are typically images held by the dominant society of non-dominant groups.

One of the biggest controlling images of Native women is the old-timey Edward Curtis[4]–style picture that leaves us in the past. So, if we are here in the academic library and not on the reservation, how "authentic" are we? You and I have also talked about Native checklists—both the ones that the dominant culture uses, and the ones that Native folks use with other Natives. I think these are controlling images of a sort.

Figure 3.1. **Paiute squaws and children. Albumen silver print, J. Paul Getty Museum.**

SK. Yes, I feel there's underlying expectations of some non-Native librarians about what a Native librarian should be and do. Are you and I not supporting Native people because we're in a university, not a tribal community? I'm so appreciative of people in our tribal communities because we need them to continue the traditions. But we also need to show Native kids anything is possible, to be *here* and be ourselves. We're not less Native because we chose to work in academia.

Because I'm light skinned, Indians usually don't know I'm Indian. This happens in my own village, which hurts, but I've learned to deal with it. And with my last name, most non-Natives ask if I'm Polish, then I jokingly say, let me explain my life story.

LT. I think this is a common mixed-race experience that sometimes you feel like you have to share your whole life history to help people make sense of you. I could always pull out my tribal ID, which states my official blood quantum. But does that actually quantify my experience in any real way?

SK. Right!?! It's complicated because, depending on the situation, I don't always feel like explaining. Especially here in New Mexico with our state slogan as a place to "experience" Native culture, I've felt people's expectations to be invited to ceremonial dances. But I don't invite everyone; I have to trust the person first because those ceremonies have to be respected.

LT. The other thing I feel like people sometimes expect from me is a tragic story. Whenever I mention Sherman, for instance. People with any knowledge of Native history know that boarding schools . . .

SK. Equal bad.

LT. Yes, true—full stop. And also . . . my grandparents met at Sherman and decided to raise their six children in Southern California. My parents met there. Both my mom and I worked there.

But, my grandma was fluent in both Shoshone and Paiute, and she didn't pass those languages along to her children—a choice also made by many immigrants. I couldn't say what my grandma experienced at the Sherman *Institute* of the 1920s that might have influenced that choice.[5] So there's definitely a loss, but not only.

SK. That's the problem of not recognizing the diversity of our own experiences. Natives also judge each other's experiences, saying someone isn't really Indian because they aren't from the rez or they don't look a certain way. Being Native mixed with some White, which is a whole other thing within Native culture that . . . (both laughing)

LT. Is not typically a good thing, dear reader.

SK. No, it's not awesome to some Native people to be part White. Though it added to my different-ness, I have always acknowledged and valued both sides of my family. Ignoring that diversity within our communities can be harmful to mixed kids. It was to me.

LT. I also have a lot of mixed relatives, and not just part White, but Tongan, Mexican, Filipino, and so on.

SK. Yet we don't often see representations in dominant culture of mixed Native people, which reinforces the controlling, stereotypical images. We have to share our experiences, especially those different from the outsider-created "norm."

A college classmate told me he heard Indians got free trucks from the government, and I told him that would be great, but no, we don't receive free government trucks. I imagine those stereotypes come from misunderstanding the relationship tribes have with the federal government and their legal trust responsibilities to us. The United States created this relationship to atone for all their policies and actions that killed us, obliterated our culture, and took our land.

LT. In return, we got commodity cheese. Which, to be fair, is delicious.

SK. Agreed.

EXPECTATIONS: OURS AND THEIRS

SK. Even though we have a fair amount of Native faculty (Natvig 2016) and students (Office of Institutional Analytics 2017b) at UNM, our non-Native colleagues are mostly unaware of how culture and identity affect our daily work lives.

Like the day I was going to my reference shift and got pulled into conversation with an elder Pueblo student. As a younger Pueblo woman, I had to listen, not interrupt, and let them guide the conversation. Then a colleague, also a woman of color, came and interrupted the conversation (ignoring the elder), scolding me for being late to my shift and left. I was shocked at her rudeness to the elder and to me as a colleague. I apologized to the elder and later my desk partner, explaining why I was late. She understood and had no problem.

To have a coworker—who apparently didn't understand the work it takes to build these relationships—not only undermine my professional efforts but also disrespect a Pueblo elder was infuriating. This incident (and others) made clear that many librarians do not recognize efforts with our communities as actual work. I believe some colleagues assume I have innate "Native" knowledge that makes it "easy" for me to engage Native people with library resources.

LT. I think this kind of work can be mistaken for just chatting or socializing—and I think this is true of a lot of the outreach work we do. But in your specific context, that assumption is particularly damaging.

SK. I advocated during a search committee (supported by three White colleagues) for inclusion of a preferred qualification of Indigenous language proficiency for a special collections position, considering our collections include many materials in local Native languages. The chair's response was, to paraphrase, any candidate who speaks a Native language should work in INLP. What I took from this was "stay in your place" and don't try to present cultural knowledge as beneficial; it is simply tolerated.

LT. I've got a bit of a long story weirdly related to that idea. Up until recently, my research focused on threshold concepts and information literacy—which became somewhat controversial. One particular critique started with a blog post written by a prominent academic librarian where he speculated that threshold concepts "probably" reflected a White, middle-class, educated perspective but ended with "I don't really know" (Wilkinson 2014). However, a different group of White academic librarians ran with this speculation and repeated or alluded to it with more force in various public forums.

My work with threshold concepts started at a public institution with an over 80 percent non-White student body, working with two colleagues to improve our teaching. By the time this "elite" criticism was floating around, our research team was half women of color, three-quarters community college librarians, and all of us working at institutions with very diverse populations. It was pretty ironic to hear our ideas being criticized as elite when we compared the composition of our group and our contexts to that of academic libraries as a whole.

As a Native woman, getting lectured about privilege, even indirectly, by White male academic librarians was annoying. Perhaps less obvious, but more provoking, was the underlying assumption that influential work not directly related to people of color topics would, *of course*, be published by White librarians.

SK. Which comes back to the idea that Native people and our talents and knowledge should stay where they belong.

LT. Yes! But that experience made me tougher. I met a bunch of engaging colleagues, and I got to travel to various cool spots to give talks—like Qatar and Bulgaria—intimidating, but worth it.

SUPPORT AND SUCCESS

SK. We revisited the difficult things so let's share why we choose to continue and how we help each other stay sane!

LT. Right! I try to support my colleagues by calling attention to the good work they do without putting them on the spot. One commonality I have found in my own experience and that of other Native librarians is a sense of humility. This is often misperceived by the dominant culture as low self-confidence or lack of pride. This can lead to problems when we are required to trumpet our accomplishments in order to keep our jobs—like throughout the tenure process.

I was also taught to share credit because there is no way I can accomplish anything without the help of my community. However, the dominant academic culture is often competitive, and some folks take as much as they can get away with.

I've also found that the dominant culture tends to favor those who always have something to say. I've actually learned over the years to speak up more frequently, but I'm not comfortable doing it.

SK. It's hard to learn the norms of academia, which sometimes seem counter to the values I grew up learning, like acknowledging the role of community in success versus individual achievement.

LT. It seems like many things that Native librarians have to learn are tacit cultural knowledge. That learning and effort typically goes unacknowledged except in the instances where we violate norms and are sometimes penalized for that rather than for our actual performance. That's why it's nice to have Native colleagues—I can relax and just be. And I love the work I get to do with *all* of my amazing colleagues—we have a lot of fun!

SK. I appreciate you and other Native colleagues because we laugh and commiserate about everything. Jody Gray (2017) shared her experience of building community as a way to succeed, and I feel we created a similar community. I would not have attempted a tenure-track position if it wasn't for the encouragement of Native colleagues, including you. This is why it's so important to make libraries and librarians reflective of our communities!

ENDING THOUGHTS; OR, WHAT WAS THE POINT?

Circling back to the beginning, we hope readers have heard in our stories the variation we have experienced as Native women librarians. Through conversation we realized our similar paths: childhoods as Indigenerds who found a place in libraries and books; the unique existence of being Native librarians in tribal schools; and regularly being viewed as outsiders within our communities. We have existed and continue to exist on the margins of multiple communities, and in sharing these stories with each other, we realized we were not the "only one." Hopefully others will recognize their own experiences in this narrative and realize the same.

NOTES

1. "Blood quantum laws or Indian blood laws are those enacted in the United States and the former colonies to define qualification by ancestry as Native American, sometimes in relation to tribal membership. These laws were developed by Euro-Americans and thus did not

32 *Sarah R. Kostelecky and Lori Townsend*

necessarily reflect how Native Americans had traditionally identified themselves or members of their in-group" (*Wikipedia*, "Blood Quantum Laws")

2. The Indigenous Nations Library Program (INLP) provides information services and academic support to the UNM community and engages in library outreach with indigenous communities. See http://libguides.unm.edu/INLP for more on this unique program.

3. Padilla (1994) says faculty of color "frequently find ourselves having to respond to situations that are imposed on us by the administration which assumes that we are best suited for specific tasks because of our race/ethnicity or our presumed knowledge of cultural differences."

4. Edward Curtis was an American photographer working around the turn of the century who became famous for his portraits of American Indians.

5. If you are interested in the history of Sherman Indian High School, they have a wonderful museum right on campus, run by Lorene Sisquoc, a great example of an amazing Native woman whose work supports cultural preservation efforts. See http://www.shermanindian.org/museum/.

Chapter Four

Moving On and Upward

A Conversation with Dexter R. Evans

On April 14, 2017, Teresa (TYN) and Jorge (JRLM) conducted a telephone interview with Dexter R. Evans (DE). A list of questions was sent to him prior to the call, which lasted just under two hours. Teresa and Jorge then transcribed and edited the conversation and sent it to Mr. Evans for his review, along with the recording.

TYN and JRLM: *Tell us about why you became a librarian.* **DE:** I really wanted to do something to help my mother and people in my community. I wanted to help find information for those I knew who just didn't know where to start or what to ask. My mother was disabled, and I knew there were a number of programs available to her that we weren't sure how to find. I just wanted to be a researcher and find the needle in the haystack.

    TYN and JRLM: *What are you passionate about?* **DE:** I'm passionate about service, education, and helping others find their lightbulb moment. Twenty years later, I still get very excited and just as electrified when it comes to sharing my thoughts, my insights, and experiences to help benefit someone else with setting their goals.

    TYN and JRLM: *What is the biggest issue you have faced/addressed in your career since 1996?* **DE:** Professionally, it was trying to put myself in a position to build and gain a sense of respect, to strengthen my aptitude of understanding new technology, and learning new concepts. I needed to keep my skills updated with the changing technology in order to help influence and contribute my insights for change with the companies that would employ me. After meeting some very charismatic leaders, a couple of librarians who were reps, and the support of my library school mentor, I thought I'd take a stab at this role for a bit. On the flip side, I always felt, two or three years, I'd be back working in a library because I would miss the students and the camaraderie. I'd also miss going into the classroom and working with faculty.

DE: [*Motivation to change the world/be a change agent?*] I've visited a number of academic sites and corporations with minimal to no online resources, no R&D (research and development) teams because libraries were viewed as a non-revenue-generating line item. There have been few librarians that have managed to maintain their jobs over the years as most libraries have downsized or closed. Corporate executives and some school presidents don't usually make the connection with the technology being used to deliver resources and provide valuable content to keep their companies or college students competitive. Being part of that as a change agent, to help educate them, has been incredible. I do enjoy making the sale, but it's more about building good relationships, filling a need, and asking myself: did I find a problem, answer the questions, and provide a solution. I'll give you a personal example.

My sister and I are very close; she's two years older than me. She works in the banking industry as a processing officer for mortgages. No one in my family, after all of these years, really understood what I do for work. She was the one who pushed me to go to college and really supported me making sure I attended somebody's school. Companies are changing, really pushing online course development, and her company was no different. Her employer began suggesting and recommending e-books to their staff, and she selected titles on self-help, self-motivation, and keeping yourself and your colleagues energized about work, time management, and work flow. [After reading three of these titles, she looked at the bottom of the screen and saw EBSCO.] "Wait a minute, my brother works for EBSCO!" She called me from work. "Don't you work for a company called E-B-S-C-O?" I said, "Yes." "This is what you do??!" I said, "Yes, Bridget, that's one of the hundreds of online resources my company provides to our customers." She said, "Ahhh, I told everybody that was my brother!" She was so proud and happy to have made that connection.

The reason this story is significant is this: we grew up in a small town in Texas of about 20,000 people, and my sister was very shy, and absolutely was terrified of the idea when I moved her and my mother and her two kids to Dallas. And thirteen years later, she has moved into four different positions, at three different banks, and each bank has reached out to hire her. **TYN:** *Does she understand how that connects to her insisting you go to college?* **DE:** Yes. She would always say, "That's who you are, Dexter. That's what I love about you; you make the complicated seem easier. You break it down for me."

TYN: *Well, the other thing is that it's difficult, I think, for people like you and I who don't have children. We still have to figure out how we are going to leave our mark. A lot of times we don't get a chance to reflect on what impact our work has had.* **DE:** We have one of our greatest humanitarians who said, "I've seen the promised land. I may not get there with you, but we, as a people, will get to the promised land."[1] Now, would he have truly known what his impact was to the world, so we have to push, forge ahead, and fight to educate and create more examples for the next generation. Your name [Teresa] is in print, your name is inked in a published work, and I can read it and share it for years to come. And that was important to me. Because when we grew up and had family reunions you could talk about uncle's, auntie's, and cousin's achievements, as family members would share those stories that we may not have known about otherwise. Many stories may not have been recorded, and many may never be told. So, in our circle of family and friends, it makes a difference to those who will be involved enough and read about this rich history. I love my family, and I love my niece and nephew very much. I just want to leave an indelible impression on them. I feel it's my obligation to share my journey with them so they may use my accomplishments as a source of strength and motivation based on my love for life, people, adventure, and culture. I will not be a statistic to them, and I rose above the conditions and challenges within my childhood community. This [book] is very important because it's OURS. It's our little circle and for those who will get a chance to read it and share it with other circles. Everyone's circle can touch and influence so many other aspiring minds and dreamers. **TYN:** *Define "our little circle."*[2] **DE:** That just means a group of individuals who believe in a similar cause or in a similar profession, wanting to affect change in a positive manner. The world is very small, and we meet people ending up realizing they know someone you know. We have to do our part to encourage each other, serve our communities, and communicate with those who can be positively affected by our words. I recognize you have to keep doing what you do to improve because sooner or later, you will collide with another circle. And your circle will grow and expand outward into the world.

TYN: *Am I in your circle?* **DE:** Yeah, absolutely. **TYN:** *Or is our circle just what's around us? And we impact, or not, in our circle, and then it ripples outward?j* **DE:** It does; it ripples outward. You made me a part of your circle twenty years ago! **TYN:** *Yeah, we're in the same circle. Now you're in my circle, Jorge.* **JRLM:** *Yeah, all of us.* **DE:** Yeah right, so now, we bring Jorge in, and he's in the circle, and he'll get from us what we share, and he'll feed his spirit outward to others, to try and create another circle. Because really, we have to rely upon each other to get that support, to share those supportive words. And sometimes you feel embarrassed, you feel fearful, you feel like someone will reject you or laugh at you if you have a different idea or different thoughts, and you want to have a circle of people that you feel comfortable with. We're adults, but I certainly need my colleagues on days I'm struggling or [when] I am challenged about something. And then when you accomplish your goals and dreams, hopefully, you know, we're always able to celebrate each other. Pulling in more people makes a bigger circle of people to influence and help so many more. That's how we keep growing. **TYN:** Do you have White people in your circle? **DE:** I share with all ethnicities, religions, [and] professions and love listening to different perspectives in my circle. It all adds to my education and continues to mold and shape my growing perspectives of life. I accept everyone who wants to share something that can be used as a tool for learning.

JRLM: *What's your proudest accomplishment thus far?* **DE:** There are two that come to mind immediately. One, at the University of North Texas library school when I graduated, I was named co-outstanding student of that graduating class. Coming from my background of a single-parent home, raising two kids in a low-income apartment community, a disabled mother with no "real job" prospects, that was an absolute blessing. My mother would say, "If you're open to being yourself and receiving love, then you will be one of the richest people in the world." And I never understood that as a child. By the time my sister and I were teenagers, we experienced that light-bulb moment. It's what pushed me to make every day count. As I was preparing to leave for college, my mother said, "Make us proud by doing well and learning what that school has to offer. Don't be too afraid." That's how [those] two women in my life really pushed me. I never lost focus and gained more confidence. The four years I spent at the University of North Texas were the most wonderful and motivating years of my life; I thought of my mother and sister each and every day when I didn't want to go to class, and when I thought I couldn't understand chemistry. [Smiles.] Even in library school when I took eighteen hours, I never thought I could accomplish completing the requirements. I had my Michael Jordan moment when I earned a 4.0 GPA during my first semester in library school after being admitted on a conditional basis. He [Jordan] was an average athlete who made a few big baskets bringing him national notoriety before becoming a pro athlete, but because he worked hard and had enough people supporting him to be better each day, once he found his rhythm and flow for each opportunity, he started to shine in every performance and never looked back. I found my place within a few opportunities to be my own Jordan and wanted to keep them coming. And I never looked back.

The second one was when I received a copy of *IOOV* 1996. That is the absolute honest truth. I swear that seeing my name in print inspired me more than ever before. I knew I probably wouldn't want to pursue being a professor, because I had other ideas, other dreams, and other goals. When I see the name Dr. Teresa Neely, I say, "I know her, and I know a part of her talent that shines during the writing process, helping all the contributors in this project find their flow to write and record their story." I'm just happy to be able to be a part of this collection of stories in print once again.

TYN: *So all through college you're still doubting yourself, even though you have two strong Black women in your corner, and then, you get to college and you have two Black men there for you?* **DE:** Yeah. Exactly, you're right. I still doubted myself until the day I was informed I achieved the required credit hours to graduate; I still didn't accept it. I continued being afraid that I would receive a letter or phone message that I was not approved to graduate. That represented the kind of doubt a few people in my childhood community planted in your head, coupled with remembering times when my mother was not approved to purchase items we wanted for our apartment or the holidays. I wished for days of the past when there was a strong support system from residents that would make it their job to encourage and outright demand from young people a sense of pride in representing the community at the next level having the privilege of going to college. As I matured, I realized the small amount of resources she [my mother] had raising me and my sister, and I was certain that if I didn't make it in college, at least I knew this; I knew how to survive. I learned and accepted that I had this ability to communicate well and negotiate opening doors of opportunities. My mentor said to me [before I registered for graduate school], "Dexter, I can help open the doors for you, my child, but you're going to have to do the work to stay there. And I believe you have what it takes to do it."

So that's why I applaud women who juggle life's events while caring for family, providing shelter, bringing home the bacon, and continuing to push for their dreams and pushing others. It excites me when I get to speak with Dr. Neely, because there's admiration and respect, to always show my appreciation, as a Black man. I have [driven] myself to make sure that I'm contributing to a circle and be looked upon as a resource of inspiration by young people especially from places like my community. Women have always set the bar for me, keeping me motivated to do better since my days in school and now as an adult in the library profession.

TYN: *In listening to what you're saying, I hear a lot of emphasis being placed on things that are carved in stone and leaving your mark and making sure that you impact people in your circle and that it keeps going. Tell me why you haven't published anymore?* **DE:** I haven't published anymore because I've wanted to pursue other avenues to make certain to build upon something tangible and concrete ahead in the future. I wanted to create a legacy to leave behind for my family, my alma mater, and to a few bright spots in my life that have budding futures ahead. **TYN:** *So you were motivated to work to make more money?* **DE:** Yes, create more resources and wealth. It wasn't just about money, but more about building resources to create wealth. Resources could open doors that created income and more opportunities to establish a structured path beyond my life. My goal has been to work hard to plant seeds that would grow to support my family, charities, foundations, and scholarships supporting people like me and those that have demonstrated a passion for life by serving others. Real estate is what drove this machine for me and the reason why I haven't transitioned back into publishing with all the challenges and stress of trying to manage it all. This machine will hopefully allow me to create equity in my portfolio so that helping to start a scholarship fund or pay a student's tuition would be the end result.

TYN: *What is it like to be a Black man and do what you do? Because Texas and Oklahoma universities are probably very White.*[3] **DE:** Very much. There are still a lot of places here in Texas that are very White, and it's still very isolating. Because once we leave most conferences after seeing a few familiar faces of color, we're back to being the only minority, in most cases, within your place of employment. That's what it feels like. And you have to have a commitment and desire to add flavor and your perspective to your environment whether in a library or as a vendor.

JRLM: *Has there been an increase in folks of color in the industry since you've been in it? Or a decrease, or has it stayed the same?* **DE:** I feel like it's been an increase because there's so many new faces of color popping up over the past few years, and it's delightful to have a new level of interaction with new blood. There are more librarians of color in library positions versus corporate vendors. However, corporate vendor roles are changing in phases with more people of color, a sprinkle of African Americans, and more women of color based on my observations. It used to be a pretty homogenous culture when I first started in the 90s, but more Latinos and international hires have become a regular occurrence. It's encouraging to see more faces that represent our nation helping to broaden this library industry.

For example, the company I worked for acquired a few strategic companies, and we added new personnel from the pool of candidates to be on our team, similar to my hiring, and they both were Black men (a VP from New York, and a director from Louisiana). The team also [inherited] three or four Black women to fill positions on our growing team. I met them all and offered my support and insight while navigating through the organization. It makes me very proud of my leadership team bringing aboard the best talent and recruiting good candidates.

TYN: *When do you think you will retire?* **JRLM:** *What is next for Dexter Evans?*

DE: I'm going to say this: I have no concept or idea on when I'll retire. One, because I have too damn much energy to not give all I have while I'm alive. I love waking up and looking forward to what I'll discover or who I'll meet on a given day that may change my thoughts. I recognize I have limitations on being able to travel by air and driving long distances as I get older;

but I tell you, when I stand up, and I see those smiles and feel the anticipation, the stage is set and it's time to give them all you have to offer! I have a tremendous amount of passion for this industry, and it has been good to me. I started out wanting to help my mother find information for beneficial services and a job and ended up becoming a librarian. The library industry has given me and my family more than I ever thought possible in my career journey.

I never had a plan. I just wanted to do what felt right. I'm always looking for new ideas and inspiration to recharge my engine so I can continue building and sharing. I just love life; it's similar to a deck of cards. And whatever card comes out, I want to explore how I can play it. It's up to me how I decide to play that card. And having a network of good, smart, resourceful people opens my mind on what makes my card powerful or influential if played right. I don't consider [what I do] mundane work because I love doing it. I've heard people say that old cliché, "If you have fun what you do every day, it isn't work." **TYN:** *And everybody doesn't have that. Most people that we know have jobs, they don't have careers.* **DE:** Right. Exactly. **TYN:** *And they definitely aren't having fun when they get there.* **DE:** I'm about nineteen years in this industry and have traveled over 90 percent of the United States and never thought I'd be in this role this long. This job has exposed me to many wonderful people and offered great opportunities for me to grow and learn my craft. This career path has given me a strong sense of purpose in being able to utilize my energy and my intellect to the best of my abilities.

NOTES

1. See Dr. Martin Luther King Jr's "I've Been to the Mountaintop" speech at http://www.americanrhetoric.com/speeches/mlkivebeentothemountaintop.htm.

2. This interview was recorded in April 2017. During the summer of 2017, Jorge began referring to the contributors to *IOOV* 2016 as the Collective. Dexter's response to my question indicates that these two concepts, the Collective and "our circle," are similar in definition despite the perceived scope/reach of each "group," physically and figuratively.

3. Dexter is regional sales manager for EBSCO Information Services in North Texas and Oklahoma. He is responsible for colleges and universities throughout a large, spread out geographical area.

Chapter Five

Boundaries of the Body—Finding My(whole)self

Rituals and Rites

Jennifer Brown

When I think about what influenced my path toward librarianship and the creative arts, I am immediately struck by the nature of what it means to *give*, to leave behind traditions and rituals that shape those we love. My mom, dad, and sister have given me many things, but chief among them were a passion for books and the encouragement of my developing a kind of boundless creativity.

When I was ten, I applied for my first library card; my mom took me to the Carson Library branch of the Los Angeles Public Library system, walked me to the circulation desk, and had me ask for an application. It was probably foolish to be so excited, hearing the staff say things like "you can check out this many books at one time" or "make sure you bring your books back before the due date, if you don't want a fine," but I was giddy. Going to the library and choosing my next adventure quickly became a ritual, a rite.

When I was twelve, I wrote my first short story: "The Bully." I know this because my mom *still* has a copy, and it's slated to go into a scrapbook chronicling memorable moments from my family's early years. Now, it's probably got plenty of flaws (like issues with characterization or inconsistent narrative voice), but it's one of the first original stories I ever told—a piece with my own style and creative flair. Telling tales became central to both discovering and expressing my voice, to understanding and pushing against the systemic "-isms" that colored my experiences. To imagining worlds where Black women were central characters; where LGBTQ teens opened portals to other realities; where neurodiverse protagonists thwarted villains and grew within the narrative. Worlds where I might see myself, and others I knew, reflected—triumphantly, *truthfully*. Where we might be seen as both worthy and whole.

These rituals felt all the more important, especially when I considered the discrimination my parents were subjected to throughout their lives; Donna and Richard Brown were first-generation students who didn't have access to the same kind of guidance or help others had when applying to colleges. It's thanks to them that I was raised with higher education as a core value in our family. There was no question whether we'd go to college; we would, but what we did once we were there was entirely up to us. So finding my way into librarianship, while negotiating my continued desire to write professionally, set up an early dichotomy that's defined my journey thus far: choosing between public service or starving artistry.

Well, here is where I posit the question: Why not *both*? This chapter will chronicle my choice to become a science librarian while dedicating myself to a time-consuming, yet soul-sustaining, side hustle as a speculative fiction writer. Woven through this larger narrative will be a focus on the things that've made this experience challenging: the Whiteness of academic librarianship and traditional publishing, and finding my voice within these realms; encountering tokenism and microaggressions within the academy; and finding ways to balance my personal and professional goals amid the loss of a parent.

MLS OR MFA: WEIGHING MY OPTIONS

A wonderfully talented librarian recently coined a term that's transformed the way I view my entry into the profession: "vocational awe." Fobazi Ettarh defines this concept as "the idea that libraries as institutions are inherently good. It assumes that some or all core aspects of the profession are beyond critique, and it, in turn, underpins many librarians' sense of identity and emotional investment in the profession" (Ettarh 2017).

Ettarh does an excellent job showcasing how this concept reinforces White supremacy in libraries, but I'd like to key in on the "identity and emotional investment" portion; it's what piqued my interest in librarianship to begin with, and what now contributes to bouts of burnout since entering the profession in 2015. When I decided to apply to graduate programs, I had just come out of working in the private sector; every waking second had gone to furthering someone else's profit margins, advocating for products I didn't identify with, and advancing an agenda that didn't seem to have any real impact on the outside world. I'd just graduated from the University of California, Berkeley (Cal), and had spent the last four years critiquing texts within media studies and English; I'd also spent that time working as a student employee at the Doe Memorial Graduate Library, where I'd come to view libraries (and, by extension, librarianship) as an extraordinary profession built upon foundations of equity. Even small encounters (like finding a book that someone desperately needed in the re-shelving area or helping someone navigate the stacks) felt more meaningful than any task I'd been performing in my private sector role. Not only that, but our student and support staff were incredibly diverse; I worked alongside other Black and Brown folks, not realizing that the profession purposefully erects barriers to define their work differently than what credentialed librarians do, and thus I believed that my work in libraries would *always* resemble that environment. I assumed the diversity I saw at the paraprofessional level would be replicated once I moved into the professional realm.

Leaving my job in the private sector was simple; it was the product of a summer internship, and though it could've been parlayed into a full-time opportunity, I opted instead to focus on finding a more fulfilling career path. For me, that meant going back to school.

When considering my options, I made two separate lists: one filled with the "top" library schools (gathered from the yearly *US News & World Report* rankings), the other brimming with the best creative writing programs in the country (according to a list published on the *Poets & Writers Magazine* website). Lists feel like wells of possibility; whether penning goals or dreams, they all seem like potential realities on paper. Weighing the pros and cons of these two choices was challenging, but I had to be honest with myself—I'd never lost the desire to hone my craft and eventually publish in traditional trade fiction markets. This initially gave master of fine arts (MFA) programs an edge over library school. What's more, I'd watched my sister complete an MFA at Mills College in Oakland, expertly crafting narratives that would go on to secure her entry into the coveted Clarion West writer's workshop and, eventually, a career as a literary agent. Watching talented Black women achieve their dreams inspires a heady kind of appreciation, but seeing Stephanie grow within this field was particularly empowering.

Still, impostor syndrome struck hard.

I didn't have a single finished writing sample ready, and I wasn't confident in my ability to craft any by the upcoming application deadlines; I hadn't published a single story, ever, in my life; and the one writing sample I did submit in undergrad couldn't earn me entry into one of Cal's coveted creative writing classes. Once, I gawked while a former friend waxed poetically about how close her family was with a *New York Times* best-selling novelist and how that author had given her advice on how to chart the publishing industry, sharing information that I could only *dream* of coming across. The business of selling books is tricky; you can be agented and still have editors reject your manuscript for not being "marketable" enough to mainstream, White audiences. However, recent efforts, such as the #We-

NeedDiverseBooks campaign, have helped make way for new voices, perspectives, and stories. By the time we were juniors, her work had already been published in literary magazines; she'd gotten into the creative writing classes I couldn't; and she was graduating a year early with exciting prospects on the horizon.

I took her prose and her privilege and weighed them against mine, believing my words and passion for the field were not enough.

Not typical enough.

Not interesting enough.

Not White enough.

I let impostor syndrome chart the course of my boat; I let it tangle about the sails, steering me away from possibility. Its compass became my own. In that entire struggle, librarianship felt like a beacon. If my stories weren't ever destined to leave my computer, I could at least spend my career collecting, curating, and recommending good books. Not only that, but I was raised with the knowledge that one needs to provide for oneself; stability is key. Writing might fuel me, but I couldn't eat those words—and the MFA didn't guarantee publication.

Thus, I thought librarianship might fulfill me personally and professionally; the research I did into programs seemed to reaffirm the field's inherent goodness while masking its many flaws, and this rooted my identity and emotional investment in the field.

GRADUATE SCHOOL

In many ways, library school provided me with powerful wake-up calls. I'd enrolled at the University of Michigan's School of Information (UMSI), and it was the first time I'd lived so far from home; it was also the first time I'd glimpsed Confederate flags hanging from balconies and plastered in windows, reminding me of my place and symbolizing much of my time there. The diversity I witnessed as a student library employee felt practically nonexistent in my program; we boasted a sizeable population of international students, but few other ethnic groups. Those of us who were interested in diversity and equity at the institution worked hard to carve space for ourselves within the academy; I went on to collaborate with wonderful peers (who, I'm pleased to say, are now wonderful colleagues I continue to work with) in UMSI's Multiethnic Information Exchange (MIX) organization. My library and information science (LIS) program wasn't entirely bad; there were faculty who took ample opportunities to make us better educators and professionals. Everything from courses like Technology and Accessibility and Information Literacy for Teaching and Learning, to preservation faculty willing to call out White supremacist practices in archives, went a long way toward bettering the overall environment. However, I was often *still* the only (or one of two, depending on how many of us were in the class) person asking my peers to be accountable, and to willingly critique our institution when it got things wrong.

To exist within this field, then, became about constantly being seen as *other*—first, and foremost.

Amid these struggles, I also underwent a serious family emergency. After finishing my first semester in library school, my family and I spent that Christmas in and out of an intensive care unit, my father's health rapidly deteriorating. His heart stopped twice, and he underwent countless tests, before doctors finally discovered the culprit: my dad had Lou Gehrig's disease, or Amyotrophic Lateral Sclerosis (ALS).

We were told he might only live for a few more months, perhaps less. And while efforts like the #IceBucketChallenge have raised awareness of and funding for ALS, there is no cure—not for my father, and not for the thousands of others currently living with this disease (ALS Association 2017).

I spent the rest of that holiday break struggling to carry graduate school responsibilities alongside the trauma of what my mom, sister, and extended family were going through. At that time, I had planned to apply for Alternative Spring Break internships, get a jump on course materials for the following semester, and prepare to return to my library assistantship in the spring.

I learned how to manage school, as a system; however, life hadn't taught me what to do if one of my parents became terminally ill. I considered leaving my program to return home and help care for my dad—ALS tends to manifest differently from patient to patient, but many end up losing vital motor functions as the disease progresses. But my mom and sister urged me to continue my studies, so we supported each other from afar.

FIRST PROFESSIONAL POSITION

Much of the librarian I am today can be directly correlated to the advice and support I received from crucial mentors; in particular, my director within Michigan's University Library Associate (ULA) program helped me understand the profession more deeply than I ever could have on my own. At the time, the University of Michigan Libraries (U-M) had a partnership with UMSI; applicants who applied for one of five ULA positions, if selected, were awarded full funding for their graduate degree and given a part-time, professional assistantship in one of U-M's academic libraries. Mine was located at the Harlan Hatcher Graduate Library, within their User Information and Discovery Services department. Under the tutelage of Karen Reiman-Sendi, and wonderful colleagues at the library's Knowledge Navigation Center, I learned the ins and outs of technology librarianship, provided instruction for undergraduates, and completed a capstone research project that investigated the use of photogrammetry as a preservation method for cultural heritage artifacts. These experiences, and their technology focus in particular, prepared me for my current role as the emerging technologies coordinator, a fairly new position at Columbia University's Science and Engineering Libraries.

Now, I never thought I'd end up in science librarianship; my background is solidly in the humanities and social sciences, so I assumed that would direct where I landed. However, what drew me to science librarianship was having an opportunity to work at the bleeding edge of discovery; I love collaborating with bright, engaged students who're shaping our technological futures, with faculty who are pioneering scientific advancements. The emerging technologies coordinator role seemed to offer all of this and more while building from the skills I'd gained in my graduate program. More than that, my institution has been incredibly wonderful about allowing me to define what this position is for myself. Because I love teaching information literacy sessions, they immediately incorporated me into the team of librarians that teach first year information literacy sessions in Columbia's University Writing Program. They've also been incredibly supportive of my involvement with larger campus bodies, such as Columbia's university-wide Race, Ethnicity, and Inclusion Task Force. I'm grateful for the freedom they entrust staff with because it's allowed me to innovate in ways that stretch beyond this role's original boundaries.

However, copious amounts of freedom can't cure the profession's ills. I've found technology librarianship, which includes everything from STEM (science, technology, engineering, and math) to digital humanities, to be largely dominated by privileged White men; when you couple this with statistics that cite librarianship is 89 percent White (Davis and Hall 2007), or with the fact that navigating PWIs (primarily White institutions) means traversing racist, segregationist, sexist, homophobic, and ableist histories, it's difficult to sustain the rose-colored glasses that vocational awe begets. And though I love crafting innovative services that advance my institution's research efforts, there's still something to be said about not seeing yourself reflected within the disciplines you serve. I don't always have the luxury of working with faculty and students who look like me or share my background.

Alongside this, I struggled to cope with my father's worsening illness while adjusting to life in New York City. While I was learning the subway system, my mom was practicing how to suction mucus from my dad's tracheal tube; while I attempted to cover groceries, my family dealt with unaffordable care facilities to support him. I called home every day, offering as much support as possible, but it didn't make living thousands of miles away, or struggling through impostor syndrome at work, any easier. I'm grateful for my extended family's help during this time; every meaningful visit aunts and uncles paid him, every home-cooked meal my grandmother prepared for my mom, and every other supportive gesture each of them made went a long way toward filling my dad's last years with love and light. But I'm especially proud of my mom for opting to become my dad's primary caregiver, personally ensuring he received excellent medical care. Because of all their efforts, he surpassed his initial prognosis and went on to live another three years. He passed in November 2016, weeks before I was scheduled to fly home for Christmas.

Around this time, life grew darker; shadows coated my every step. So I returned to the one place where expressing every part of myself felt safe: within my art. I spent entire lunch breaks plotting out novel ideas; I meditated on my grief by crafting characters who'd overcome theirs. I lost myself in worlds filled with light, and returned to work more enthusiastic *because* I let myself exist wholly outside of it. These precious moments made me realize how valuable my time is; that if I was willing to spend evenings and weekends crafting lesson plans for information literacy classes, then I ought to be willing to put the same energy into a craft that is completely for *me*.

I started by carving out chunks of time, both before and after work, to pursue my craft. Then, I gradually challenged myself to extend, grow in the same way I would when learning something new for work. I enrolled in a creative writing class, where I survived my first workshop critiquing experience; I submitted a short story for publication and began lining up future writing workshops to apply for. I allowed myself time for healing, to rediscover the boundaries of myself in ways I'd never tried before. Doing so has aided in shirking the same kind of vocational awe that made me feel as though my emotional investment in work should surpass what I invest within myself.

STRATEGIES FOR FINDING YOUR(WHOLE)SELF

Finding fulfillment within this profession, for me, has been about finding myself outside and beyond it. Whether artistic pursuits are your thing, or you have some other meaningful hobby, I'd now like to share the strategies that've helped me thrive within this profession, with the hope that they help you, too. I cannot stress enough:

Find Your People: What's made the process of working (and, honestly *staying*) in this profession easier has been finding my people. Living in New York City, I'm exposed to a vibrant and diverse set of LIS professionals who span the boroughs; I've connected with a number of folks who've kept me sane as I navigate the field. Additionally, I've met wonderful people at other institutions, sometimes in other states, who've also provided me with great support systems. There are currently a number of spaces cropping up to support marginalized voices in LIS; Jenny Ferretti and Sofia Leung currently run We Here (We Here 2017), an online Facebook group and Slack channel that anyone can participate in, regardless of geographic location; they also host monthly video chats for participants to confer and offer solidarity as we struggle together.

Feed Your Passions: I encourage anyone who's entering their first full-time position to explore who you are *outside* those confines early on. Find meaningful ways to spend your time outside of work, and try your best to erect boundaries between where your library efforts end and *you* begin.

While I highly encourage marginalized folks to consider librarianship as a profession, I'd be remiss not to shed light on the many problems I've seen within it. The honeymoon phase has ended; the vocational awe that drew me to the profession quickly dispersed—libraries aren't neutral places, and the profession isn't some magically equal environment. There are wonderful things about it—the public service aspect has and continues to keep me pushing through rough days. However, I have experienced too many "-isms" firsthand to call this profession a safe place for us. We've had to literally *carve out* a place for ourselves at too-White conferences, to endure anger and frustration from those who claim they'd like to do this work alongside us. But this work is rewarding when surrounded by the right opportunities and colleagues. More than that, I think any profession becomes more bearable when you allow yourself the right to be, in whatever way feels right for you.

Chapter Six

Do It for the Culture

My Life as an Archivist

Rachel E. Winston

Bring me all of your dreams,
You dreamer,
Bring me all your
Heart melodies
That I may wrap them
In a blue cloud-cloth
Away from the too-rough fingers
Of the world.
—Langston Hughes

I never set out to be an archivist. Or a librarian. Or any kind of information professional or dream keeper, for that matter. As best I can describe it, it just happened. And as I consider the journey to this point, the idea of being led by chance completely gives way to the fact that I have been led to do this work because it is my calling. As an archivist, each and every day I operate out of a fierce love I have for my people, and that guides the work that I do. Certainly, I would not be where I am today if it were not for my parents, whose love continues to sustain me and makes things possible. I would also be remiss if I did not acknowledge the impact individuals like Makiba Foster, Virginia Toliver, John Hunter, Wanda Williams, Clara McLeod, Trevor Dawes, and Meredith Evans had in encouraging me into the field and in helping me realize that I could exercise my interests and strengths within the profession, and more important, make a real difference. [1]

Though archives and librarianship now lie at the heart of what I do, I prefer to consider myself an information professional in the GLAM (Galleries, Libraries, Archives, Museums) field. This lens allows me to articulate both my experience with, and dedicated interest in, cultural institutions of various types, even if my specific interest within them revolves around managing collections and working with archival material. In a way, it also helps me remember how and why I became an archivist to begin with—by way of museums.

Growing up, on every family trip anywhere, museums were a part of my family's itinerary. Children's museums, history, art, science museums—if it was there, we would go. Similarly, public programs and special exhibitions at local cultural institutions were regularly incorporated into our weekend activities, including plays, festivals, and other cultural activities. So, museums and culture have always been a part of my life. While I wish I could say my feelings toward museums have been amorous from the start, that is simply not true. I have countless memories of trudging through exhibition galleries, hot, bored, and annoyed. Or, at the mention of another inevitable museum visit, responding with an eye roll and a complaint in protest.

The change occurred for me in high school, when I began to see museums as not just someplace I *had* to go to learn about *stuff*—but rather, as a place I could go to see myself. A place to bear witness to the lived experiences, history, and culture of people who look like me represented in a fullness I did not experience in my everyday life. I grew up in predominantly white[2] neighborhoods and attended predominantly white schools, so being one of a few Black people, if not the only one, in any given situation was my normal. In the years I was learning to understand my Black identity within such a white context, museums became a place I could go for answers and for refuge. Exhibitions told me things that textbooks and teachers did not. Cultural institutions affirmed and celebrated my Blackness—something that I just could not achieve in the white communities where I spent most of my time. Knowing there were people actively dedicated to preserving my history and culture provided me with a sense of peace in what would prove to be a challenging stage of adolescence, as I came to reconcile my and my family's Black identity within the context of our very white surroundings. It was at this point that museums became part of my revolution.

For me, the excitement lies in that interaction between oneself and the museum object. This certainly was the case for me as a teen, and remains true now that I find myself on the other side of things, creating these opportunities for others. The interaction—the confrontation of documented history—is where the interpretation, reconciliation, and sense making happens, and it has the potential to be a very meaningful and vulnerable moment. I remember visiting the Schomburg Center for Research in Black Culture[3] while in high school, and seeing a selection of Malcolm X's handwritten speeches and notes on display. While I cannot remember the specific speeches I saw or what the notes described, I do remember how seeing these things made me feel. I was overcome. The opportunity to engage with a man whose legacy was so big in my mind, and in my heart, in real time brought me to tears. Similarly, I recall the first time I saw a Ku Klux Klan robe and paraphernalia on display at the Birmingham Civil Rights Institute,[4] in Birmingham, Alabama, and the shock it sent through my body. I recall seeing several costumes belonging to Black dancer and social activist Katherine Dunham on display at the Missouri History Museum[5] and feeling compelled to claim my hometown in a way that I had not been interested in doing before—if she is considered to be one of the region's own and greatest, why shouldn't I? Truthfully, I could go on and on. The ways in which objects that represent history impact our present lives in real time is something that continues to impress me.

The goodness fed to me in these years by museums fostered the strong commitment I have to celebrating and preserving our history, our culture, and the dreams of our people. As I grew into this commitment, I began to see the need for not only museums but also qualified, dedicated people to work in them. After high school, I attended Davidson College, in Davidson, North Carolina, where I studied anthropology and French, and even designed an independent study course in museum studies with my advisor, Dr. Nancy Fairley. While in college and in my postgraduate years, I held various jobs— mostly project based, grant funded, or volunteer—at museum institutions across the country. In these experiences, I helped develop and execute programming and thoroughly enjoyed it. In fact, for a period I was convinced I was destined to work in museum education. It wasn't until I became involved at the St. Louis Soldiers Memorial and Military Museum (SMMM) that I was exposed to collections management and archives.

Because the SMMM staff was small, I had the opportunity to take on roles with significant responsibility—including conducting oral histories with local veterans, designing exhibitions, facilitating public programming, managing social media, monitoring museum facilities, and spending a significant amount of time in the collections. During particularly slow times, I could be found in the museum's collection, examining old photographs and reading letters written by servicemen to their families back at home. The time I spent in collections was extremely telling, as I was really able to understand just how powerful a role those who steward collections play. Collections, and the archives contained within them, are the lifeblood of cultural institutions. If our collections document our existence and represent our legacy, then those who steward them must be capable of taking care of them to ensure they are accessible for future generations.

My time at SMMM motivated me to expand my skill set in order to be more knowledgeable about managing the materials I worked with. I became interested in pursuing graduate school out of a desire to improve my professional abilities and best serve both the collections and the community members who entrusted us with their materials—much of which included contents that were deeply personal, and included items like memorabilia of family members lost during war, letters, and keepsakes of deceased loved ones. While I could have achieved this with an advanced degree in museum studies or a related discipline, I found library and information science to be the most advantageous. Coursework for an information science degree would equip me with what I needed to work with archival material, in addition to providing me with the knowledge needed for effective collections management, cataloging, reference, and things of that nature. I believed compounding these transferable skills with archival knowledge would position me to be able to work in a variety of institutions, which continues to be true.

I began graduate school in 2013 at the iSchool at the University of Texas at Austin (UT), and earned my master's degree in information studies with a graduate portfolio in museum studies in 2015. My coursework focused largely on archival enterprise and the management of cultural programs and institutions. By design, my graduate studies were very interdisciplinary. I became involved in various schools/colleges and departments outside of the iSchool by way of courses, employment, and events in art and art history, public affairs, social work, and Black studies. The intentionality behind pushing my archival learning beyond the information discipline was a direct result of my exposure to the inner workings of cultural institutions and having seen the varied perspectives and stakeholders involved in sustaining successful cultural programs.

Spending such a significant amount of time outside the iSchool earned me curious glances from my colleagues, given that it was not the norm. Not only was I the only Black woman in my cohort, I stood out especially as one who did not follow a specific course geared toward a specific type of institution (e.g. academic library, archive, museum). In other words, I crafted my own path based on my deeply held convictions. I stayed motivated in the face of side eyes, doubting questions, and feeling unsupported at times by the iSchool and by finding allies and holding firm to the fact that I was giving into a need that actively exists—that is, the need for trained stewards in the Black community ready to do the work of preserving legacies and telling our stories.

With ever increasing advances in technology and information access, the traditional role of archives and established practices of preservation are being called into question by changing demands. We have reached a point where we are losing the generation of elders who lived through Jim Crow and other periods of anti-Blackness on both a local and international scale, and on whose sacrifice we directly benefit from today. Negotiating these issues of medium and preservation with a rapidly decreasing source of knowledge lies at the heart of what motivates me. If we do not act intentionally from a place of care and concern, we are in real danger of losing crucial parts of our legacy. This work is big and important, and cannot be done in silos. Thus, when graduate school presented me with the space to build my personal capacity in working collaboratively across disciplines in a self-directed way, I took advantage of the opportunity—and it paid off.

Upon graduating, I was brought on by the Department of Black Studies at UT, and specifically by Drs. Daina Ramey Berry and Cherise Smith, to do archival and registrar work. In this role, I managed the department's incredible art collection, helped develop archival projects, and also assisted with coordinating activities of the programming arm of the department, the John L. Warfield Center for African and African American Studies. It was during my tenure in Black studies that UT began recruiting for a brand new Black Diaspora archivist position in UT Libraries. I successfully applied, and joined the Nettie Lee Benson Latin American Collection (Benson) staff as the inaugural Black Diaspora archivist in the fall of 2015.

In my role as Black Diaspora archivist, I am responsible for managing the Black Diaspora Archive (BDA), which is a new, collaborative project among UT Libraries, the Benson, and Black studies. My position is a special one—not only is it the only one of its kind, but also the element of collaboration that grounds the project and guides both the quotidian and visionary work that I do to support it strays from the job description of a typical archivist. Though it may be untraditional, it suits me, and in a very real way I feel as though I was preparing for this position before it even existed.

One of my first responsibilities after assuming this position was to establish the BDA's mission, which is to collect documentary, audiovisual, digital, and artistic works related to the Black Diaspora—that is, people and communities with a shared ancestral connection to Africa. While the geographic collecting area for the Black Diaspora is global, this archive is currently focused on materials documenting experiences from within the Americas and the Caribbean, building upon the Benson's existing strengths and overlapping areas of interest among students, faculty, and staff in both Black studies and Latin American studies. In addition to collecting, the BDA aims to promote collection use and research through scholarly resources, exhibitions, community outreach, student programs, and public engagement.

As the primary manager of the BDA, my ultimate charge is to provide a deeper understanding of the Black experience throughout the Americas and Caribbean with primary sources. At its essence, this necessitates the acquisition, collection, preservation, and accessibility of archival records. How that actually translates, however, is more complex. As an archivist, and particularly as an archivist building a new collecting area at an established institution with international renown, the work that I do not only communicates the narrative of my institution and its collecting interests and abilities but also contributes to memory making and the remembering of history on a larger scale. In this way, my efforts help preserve legacies, uncover truths, and facilitate access between these materials and people who are interested and capable of doing the work. The very thing I set out to do!

Since the Benson has been collecting on Latin America for nearly a century, the collection inevitably includes Black representation. However, it wasn't until the creation of the BDA that this kind of collecting was done in an intentional, sustainable way. Thus, another part of my charge includes reevaluating current holdings with a perspective that centers the Diaspora and privileges the perspective, voice, and contributions of these populations, as opposed to a gaze that examines them as subject.

A routine part of my job responsibility at the Benson also includes providing reference, outreach, and instruction. This incorporates working with undergraduate and graduate students, classes and groups, domestic and international outside researchers, faculty, and other campus entities to provide information on using archives with particular focus on the archival resources available in the Benson collection. I take this part of my job very seriously, mainly because I enjoy it so much. Honestly, I'm grateful for every opportunity I have to share my passion for archives and the BDA, and more important, encourage people to feel invested in and empowered by the archive. I feel this way particularly when working with students otherwise labeled as marginalized, who may not normally think to see themselves represented in archival institutions—especially one located within a large, predominantly white research university.

When I consider the work that I do as an archivist and the vocation of librarianship within which it is situated, I find it all too fitting that I am in a professional field of long-standing importance in the Black community, and further, one with a rich and wonderfully documented history.[6] As I continue to strengthen my professional capacities, I remain confident that meeting information needs and advocating for appropriate representation will be central to the work that I do. I am genuinely excited by the ways in which my professional efforts and personal interests complement one another in GLAM institutions and, ultimately, work toward the benefit of preserving the legacy of Black people in both a local and international context.

Looking to the future, I only see the role of archives strengthening. In order for this to happen, however, archivists must be willing to take more creative, collaborative, and political approaches to our work. Rather than preserving documents just for preservation's sake, our profession must look to the ways in which archival records not only reflect the past but also engage both the present and the future. We must be motivated by the opportunity to counter narratives, address/redress injustice, and demonstrate the fullness of the lived human experience with compassion. By no means is this charge easy, but it is one I will continue to embody and embrace. Even on my most challenging days, I cannot deny that I have found my dream job. I am invested in something much bigger than myself. But truthfully, it's not about me. Rather, it's about what I can do—for the present and past livelihoods, legacies, and dreams of my people. I do it for them, and I do it for the culture.

NOTES

1. I came to know many of these individuals while living in St. Louis, Missouri, and others by attending the American Library Association's Black Caucus meeting in 2014.

2. In reference to race, I capitalize *Black* and do not capitalize *white* as a comment on the inequality Black people continue to face within a global context. For similar reasons, I capitalize *Diaspora* when referring specifically to the Black Diaspora.

3. The Schomburg Center for Research in Black History and Culture is a research unit of the New York Public Library located in Harlem, New York. See www.nypl.org/locations/schomburg.

4. Birmingham Civil Rights Institute, www.bcri.org.

5. Missouri History Museum, www.mohistory.org.

6. See, for example, Josey (1970), Josey and Shockley (1977), Neely and Abif (1996), Josey and DeLoach (2000), and Jackson, Jefferson, and Nosakhere (2012).

Part Three

Strength

STRENGTH

Chapter Seven

You Are Not Alone

Joanna Chen Cham

As a second-generation Taiwanese American who grew up in beautifully diverse Los Angeles, I am lucky to have grown up and lived in a time and place where I can fully live both of my identities as Asian and American. The reality, however, is that much of the rest of the nation, and my chosen profession, is still catching up. In this chapter, I will share my experiences growing up in a predominantly Asian American suburb and attending the University of California, Berkeley (UC Berkeley) and as one of a handful of Asian Americans in my master's cohort, one of less than 3 percent of Asian Americans in museums (American Association of Museums 2011), and one of only 1 percent of Asian American archivists nationwide (Walch, Yakel, Bastian et al. 2006), and finally, as one of roughly 4 percent of Asian American librarians (American Library Association 2012). I will also share the ways in which mentorship, diversity initiatives, and professional development allowed me to find encouragement from professionals who came before me; like-minded colleagues and friends who both understand and challenge me to fight for diversity; and opportunities to engage as an activist and advocate for a library, information, and archival landscape that better represents people from all races, backgrounds, and identities. Mostly, though, this chapter seeks to share just one of many complex experiences of being an underrepresented minority in the information profession in hopes of giving voice to our far too unseen experiences and to identify ways in which we can move forward together.

When I was first asked to contribute to this book, I was excited. But I couldn't imagine how daunting the premise of writing in my own voice would be. But we all have to try. This is my story.

If you had asked me what it was like to be an Asian American back when I was a child, growing up in the 1980s and 1990s in the predominantly Asian

American suburb of Arcadia in Los Angeles, California, I would have said it was fine. The truth is, I'm not sure I would have really understood your question.

I am a second-generation Taiwanese American. My parents are from Taiwan. All four of my grandparents grew up under Japanese rule in Taiwan, and my maternal grandparents moved to Japan when my mother was in high school. I grew up speaking Taiwanese at home and English at school, and picking up bits and pieces of Japanese in the summers I spent visiting my grandparents. I recall reading *The Joy Luck Club* (1989) after fourth grade, because it was the only book I could find in English while I was in Taiwan that summer. I remember thinking contentedly to myself how I could not quite relate to the daughters of the novel. Unlike them, I felt no pull between having to identify as Asian or as American, and I only realized much later how lucky I was to have grown up in a time and place where people looked like me, whose parents' stories were similar to mine, whose culture and values and food were like my own, so much so that I had so little to explain, because those around me were also primarily second-generation Asian Americans, many of whom were Taiwanese Americans as well. Our numbers in the ethnic enclave of the San Gabriel Valley allowed us to be comfortable in our own skin, to be both proud of our heritage and proud to be American.

The truth is, surrounded by people like me, I felt comfortable in my skin but unaware both of others' experiences and of what it would be like to be Asian American outside my own communities. Because my parents were born in a foreign land, and because Asian Americans were only a footnote, if they appeared at all, in our history textbooks or in the literature we read, I knew little of the long history and struggles of Asian Americans in this nation. I was both surprised and incensed the times I encountered racism explicitly, and I can still hear the ringing in my ears the first time someone said "ching chong" to me while I was, ironically, looking out at Lady Liberty while visiting my brother in New York. But I had not yet developed a language for why it bothered me. I knew only that it was hurtful, that it mocked my parents' native tongue, and assumed something of me because of the way I looked.

If you had asked me what it was like to be an Asian American back when I was a college student, coming into my own on the diverse campus of UC Berkeley, I still would have said it was fine. The truth is, I would have only just begun to understand what it was like to be a person of color in these United States.

I encountered for the first time Asian Americans whose families had been here for generations. I realized that when I said that I spoke Mandarin poorly, what I meant was that I actually could understand and engage in basic conversations, thanks to all those years of Saturday Chinese School, and not that I only knew a few words, which was what my third-generation Chinese

American friend meant when she said she barely spoke Mandarin. My room-mates were Chinese American, Indian American, Japanese American, and Filipino American; my Taiwanese American–founded church was led by a Korean American pastor and his Japanese American wife; and for the first time I was introduced to a much broader experience of what it meant to be Asian American. Yet I remember thinking how, while my social life con-sisted of cultural heritage nights and talks about the intersections of faith and identity and social justice, my history classes rarely seemed to intersect with my own experiences. While I certainly did not expect to discuss the Asian American experience in my Holocaust history and Jewish studies courses, it is only now in retrospect that I realize how little the Asian American experi-ence was incorporated into my California history, civil rights history, American history, and World War II history courses. Do not get me wrong— I absolutely loved UC Berkeley and I am a proud Golden Bear. I loved the historic campus, my amazing professors, and the opportunities I had to ques-tion history, politics, and the state of civil and human rights. I just wish that Asian American history was represented in textbooks and conversations as well.

The truth is, surrounded by people like me in my social circles, but not in my academic life, I felt comfortable in my skin, but without even the vision to dream a different reality in which my communities' and families' history were not relegated to footnotes and considered as the responsibility of ethnic studies, and where I would see Asian American history faculty, graduate students, and librarians. It is actually only now, upon reviewing my tran-script, that I realize for the first time that the only Asian American faculty I had in my entire undergraduate career were in my Japanese language courses. I suppose it was a glimpse of what it would be like to be a person of color in academia.

If you had asked me what it was like to be an Asian American a decade ago, working in museums and archives for the first time, and studying archives and digital humanities in my master of library and information science program (MLIS) at the University of California, Los Angeles (UCLA), I would have said it was interesting, that it was both lonely and empowering. The truth is, I would have finally understood your question.

Although I still lived and worked in the wonderfully diverse city of Los Angeles, I was still always only one of a handful, if even, of Asian Americans and/or people of color in the museum and archive field. I distinct-ly remember attending my first professional museums conference out of state in Philadelphia, while I was working at the Los Angeles Museum of the Holocaust, and realizing slowly that I was literally the only Asian American among the five hundred attendees. The experience repeated itself years later when I attended my first archives conference and realized there were only a handful of Asian Americans, a few Latinx, and no African American or

American Indian archivists that I saw throughout the conference. It was then that I learned that Asian Americans were only 1 percent of archivists nationwide (Walch, Yakel, Bastian et al. 2006). It makes me wonder about whose stories we are missing in archives across the nation.

Even though I was surrounded by my incredibly supportive family, in particular, my parents and my husband, Matthew, and my many wonderful colleagues in the field, it was the friendships, the mentorship, and community spaces carved from the various diversity initiatives and fellowships I was privileged enough to be a part of that made me feel like I belonged in the professional communities that did not look like me. I was surrounded by wonderful mentors and colleagues in the profession, many of whom I keep in touch with to this day.

The truth is, I still felt this way.

The truth is, surrounded by rooms full of people who did not look like me, I felt uncomfortably aware of myself and of my differences, not only in how I stood out, but in the ways it began to feel like the profession was not meant for me, in the ways where I felt the uneasiness of being one of a handful of people of color in the room, in the ways where I subconsciously felt the weight of representing, well, all people of color, or of Asian Americans, or of Taiwanese Americans, depending on the makeup and nuances of the crowd, in the ways where I felt like my history, my culture, or my background would never quite be represented in exhibitions, in collections, or in the profession. It reminded me of how we invariably played the "Look! There's an Asian!" game whenever we watched television because of how rare and surprising it was to see ourselves reflected in the media.

I am forever indebted to the Association of Research Libraries (ARL) Initiative to Recruit a Diverse Workforce Fellowship (Puente 2013), the ARL/Society of American Archivists (SAA) Mosaic Fellowship (Puente 2014), the American Library Association (ALA) Spectrum Fellowship program (Prellwitz 2013), and the many other diversity scholarships and fellowships that helped me get to where I am today. Through these fellowships and initiatives designed specifically to recruit a more diverse workforce for libraries and archives, I received generous financial assistance that allowed me to pursue work full time, more freely pursue valuable and practical professional experiences like my fellowship at University of Southern California Special Collections, and attend numerous conferences such as the ALA annual, SAA annual general meeting, and the National Diversity in Libraries Conference (NDLC). I was matched with mentors, women of color who were also amazing archivists and librarians, whom I know I can call and confide in or meet over coffee and tears. I was given the opportunity to attend conferences and learn about librarianship and archives, and I was given advice and insights into the job market and interviewing process. Perhaps most important, though, I had a group of people to whom I belonged, a group of people with whom I shared the experience of being underrepresented in the broader profession, a group of people I could count on and stand alongside in fighting for diversity, inclusion, and equity.

If you asked me now what it was like to be an Asian American woman/ librarian/archivist/digital humanist existing in Trump's America, in a time where racism, sexism, and discrimination feel so alive and strong, I would tell you that I have never felt so heartbroken, so disappointed and disillusioned, so tired and sad, and so angry and invalidated as a woman of color and daughter of immigrants. The truth is, I would have been waiting for you to ask that question, for someone who genuinely wanted to know what my experience was like, for the world to not just pretend that everything was fine.

I am a Los Angeles–born and Los Angeles–raised Taiwanese American, daughter to two incredibly loving, hardworking, and self-sacrificing immigrant parents from Taiwan to whom I owe the world. I am a second-generation Asian American who knows more about my parents' home country than I do about the Asian Americans who have fought long and hard for our rights in this country. I am one of the few (of my Asian American MLIS cohort), one of the one percent (of Asian American archivists nationwide), one of the roughly four percent (of Asian American librarians across the nation). I am both part of a model minority myth and a community that has at times aligned itself with Whiteness and anti-Blackness, yet is alternatively pegged as a perpetual foreigner at best, and dangerous other, at worst, often excluded from American conversations on race, as if the conversation was only binary: Black and White or not Black or White or Latinx or Asian American or American Indian. I am an Asian American woman/librarian/archivist/digital humanist who has been told by a colleague that my hometown had an "Asian invasion," whose professional opinion and lived experiences have been dismissed, who is the only woman of color in the room. I am an Asian American Christian academic librarian—my worlds at times intersect, but more often than not, collide as the closest of families and friends range all across the political spectrum, both in ways I can understand and never understand, in ways where it has felt my faith has betrayed me and yet where it has felt I must remain a bridge. It has been an interesting time to be an Asian American in Trump's America.

And so I know what it's like to feel alone. To feel so ironically alone and disempowered and just tired, despite faith in a good and just God, despite supportive family and friends, and despite the best allies, even in places where the rest of the institution and city looks like me.

The truth is, there will be days where you will feel the crushing, nearly unbearable, completely unbelievable weight of being a young person of color in this profession. There will be days when—even in the hallowed halls of ivory towers, where the pursuit of knowledge is held high; even in the sacred stacks of treasured histories, where the value of all voices is held tight; and even in the heart and hub of the city center, where the freedoms of all are held onto—the minds and bodies and voices and hearts of people of color in this profession will be told that their professional assessments and lived experiences do not matter. That they do not have the knowledge, the understanding, or the position to challenge those unfettered claims and wistful wishes for diversity and social justice, which only fly away without enough substance to weigh its wearied claims down. On those days, which will inevitably come, know that you are not alone.

You are not alone.

The reason I'm still here in this profession is because I've surrounded myself with mentors and colleagues and spaces where I can be myself, where I can simply exist or share knowing there is understanding and empathy waiting for me among other people of color who get it without an explanation, whom I can text at a moment's notice, whose offices I can escape into, whose shoulders I can cry on, and whose ears I can confide in. I AM NOT ALONE.

I'm here to tell you, my friends, you are not alone, either. You are not alone. You are not alone. You are not alone. This is as much a reminder to myself as to you. You are not alone. These small handfuls and percentages of us in each room, in each university or archive or library—we make up hundreds, thousands, even. There are those before us who are paving the way slowly, and there will be those who come after us. We are a text or a call away; a Facebook group or online chat ready to listen; or communities of people locally, socially, or in our cohorts or ethnic caucuses ready to be rallied. The stories do not end here. They continue in conversations, conferences, and closed communities. There will be times when you will feel like you failed, or that you are utterly alone, or when you are completely dismissed and invalidated in micro- or macroaggressions. Know that you are strong, that you are not alone, that it is not right, but that you will stand again, even if it means leaning on each other for a while. We need each other.

So now I invite you to share your story. If I were to ask you, what is it like to be a person of color in the information profession today, what would you say?

Chapter Eight

How I Got Over

Evangela Q. Oates

On the afternoon of June 6, 2005, I received an e-mail from the coordinator of the search committee extending an invitation for a telephone interview. I was excited as I had not received any promising leads in my job search thus far. In fact, I had not received any interest from public or academic libraries. So, I was pretty stoked for the opportunity, and even more, because it was a research institution in New Mexico. New Mexico? That is between . . . Texas and Arizona, right?

I was just finishing up the last course of my library science program at North Carolina Central University, and after a year of being a full-time student, I was ready to put my skills into practice. Months before, I had applied for this position—and many others—with great expectations that I would be employed soon after. At this point, I was still optimistic about employment opportunities, although looking back, there was not much reason for such confidence. Our instructors had warned us about the difficulties of entering academic librarianship, but never spoke of the extra burden for people of color. My most prominent worry was if there were any Black people employed at the library, and if someone was going to ask me about my hair. More on that shortly.

I had the phone interview, a campus interview, and subsequently was offered the position by Camila Alire, then dean of the University New Mexico (UNM) University Libraries (UL). She called me on a Sunday evening—yes, Sunday—and I accepted her offer in about four seconds flat! I was such a novice to negotiation! But hey, when opportunity knocks, you have to answer. In that moment, I secured my first professional position in an academic library as the resident in public and research services at the UNM UL. With this position, I would have faculty status, an office, a salary, and most important, flexibility to make mistakes, as it was a residency program.

Now, about the hair thing. This requires a little backtracking as it refers to my first encounter with my would-be supervisor, Dr. Teresa Y. Neely. As many Black women will attest, our hair often holds political, social, and/or spiritual implications. Wearing one's natural hair texture subjects you to unsolicited comments—some positive, some negative, and some downright offensive. In addition to comments, we often prepare ourselves for how we will respond for the inevitable day when a stranger, without permission, touches our hair. It *will* happen! So, one can imagine my relief when I saw this little Black woman with locs holding a sign with my name on it. She had volunteered to pick me up from the airport for the on-campus interview. I was not sure if I would be offered the job, but I knew that her presence meant that she had already fielded most of the inquiries and comments about our hair. Suddenly, there was one less thing to be concerned about. Many thanks to Dr. Neely for taking one for the team.

MENTORING

During my career in librarianship, I have been mentored at every step, exclusively by one person. My mentor was once my supervisor; however, our relationship developed from a direct report to a "professional ally." I have not asked her why she still takes interest in my career, but I guess it would have something to do with her commitment to seeing the profession hire and retain people of color. Sears (2014) affirmed the importance of mentoring for minority librarians, writing, "mentoring should be a component of the program" for libraries seeking to diversify their rank (Sears 2014, 128). I describe my mentor as a professional ally as she has been an observer and participant, listening and/or giving advice on how to navigate organizational challenges. There have been several times when her guidance shielded me from disastrous situations. I was not able to avoid all pitfalls but was able to survive them because of her foresight and my ability to formulate a plan.

Our relationship also formed through our shared experiences of often being the only Black person in the room. With so many negative and manufactured perceptions of the *angry Black woman*, it was essential to have someone who could provide balance in situations where I knew I might be unfairly targeted. I did not have to convince her that I was not angry, aggressive, or any of the usual terminology that is frequently used to describe ordinary, uneventful interactions between Black women and their peers. She may have given suggestions on how to better respond, but there was not an immediate assumption of unprofessionalism or accusations of intimidation. I can only imagine there were other complaints that I will never know about since she was able to filter them.

In thinking about my experiences with other supervisors who were not people of color, there have been times when I needed to defend myself from unfounded allegations. I call them the *bag of PETTY*, where pettiness reigns supreme. In the case of one performance evaluation, one supervisor listed a number of complaints he had received from colleagues outside of my department. When he was finished, I remember thinking, "Now I have to say hello and smile to everyone in the hallway." Who else has to constantly wear a smile in order to make others feel comfortable? And without fail, the dreaded "they say you are aggressive" comment was given. To his astonishment, I finished his sentence. What he failed to understand is that I know Blacks are always described this way. In a 2016 interview with Oprah Winfrey, in response to a question about how she felt about being labeled this way, Michelle Obama responded, "You think . . . this isn't about me, this is about the person or the people who write it" (Liptak 2016). Assertive behavior comes across as aggression. One's authority is viewed as oppressive. I do not care how much I smile (which is exhausting, by the way), because I am a Black woman, my very presence can be perceived as troublesome. For this reason, one will most certainly need the support and guidance of more experienced professionals. I have been fortunate to have someone who understands, and is able to give constructive criticism of my work, without penalizing me for my race and gender in the process.

As a Black woman, my mentor is able to understand racial microaggressions as she has experienced them, and has been witness to them. However, for many White people, these instances just do not exist. Alabi (2015) wanted to know if "White academic librarians observed derogatory exchanges directed at their minority colleagues." She found that little to no White people had observed these behaviors, far less than their minority colleagues. How can this finding not be important for the retention of librarians of color? When no one sees or acknowledges offenses against you, or people who look like you, you are not likely to remain in that place or that profession. Isolation, specifically cultural isolation, can be very difficult for minorities. Zambrana and her colleagues investigated mentoring experiences of minorities at research institutions and found that "many participants reiterated this sense of isolation and spoke of the need for senior scholars who understood what it meant to be an underrepresented minority in the academy" (Zambrana et al. 2015, 55).

In my current position, as the director of library services at the SUNY Sullivan campus of the State University of New York system, I am the only Black librarian, and that has been consistent at two of the four academic libraries where I have worked. I should be clear that having other librarians of color on staff does not ensure collegiality; however, it does give our colleagues the opportunity to have interactions with more than just one minority group. As I mentioned earlier, having a Black woman on the faculty prior to my arrival made it so that it was not so unusual to see us, collaborate, and learn about us as individuals. Black people and other racial minorities are often judged as a group. Even though many White people claim they have "friends that are . . . ," many of their comments reveal that many of these friendships are merely loose associations (Ingraham 2014).

My earliest experiences in librarianship cultivated a strong desire for professional development. Whenever there is a chance to enhance my skills/ knowledge, I pursue it. My residency at the UNM UL encouraged me to seek as many opportunities for professional improvement as possible. In the non-tenure-track resident position, I was able to explore different aspects of librarianship, including research instruction, projects, and reference, which allowed me to identify the area I was most passionate about. At the time, the structure of the residency was not well received by other librarians in the department. Many felt as though it was a wasted hire and would have preferred a tenure-track position given the perceived lack of available people to do instruction and reference work. More important was the lack of influence they had in the day-to-day schedule of the resident. Their limited authority could be attributed to the misuse of former residents. Without the structure of what I called the "resident bible," and a philosophy of the nature of a residency, former hires had less than stellar experiences in the program. However, my mentor created the bible/guide to ensure a vibrant, learning-centered introduction to academic research librarianship. One can see parallels in how library faculty of color navigate the tenure process.

According to Damasco and Hodges, librarians of color often have difficulties in promotion and tenure. In looking at the distribution of workload, they found that teaching faculty of color "engage in high levels of service activities, despite the fact that service is often given less weight than research and publication when it comes to tenure or promotion." Many of their respondents reported they were asked to fill in for various committees, while others sought these experiences as they found them to be quite fulfilling (Damasco and Hodges 2012, 290). Perhaps having a mentor who has gained tenure would have been beneficial as they may have been able to help them find balance in service and research responsibilities. Regardless of ethnicity/ color, many professionals find it difficult to refuse invitations for service (to the institution). My time at UL of UNM taught me how to politely refuse projects, so much that I have never felt guilty for not accepting more projects/service than I could handle. Too, I have witnessed the consequences for junior faculty who give more time to service than publication. Tenure committees and departments seem to forget the impact of service when it is time for promotion.

PROFESSIONAL DEVELOPMENT

As a resident, my position was limited to two years; however, I was able to cultivate strong and lasting relationships with my colleagues. Some of them wrote letters of support for the American Library Association's Emerging Leaders Program for newer librarians.[1] I was accepted as part of the inaugural cohort and was able to meet other up-and-coming librarians from many different backgrounds and ethnicities. As with the profession overall, my fellow attendees were mostly White, but definitely more people of color than what I was used to. The Emerging Leaders Program aims to create a loose model of group mentoring that, according to Johnson, "shares characteristics with learning communities and communities of practice" (Johnson 2007, 406).

My cohort was assigned a mentor for support, but we were responsible for moving the project along. I had a very positive experience and, consequently, developed more interest in leadership in the profession. After my time at UNM, while employed at another institution, I applied and was accepted into the Association of College and Research Libraries (ACRL) Information Literacy Immersion Program.[2] What an intense program! It was expensive, in terms of time and money; however, it was well worth the expense. I negotiated my participation in the program when I was offered that particular position. Even though I had not yet been accepted into the program, I knew it had to be a part of the package for my next position. Negotiations are often the most challenging part of the interview process. Very few new(er) librarians will feel comfortable negotiating for professional development as a requirement for employment; however, I had been groomed to understand that good employment experiences require both parties to feel like they have not compromised. Having a mentor, whether formal or informal, empowers one to feel better prepared for obstacles (Oates and Neely 2011).

LEADERSHIP IN THE PROFESSION

These days, with more than ten years of professional experience, and a wealth of lessons learned from participating in professional development opportunities, I feel I have come into my own as a leader. Because of my experiences, I feel adequately equipped to handle most situations. Before deciding to become an administrator, I was the head of reference and instruction at a small, private college in New York. I was able to develop as a leader as I supervised part-time reference librarians as well as managed the education library. For someone who had always been responsible for my own actions, I was now in charge. I adapted well to my new responsibilities and realized how much I enjoyed being a part of the development of new librarians as well as learning from those with many years of experience.

One of my most rewarding experiences was serving as an internship coordinator. A student on campus, who was in the final year of her program, had contacted the campus career center for placement in a library. Initially, she thought she would work in a public library, but the director suggested that she consider the college library. When I was told about her interest, I immediately volunteered to coordinate the internship. I called Dr. Neely to ask her to send me a revised copy of the bible so that I could model the internship with some of the things that made mine so successful. I used the key components of focused projects, journaling, shadowing, and providing reference services as an introduction to academic librarianship. By the time her internship had ended, she seemed like a part of the staff, and her departure was bittersweet. This opportunity to mentor revealed the depth of my passion for mentoring others, helping them grow into the professionals they had hoped to be, but may never have thought possible.

One thing I have learned about management/leadership is that knowing what *not* to do is just as important as having the right answers, which can be subjective and relative. By this point in my career, I had seen plenty of examples of poor management and leadership. Bad experiences have powerful lessons in them, too. Do not remove them from your repertoire. Instead, find a way to frame them so that you can acknowledge your strengths and the areas where you need improvement.

So, what kind of leader am I? That depends on the organization, and sometimes, it depends on the day. In addition to being the director of a library in the SUNY system, I am also a doctoral student in educational administration at the University of Nebraska–Lincoln. As an administrator, I try to remain a strong advocate for my staff. Because I have had such great experiences, I want to model that for other librarians, especially those new to the profession. As a part of my introduction to the library, I always mention that we are the largest employer of students on campus. A couple of students from that same group decided to apply for work at the library, and one of them was hired and stayed for all four years. She continued to work after graduation and ended up getting a full-time position as staff. She has not explicitly expressed an interest in becoming a librarian but perhaps that may change in time.

One important question for me to consider would be my ability to attract young Black men and women to the profession. Besides work-study or part-time students, no one from that demographic has expressed interest in librarianship as a profession; however, I know that my presence has changed the way many students of color think about it. When I am asked about my career, I emphasize how the profession has given me lots of mobility and a chance, through professional development, to travel across the country. Rarely do they expect that a librarian could have opportunities to live in different time zones.

One last thing that I should point out is that it is never too late to become a mentor. For every stage of your career, you may need someone with wisdom and experience to help keep you on your desired path (Sears 2014). Mentorships do not have to be formal, and you should not wait to be appointed one. Seek out those who have the energy, knowledge, and desire to help someone else grow. It may be someone with a legacy of mentorship, or it could develop out of casual interactions. Whatever the case, do not let opportunity slip through your fingers as they are not certain to come around again. Believe in yourself, work hard, and when you get the chance to help and inspire someone, rise to the occasion! Remember, there are folks coming behind us, and we have to make things better for them, just as our elders did for us. Power to the people!

NOTES

1. ALA Emerging Leaders Program, http://www.ala.org/educationcareers/leadership/emer-gingleaders.
2. ACRL Information Literacy Immersion Program, http://www.ala.org/acrl/immersion.

Chapter Nine

The Jackie Robinson of Library Science

Twenty Years Later

Teresa Y. Neely

"As the sole African American librarian in my present place of employment, the fact that I am a Black woman has never been more apparent, if not to my colleagues then most certainly to me . . . the legacy of my birth is brought to fore every time I sit down in a meeting, [or] converse with a colleague"— Teresa Y. Neely, "The Jackie Robinson of Library Science"

In the twenty years since *IOOV* 1996 was published, my journey as an academic research librarian has taken some unexpected turns, geographically and otherwise. I successfully completed my comprehensive exams and defended my dissertation proposal in the fall of 1997 at the University of Pittsburgh's (Pitt) School of Library and Information Science. Upon returning to Colorado State University (CSU), the tenure-track clock that had been paused when I left in August of 1995 to pursue the doctorate started back up again. Between 1998 and 2001, I was the acting coordinator of reference services—instruction, outreach, and staff training. When the search for a permanent coordinator was held, I applied and was not granted an interview. It was then that Dr. Camila Alire, who had become dean of libraries at CSU while I was away at Pitt, advised me, "If you want to move up, then you will have to leave." It was sound advice that I took to heart.

In 2000, I completed the PhD degree and, shortly thereafter, left CSU for a position with more responsibility at the University of Maryland, Baltimore County (UMBC), just prior to September 11, 2001. My time at UMBC was not good for me, physically or mentally. I was the head of the reference department when two of the reference librarians were dealing with issues that significantly impacted their work lives. Supervising them soon consumed the majority of each day. I was extremely unhappy in this position and was very close to burning out. I needed a fresh start. During the summer of 2004, the unexpected invitation to apply for a position that I did not know existed was exactly what I needed.

In 2005, I accepted the offer to be become the director of Zimmerman Library (Chapa 2015), the largest library on the main campus of the University of New Mexico (UNM) in Albuquerque. March 2017 marked my twelfth year of continuous employment at UNM.

During my academic career, I have worked at three institutions, two of which are predominantly White institutions (PWI) (Brown and Dancy 2010). My current institution, UNM, is an Hispanic-Serving Institution (U.S. Department of Education 2016); however, the demographics of the library faculty and staff of each of the libraries I have worked at were, and remain, primarily White, as are the demographics of the profession of librarianship overall (Godfrey and Tordella 2006; Davis and Hall 2007).

I have never held a post-MLS position at an institution that included another Black degreed librarian at similar rank in a faculty position during my entire career. Twenty-four years later, I am still the only one. And just to be clear, the only one means, the only Black faculty member and the only Black woman faculty member. The most recent *ARL Annual Salary Survey* (2015–2016) reported on sex and race demographics of ninety-nine Association of Research Libraries (ARL) libraries in the United States (Morris 2017). Responding libraries, including UNM, reported there were 1,328 (15 percent of 8,899) minority professional staff employed in university, law, and medical libraries (Morris 2017, 2–3).[1] For the time period covered, Caucasian/Other (85 percent) librarians made up the majority of those employed in ARL libraries, followed by Asian/Pacific Islanders at 7 percent, Black professionals at 5 percent, Hispanic professionals at 3 percent, and American Indian/Alaskan Natives at less than 1 percent (2017, 2). Based on these findings, if I want to continue to work in ARL libraries, at an institution with other Black librarians, I need to consider a position in the Middle Atlantic, East North Central, or South Atlantic where there are seventy-one Black librarians (237 total minority librarians), seventy-five Black librarians (203 total minority librarians), and 122 Black librarians (255 total minority librarians) employed respectively (2017, 3). Across ARL libraries in the United States and Canada, women outnumber men, nearly two (63.6 percent) to one (36.4 percent) (2017, 3). In ARL libraries in the United States, White women account for 62 percent of the total population (2017, 4).

In past publications, I have written at length about the lack of diversity in the profession, specifically in academic libraries; however, over time, the percentages quoted by myself and others have, at the very least, remained fairly consistent (Neely 1998, 1999; Neely and Peterson 2007; Cawthorne and Neely 2015). In "Diversity Counts," Davis and Hall (2007) reported that, in all library types and positions (librarians, technicians, and assistants), across the board, the majority of librarians (credentialed and not credentialed) were White, female, aged 40–54, with no limiting disabilities (2007, 5). In the 2006 and 2009–2010 data sources analyzed, White women made up 73 percent of credentialed librarians. Based on these and other findings, the authors concluded that the profession is heading for "a proportionally less diverse library workforce" in the future (2007, 18).

In my *IOOV* 1996 chapter, when discussing my decision to move to Fort Collins, Colorado, despite the lack of Black people living there, thirty-year-old me wrote, "I was hesitant about moving to a place that was predominantly White and where I would have to board a plane each time I wanted to see a familiar face" (Neely 1996, 174). Not much has changed, except, on rare occasions, my people will board a plane to come and visit me, because, by choice, I moved to Colorado and New Mexico, two states with considerably less populations of people with African ancestry, to move up in my chosen profession. The demographics of my workplace did not change very much when I moved to Maryland to work at UMBC, and again, I was still the only credentialed one. It is unfortunate that there aren't more people in my profession or in my workplace(s) who look like me, and, honestly, I don't believe it will change any time soon. The struggle comes in learning how to live, thrive, and be successful within those systems "with people . . . who have learned to mistrust my kind or me," and where I often feel "isolated, out of place, outnumbered, unheard, held at a distance, or feared" (McIntosh 1986).

TRAUMA: PERSONAL AND PROFESSIONAL

Upon arriving at UNM in the spring of 2005, I decided to take each of my direct reports out to lunch for some one-on-one time to get to know them individually. One of my White colleagues who was reporting to me half-time informed me that, with the exception of my doctorate, he was more qualified than I was to hold the position of director of Zimmerman Library. This happened in my first week. I later found out he had applied for the position but had not been granted an interview.

Things were tense all around, and the massive reorganization that occurred in the summer of 2005 did not help. Departments were completely deconstructed, and some service desks disappeared. The four branch directors had more responsibility and authority than we previously had. Emotions ran high. By the time the entire library staff was brought together in a neutral, nonlibrary space to announce the new organizational structure, most of the people whose jobs had been directly affected had already been told, and what hadn't been said had fanned the rumor mills. People were stressed and on edge. The announcement was devastating to some; people left that building in tears.

In January 2005, my father passed away at the age of sixty-six. A little more than a year after I started work at UNM, on Sunday, April 30, 2006, Zimmerman Library suffered a devastating fire in the basement that destroyed an estimated thirty thousand volumes of journals and other serial publications (Schultz and Neely 2010). Eight days later, in the midst of recovery and attempts to get services back online for students preparing for finals, I lost my oldest sister. She lived forty-three days after her forty-fifth birthday. In August 2007, eight days after her forty-fifth birthday, my maternal first cousin passed away suddenly, leaving her seven-year-old daughter motherless.

On Halloween 2007, Zimmerman Library's newly renovated basement flooded when the new riser room equipment failed (Castillo-Padilla et al. 2010). All total, between 2005 and 2007, including the cross-country move from Baltimore to Albuquerque, I experienced six traumatic life and work events. The American Psychiatric Association and the Centers for Disease Control (CDC) define traumatic events as ones that "cause a lot of stress," and are "marked by a sense of horror, helplessness, serious injury, or the threat of serious injury or death. Traumatic events affect survivors, rescue workers, and the friends and relatives of victims who have been involved. They may also have an impact on people who have seen the event firsthand or on television" (American Psychiatric Association 2017; Centers for Disease Control 2017). Although I have never been officially diagnosed with PTSD (posttraumatic stress disorder)[2] or depression, during a routine doctor's visit, my primary care physician once asked, "Now what are we going to do about this depression?" Prior to that, I had never even given consideration that I might be depressed. However, reflecting on this period in my life now, I do not know how I made it through without some type of intervention—biologic or therapeutic.

In April 2008, just when I thought there had been a slight reprieve, both personally and professionally, we lost my father's older brother. Later in that year, my physical health began to decline, keeping pace with my mental health, no doubt. I had my first hip surgery in 2008. About a month after the first hip surgery, I thought I was recovering well, until I woke up in the middle of the night with both hands feeling as if they had been thrust into a furnace. Eventually, this resulted in a diagnosis of severe carpal tunnel syndrome in both hands. In 2010, I had a second surgery to remedy previously unknown issues revealed in the MRI (magnetic resonance imaging) of my hip. In early 2012, I realized the progress I was making physically with my hip wasn't really progress at all. In 2009, I had discovered antigravity yoga, and while I was amazing in the hammock, I couldn't walk worth a damn. Picture one of the Weebles roly-poly toys released by Hasbro's Playskool in

1971, recall the catchphrase, "Weebles wobble but they don't fall down," and you have the image of what I looked like walking (*Wikipedia*, "Weeble"). I finally decided to visit my primary care physician who agreed I was a little uneven and probably needed a chiropractic adjustment, and that an x-ray was in order. The results were astonishing. The image showed my left hip in perfect condition, smooth and beautiful. The right hip was several inches higher than the left and looked as if it had been beaten with a hammer. About an hour after I left the doctor's office, she called me with the results. "You don't need a chiropractor; you need a hip replacement." We ended the call, and she called back almost immediately with an appointment for a surgical consult the next morning at 8:00 a.m. Things were moving fast. According to his physician's assistant, the first surgeon had been in the military for twenty-six years. He looked at my x-rays for a long time and finally told me he did not know if he could fix it. He also noted the injury I had looked like the type of injury professional football players get. Note to self: Always get a second opinion. In August 2012, at the age of forty-five, I underwent a hip arthro-plasty of my right hip, also known as a total hip replacement (THR). The surgery, although wildly successful in eliminating my pain and returning me to hopes of full and unfettered ambulatory mobility, triggered pulmonary embolisms, also known as blood clots in the lungs. Two years later, when I began my genealogy work on my family tree, I discovered that I was not alone with this particular condition. I just hadn't died yet.

Ancestors on both sides of my family (my paternal great-grandmother, paternal grandfather, maternal grandmother, and my maternal grandfather) all have similar causes of death listed, as do my two sisters and my maternal first cousin. I'm not sure what it is called when you think you are going to eventually die from what many others in your family have died from, but it is an extremely stressful reality.

WORKING WHILE BLACK:
MICROAGGRESSIONS AND MENTAL HEALTH

Being the only person who looks like you and/or identifies the same way you do—in these states of an America, which are not particularly united in my view—contributes to the significant decline in one's mental health. You are perpetually unwell and emotionally unstable. I spend all day, every day, in an environment where I do not see anyone who looks like me until I look in a mirror. This takes a considerable toll. "Working while Black" in a predomi-nantly White environment is akin to severe psychological trauma (Louie 2017; Donovan, Galban, Grace, Bennett, and Felicié 2012; Sue, Capodilupo, and Holder 2008; Constantine, Smith, Redington, and Owens 2008). In 2012, Donovan et al. found that the prevalence of perceived racial macroaggressions (PRMa) and perceived racial microaggressions (PRMi) were "common occurrences for Black women and are associated with negative mental health outcomes, with PRMa being the less common but more detrimental of the two" (2012, 185–86). A 2014 blog post on the Crunk Feminist Collective website shares some of the microaggressions experienced by Black people in the workplace. Dr. Robin M. Boylorn, a Black woman and tenured associate professor of interpersonal and intercultural communication at the University of Alabama, writes about her personal experiences, observations, and things that have happened to non-White people she knows and have communicated with. It is as affirming and comforting to read her post as it is horrifying to know that, even while successful, you remain a target for those who are less confident, threatened by your presence, ignorant, and hostile.

> Racial microaggressions are real and while they are sometimes felt and experienced tangentially, folk of color are marginalized in similar ways simply because they are of color. Prestige of position is not protection. (Boylorn 2014)

On Boylorn's Microaggression list, number two speaks loudly to me. It is the culmination of many of the things I have been told repeatedly throughout my career and are classic "go to" phrases that are often trotted out when the use of *angry Black woman* is not appropriate. It is perfectly acceptable to have hostile, aggressive, angry White people project that on you, but when you respond, you become the aggressor, the one harassing or bullying your colleague.

> You are routinely accused of being hostile, aggressive, difficult and/or angry. You are told that your colleagues/students/co-workers/customers are intimidated by you and are afraid to approach you. You are encouraged in evaluations to "smile more," and "be more friendly." You practice a fake ass smile in the mirror on your way out the door and practice all the way to work. You fear that your resting face pose makes people think you are mean. (Boylorn 2014)

Several years ago, in a faculty meeting of mostly White colleagues, I responded to a White male untenured colleague, defending myself and my position in the discussion. Afterward, the interim dean, who was White, male, and gay, told me that he had heard from my colleagues who were concerned that I, a tenured faculty member, was publicly bullying an untenured junior faculty member. I stumbled out of his office barely able to conceal my tears. I could not believe the accusation. Were they in the same meeting? Did they hear how he had spoken to me? Did they see the look on his face? His body posture? On multiple occasions, I have been verbally abused by White male colleagues I still have to work with on a daily basis. The one I allegedly bullied actually tried to apologize, on two occasions, for the aforementioned event and another outburst aimed at me, but I ignored his attempts because he wanted to absolve himself by admitting his wrongdoing while no one else was around. I wasn't having it.

To be fair, I recognize that not all my White faculty colleagues are racist; however, I feel fairly confident in labeling their utterances, silences, and behavior as ignorant, insensitive, and uninformed. McIntosh cautions that her White Privilege Papers[3] are about her experiences and "not about the experiences of all White people in all times and places and circumstances" (McIntosh 1988, 15). Her clarifications notwithstanding, McIntosh's words speak loudly to many of us. In his 2012 history thesis from Georgia State University, Jacob Bennett explored the history of the concept "White privilege." Prior to McIntosh's White Privilege Papers, the terminology was used "to describe the structural and governmentally organized systems of discrimination perpetuated under segregation in the United States. The spike [increase in use of White privilege as a concept in American literature] in the 1980s corresponds directly with McIntosh's publication of her hypothesis about psychological privilege being perpetuated unconsciously in American society" (Bennett 2012, 3).

In her original 1988 work, from which "White Privilege: Unpacking the Invisible Knapsack" was excerpted, McIntosh listed forty-six realizations in an effort to identify some of the ways White privilege affected her personally on a daily basis (McIntosh 1988). Most of the use of her work has been limited to the twenty-six realizations that were included in the 1989 excerpt. In 2017, as I write this, and keeping my perspective on my personal journey, I am not surprised at how relevant McIntosh's realizations are to me. What follows are my responses to a few of her experiences, in the place that I work, primarily with faculty interaction.

- "I can, if I wish, arrange to be in the company of people of my race most of the time." Where I work now, and in my two previous professional library positions, this could never happen.
- "I can avoid spending time with people whom I was trained to mistrust and who have learned to mistrust my kind or me." Although I have not been trained to mistrust people, I cannot ever avoid spending time with people whom I've learned to mistrust through their words and actions toward me.
- "I can turn on the television or open to the front page of the paper and see people of my race widely and positively represented." The people are minimally visible and the majority of those are not positively represented. "In too many places, Black boys and Black men, and Latino boys and Latino men, experience being treated different under the law" (Obama 2015). This is "a definitive record of people killed by police in the U.S." In 2015, nearly 30 percent of the people killed by the police were Black, and many of those deaths were captured on video, shared across social

media platforms, and played in grisly detail, over and over, on the international news. In 2016, nearly a quarter of people killed by the police were Black (*Guardian* 2015, 2016).

- "When I am told about our national heritage or about 'civilization,' I am shown that people of my color made it what it is." This has never happened, unless the "founding fathers" were "enslaved immigrants"[4] (Lartey 2017). Recently released movies that document the contributions black people made to the space program (*Hidden Figures*, 2017) and to medical research (*The Immortal Life of Henrietta Lacks*, 2017), and the contributions of other impactful Black people are rarely used as examples. More common is someone screaming at you to "go back to Africa," enthusiastically proposing how to "Make America Great Again," telling you we need to keep "America first," and/or pushing a White nationalist agenda (Yan, Sayers, and Almasy 2017; *Wikipedia*, "Unite the Right Rally").

- "I can be fairly sure of having my voice heard in a group in which I am the only member of my race." I have had my ideas and suggestions ignored and essentially dismissed, and then appropriated and attributed to someone else in the same meeting. And no one ever bothers to correct the mistake or even noticed that it had occurred. The terms *manterrupted* and *bropropriating* appeared several years ago to define what happens to [White] women in the workplace dominated by men. I am not sure what it is called when White women treat non-White women the way men treat them.

- "I can speak in public to a powerful male group without putting my race on trial." I couldn't even type this with a straight face, because any speaking out at all to a White male colleague gives me a lifelong membership to the angry Black woman's club. I mean, currently I am the president, CEO, and only member up in here.

- "I can take a job with an affirmative action employer without having my co-workers on the job suspect that I got it because of my race." Thirty-year-old me wrote, "I would be foolish to believe that I was hired to satisfy affirmative action quotas. The rigorous lengthy interview process that one must endure in academia is not something that you can just wing with a smile and a face of color" (Neely 1996, 178).

- "If my day, week, or year is going badly, I need not ask of each negative episode or situation whether it has racial overtones." Please. This happens on the daily. See the section "Working while Black" earlier in this chapter. All negative situations and episodes do not have racial overtones, but it is taxing to feel the need to have to figure that out, each and every time— particularly when that person(s) has made inappropriate statements before.

- "I can be late to a meeting without having the lateness reflect on my race." So many inappropriate things I can say about this one. However, Black people are not the only ones who are perpetually late. I will just leave that right here for now.

- "I can expect figurative language and imagery in all of the arts to testify to experiences of my race." The art in my workplace generally sticks to offending other people who are not White. My race is generally not represented, considered, or discussed unless it is from a more global perspective, coupled with another groups' experience in the diaspora.

LOOKING FORWARD

When I came to UNM in the spring of 2005, I was hired at the rank of associate professor with tenure. In the fall of 2016, I submitted my dossier for consideration for promotion from associate professor to [full] professor. My dossier, a fifty-eight-page distillation of my twenty-three-year career as an academic research librarian, only reveals the part of my story that can be documented and reviewed for academic promotion purposes. The remaining part *could* have been documented with grievances, and allegations of violations of academic freedom or discrimination; however, the culmination of actions and verbalizations by my colleagues of what I can now name as microaggressions, ultimately, do not collectively constitute a hostile work environment, at least that's what I've been told. Although most days feel pretty hostile to me.

In June 2017, I achieved the rank of full professor; increasing the number of Black full professors at UNM to four (OIA 2016). Upon reflecting on my career, I concluded that the things that have always mattered and continue to matter to me are "diversity of people, recruitment to the profession, developing leaders within the profession, an information literate citizenry, and library as place—virtual and physical."[5] Thirty-year-old me wrote, "I have made a personal commitment to recruit as many ethnically diverse persons as possible to the profession" (Neely 1996, 66). I didn't recall writing that way back when, but I am glad I somehow managed to stay on that path.

In October 2016, I turned fifty years old, a significant milestone for me. I do not know what the future holds for me in this profession or personally. At one point in my journey, I was happy to tell anyone who listened that I would never get a PhD, likewise for an administrative position. I try to be careful about absolutes when thinking about where my next position will take me. I remain single and unencumbered and have always had plans to move closer to my family. That hasn't changed; I just haven't figured out when that will be, where I will go, or what I will be doing. In my current position as assessment librarian, I am learning a lot, and I am excited about the opportunity and the possibilities. When I first started at UNM, I would work late into the night e-mailing and communicating. I always volunteered to take notes or to chair this group or that one. Then reality set in: there was a fire, I lost a lot of people, there was a lot of water inside the building, then I had a new hip, and I realized that, if something happened to me, it would be relatively easy for me to be replaced at work. I needed to adopt a more Teresa-centric mentality. I needed to move through these spaces and this world at my own pace, on my own terms, and I needed to own my accomplishments, my successes and failures, equally. I think I've done that, and for now, I'm good. I'm still here and it's all good.

NOTES

1. On professional staff, the Association of Research Libraries notes, "Since the criteria for determining professional status vary among libraries, there is no attempt to define the term 'professional.' Each library should report those staff members it considers professional, including, when appropriate, staff who are not librarians in the strict sense of the term, for example, computer experts, systems analysts, or budget officers" (Association of Research Libraries 2015).

2. Posttraumatic stress disorder is defined by the American Psychiatric Association as "a psychiatric disorder that can occur in people who have experienced or witnessed a traumatic event such as a natural disaster, a serious accident, a terrorist act, war/combat, rape or other violent personal assault" (American Psychiatric Association 2017).

3. Peggy McIntosh's White Privilege Papers are discussed at the National SEED Project, https://nationalseedproject.org/about-us/white-privilege.

4. In March 2017, Ben Carson, a Black man and housing and urban development secretary, referred to African slaves as "other immigrants who came here in the bottom of slave ships and worked even longer, even harder for less" (Lartey 2017).

5. Teresa Neely's "Statement of Librarianship," submitted as part of the requirements for full professorship at the University of New Mexico, 2016.

Chapter Ten

"The Shoe Is Too Small and Not Made for You!"

Racial "Covering" and the Illusion of Fit

Silvia Lin Hanick

There is a part of the Cinderella story that has always baffled me. Cinderella spends a magical night with the prince at the ball, and he is ready to propose. Yet, when he next sees Cinderella, he does not recognize her until she puts on the slippers. Wasn't there something innate in the curve of her smile or the sparkle in her eyes that made her worthy? Nothing? The slipper, then, must have been much more powerful than it was decorative, if it could reveal her to the prince and transform her from a scullery maid to royalty. My career as a librarian has been defined by a search for something similarly powerful. Like Cinderella in front of her prince, I wanted to be transformed and recognized—albeit as a librarian and not a princess.

When, as a graduate student, I struggled to shake off constant insecurity about my own abilities, I looked to the master's degree in library and information science (MLIS) as my magical slipper. "Once I am a real librarian," I told myself, "it will feel different." Feeling like a real librarian, however, turned out to be a moving target. At first, being real meant earning an MLIS. Then, getting hired. That wasn't as real as being a tenure-track faculty librarian or a liaison with a second master's degree. Still, how could that compare with librarians who taught semester-long classes, just like real professors? With each step of my career, realness remained elusive. In the Brothers Grimm version of Cinderella, the two stepsisters are able to briefly dupe the prince by cutting off part of their feet to fit into the slippers. My complicated relationship with legitimacy has a lot to do with the sneaking suspicion that I am more stepsister than Cinderella, desperate enough for a stolen crown that

I would slice off a toe. A talking bird could out me at any moment, chirping "the shoe is too small, and not made for you!" (Grimm 1826). Then, the prince would toss me aside for being an imposter.

There is this unwritten rule that aspiring librarians quickly learn: do not talk about how much you love books, if you don't want to be outed as an imposter. In library school, that was the difference between the people who wanted to be real librarians and everyone else. When asked about what drew you to the profession, you should talk about your commitment to community building, your interest in creating and understanding organizational systems, or your dedication to the life-saving powers of information literacy. Real librarians should be so much more than their love for books. Everyone loves books. What else have you got? Once I discovered this distinction, I did as I always have. I took note of what the correct answer should be and repeated it until I sounded convincing. Then, I stopped talking about books. Here's the thing, though. I love books *so much*. I'm a librarian because, well, books. I made up all the other reasons to sound smart and to fit in. See? I am no better than a stepsister trying to claim a slipper. While books were the last toes I gave up to fit into the slipper, they were not, however, the first.

* * *

Sleepovers, sledding, ballet classes, and s'mores. Growing up in Southern California's Inland Empire, there were so many things I knew and lived and loved only because I read about them from the inside of my mother's closet. On nights when she worked the dinner shift, my brother Joe and I would hide in her walk-in closet. According to the information network of Taiwanese aunties, children could not legally stay at home alone until they were twelve years old.[1] There's no fear of the law like a first-generation immigrant's fear of the law, though, and my mom was certain that a neighbor would see a light on in the living room, realize she wasn't home, and Child Protective Services (CPS) would be on our doorstep before the night was over. So, the closet it was. With the coats pushed aside, the floor lined with blankets, Tupperware containers of noodles, and, most important, the haul of books from our weekly visit to the public library, the closet felt like the kind of clubhouse where normal kids might spend their Saturday nights. If I had to pinpoint one instigating reason for my life as a reader, this would be it. I think about this memory with fondness. As badly as I wanted to watch *Grease* while lying in a sleeping bag at a friend's house, I never resented the nights spent with Joe in our reading cave. I don't remember feeling ashamed about hiding from CPS in a closet, but I also can't recall having ever told anyone this story.

* * *

In *Covering: The Hidden Assault on Our Civil Rights*, Kenji Yoshino (2006) argues that given the increasing diversity of this country, there are more ways than ever for us to feel out of place. As a result, "everyone covers . . . to fit into the mainstream" (ix). Covering, explained by Yoshino, is anything an individual does to hide a disfavored trait. For instance, an African American woman in a corporate office might straighten her hair rather than wearing cornrows; mothers may avoid taking time off during the day; or queer couples may refrain from attending work events together. While contemporary civil rights laws protect individuals against discrimination for traits they cannot change (race, gender, sexual orientation), many of the traits people cover have been dismissed as necessary or innocuous assimilation. Under closer examination, however, we can see that the cost of fitting in is not the same for everyone. After all, Yoshino writes, "the reason racial minorities are pressured to 'act white' is because of white supremacy. The reason women are told to downplay their child-care responsibilities in the workplace is because of patriarchy. And the reason gays are asked not to 'flaunt' is because of homophobia" (xi).

Though he is a legal scholar, Yoshino does not believe covering can be resolved by the law. Instead, people who are asked to cover should be brave enough to start conversations with their friends, neighbors, supervisors, and strangers about why they are being asked to cover. Here, I think about Claudia Rankine (2014) asking "what do you mean?" in *Citizen* when a colleague implies she is always on sabbatical (47). I side-eye Yoshino's optimism that "these conversations will help us chart and stay the course between the monocultural America suggested by conservative alarmists and the balkanized America suggested by radical multiculturalists" (Yoshino 2006, 195). Though, if the person asking you to cover is, well, you, that is a different conversation. In 2015, Yoshino was the keynote speaker at the CUNY Faculty Diversity and Inclusion Conference; as he outlined his theory, I felt a shiver of intellectual excitement (this is so interesting!) followed by anxious recognition (oh, no, this explains my whole life). During the Q&A segment of the keynote, someone asked him to comment on the hidden bias that comes up in search committees. "When institutions say they're looking for a good 'cultural fit,' isn't that code for 'someone just like the rest of us'? How is someone who is unlike the rest of them supposed to stand a chance?" While I don't remember Yoshino's surely eloquent response, the question lingered with me for years because I was caught off guard by my own answer: cover everything different about yourself until you are the perfect cultural fit.

In a report about inclusion produced for the consulting firm Deloitte, Yoshino and Christie Smith (2013) divide covering into four axes: appearance based, affiliation based, advocacy based, and association based. I have built permanent, well-furnished homes in each axis. Appearance-based covering has to do with how you present yourself, from grooming to mannerisms. I think about my preschool teacher asking my parents to give me a chance to fit in by never speaking English with me so I wouldn't pick up their accented pronunciations; about sneaking razors out of airline toiletry kits to shave my legs; about answering "yes" when a friend asked if my dress was from Free People[2] when it was actually made by my mom. In affiliation-based covering, you avoid behaviors stereotypical of your identity. I remember talking about how bad I was at math, casually agreeing to split the check even as I calculated the cost of the drinks I didn't have, and insisting on bringing sandwiches instead of fried rice for lunch. Advocacy-based covering comes into play when you do or do not decide to stick up for your group. I laughed along with everyone else when an upperclassman asked me if I had a sideways vagina, stayed silent when a library school professor referred to the Orientals and Wetbacks who came into her public library, and let countless people mock the kind of broken, English-Asian accent with which my mom speaks. Finally, association-based covering dictates how you interact with your group members (Yoshino and Smith 2013, 4). I think about the way I avoided my college Asian student group, about the absence of even a single citation for an Asian or Asian American author in any paper written for my BA or MA in literature, and about trying to manipulate the mentor/mentee selection process so I wouldn't be matched up with the only other Asian graduate assistant.

Tooms, Lugg, and Bogotch (2010) agree that the pursuit of "fit" for marginalized individuals seeking positions in education is necessarily all encompassing. "The social construction of what a leader is can be based on skill sets as well as visceral perceptions of what a leader looks and acts like," and candidates end up altering their style of dress or taking up golfing to meet those expectations (109). Fit, after all, "does not begin or end with recruitment, selection, hiring, or evaluation; rather, forces that drive 'who fits' and 'who does not fit' in terms of leadership are embedded in every aspect of society" (118).

"I always forget you are Asian," my friend says, as I set down a kale Caesar, my contribution to the potluck.

"Your English is really good," my landlord says, as I sign my lease.

"I would never have said that if I knew about your mom," my sister-in-law says, apologizing for calling immigrants job-stealing freeloaders.

* * *

Here's another story I rarely tell about myself, though it's really my mother's story. My mother, Yuen Su, immigrated from Taiwan to the United States in 1984 when my father was accepted to the University of Central Missouri. Soon after my brother and I were born, they moved to California. My father left our family before my sixth birthday. My mother committed to raising us alone even though she spoke limited English, had no family in the country, and traded alimony and child support for full custody.[3] To do so, she would sew all day in a factory, waitress in the evenings, and then work on alterations for neighbors into the early morning hours. The first year, the three of us lived with her boss, sleeping horizontally across a mattress on the floor. Joe and I entertained ourselves by putting together those pouches of extra buttons and thread that come with your new shirt and hiding in racks of clothes. Later, when we moved into our own place, my mom brought two industrial sewing machines with her so she could take in bulk sewing, earning twenty cents or so for each piece she completed. In retrospect, she must have been tired all the time. Still, twice a week, she would take me and Joe to the Upland Public Library so we could load up on books while she met with her adult literacy tutor. In a childhood that was marked by frugality, coming home with a pile of library books always felt like wealth.

My mom often laughs to her friends about the irony of my being a librarian when she still needs me to translate the operating instructions for her pasta machine. "I'm just not sure how it happened," she says. This from the woman who hangs laundry out to dry to save on the electric bill, but always gave me a hundred dollars to buy books at Christmas; who signed me up to volunteer at the public library as soon as I was old enough to do so; who indulged me in my collection of large-print back issues of *Reader's Digests* purchased from the Friends of the Library bookstore (I had the entire run of issues from 1990 to 2000); and who turned her closet into a reading cave.

* * *

As I was starting library school in 2008, the textile industry in Southern California was rapidly outsourced, leaving my mom with few employment options despite her degree in fashion and decades of experience. My plan for my master's in library science quickly shifted from "following my dreams" to "find a job, help my mom." Though I planned to specialize in youth services, I abandoned that path after seeing competent classmates repeatedly getting offers for under $30,000 a year. I loved the six years I spent volunteering in the Children's Department at my local library, the tactile delight of preparing craft supplies, and working with students in my reading comprehension group; I even loved the time I was drenched in toad urine while assisting a Summer Reading Program performer. Still, academic librarianship seemed to be the more stable and comparatively lucrative option, offering a safety net for my family.

It was also, however, populated by seriously intimidating, very accomplished Adult People who knew what they were doing. It felt like I showed up for a race three miles from the starting line. One of my friends left her job as a grant writer to go to library school and volunteered for Planned Parenthood. Another taught courses on fairy tales while earning a master's degree in English. A third had a job lined up with the National Archives months before graduation. I was twenty-two years old, microwaving tater tots for most meals, and treading water on the daily to avoid being found out as a fraud. I wonder now what would have happened if I had just said, "I have no idea how any of this is supposed to work. I've never heard the word *tenure* before today. It's crazy that I am supposed to know how to teach after one class." Instead, I put on a "hey, I'm competent just like the rest of you" mask and kept it on for the entirety of my degree, through the job search, and the four years I spent at my first institution.

In 2010, the University of New Mexico hired me as an access services librarian right out of library school as a nontenure-track faculty member. I will always be grateful for the supportive mentors who gave me every opportunity to experiment, grow, and succeed, and for everyone in access services for their patience and friendship. As hard as I worked to conceal my inexperience and to make my background irrelevant, however, there were limitations to the illusion. I could hardly hide the fact that I was the youngest faculty member by at least a decade, nor the fact that I was, at hire, the only Asian librarian on a faculty with only a handful of people of color (POC).

One of my White male colleagues, a full professor, decided to ignore me for over a year. Like, straight-up-silent-treatment, deaf-to-my-greetings, walk-past-me-like-I-was-invisible, ignore me. I don't know what I did. If you asked him if my age, gender, or race factored into his animosity, I am certain he would deny it up and down. Still, I wonder if he would have been able to pull off the same behavior toward someone he considered an equal. I would also be curious about the demographics of the sorts of folks he would consider his equals. I have the same thought about another White male colleague, hired after me, albeit on a tenure-track line. In a bizarre turn of events, a cell phone was found, turned into the reference desk, and then given to someone other than its rightful owner. I was uninvolved until things went wrong. As I was about to file a report with campus security, my colleague, who worked in a different branch, came into my office and closed the door behind him, blocking any escape route. "I need to talk to you about the way you handled that," he said. "It was bad management, and your staff is out of control."

"They're not my staff," I said (because they weren't), "and I'm not their manager. I *am* trying to fix the problem, though."

"It's not enough," he said, and proceeded to lecture me on professionalism. To be clear, this person, who was not my superior in any way, just wanted to make sure I knew I had disappointed him, and that I had fallen out of line. "Maybe this wouldn't have happened," I thought, "if I were in a tenure-track position." Without the seemingly innate confidence and power granted White men, I looked to tenure and rank to legitimize myself.

Then there was the time, at a large meeting, when a White colleague made a joke suggesting all questions unaddressed by our knowledge base and FAQ be directed to me. "For a good time, call Silvia!" she quipped, to collective laughter. I was far from the only single person in the room, though

I was the only young, single, Asian woman. Is this why a room full of my colleagues laughed at the joke? Hadn't I covered up all the ways you could associate me with the sexualized, fetishized, "me love you long time" stereotypes? "They would never have said that to one of the subject librarians," I thought. Like one of Yoshino and Smith's (2013) respondents, though, I wondered "how far I [could] go—personally subsuming my personality in pursuit of success. I [felt] like I [was] being asked to choose between being a three-dimensional authentic person and a two-dimensional cardboard cutout" (13).

* * *

After long days and nights at the factory or the restaurant or at her sewing machine, my mom would spend the late evening hours working her way through stories assigned by her adult literacy tutor, underlining new vocabulary words and penciling in Chinese definitions. I read next to her, engrossed in self-education of a different sort. I studied up on summer camps and makeovers via *The Babysitter's Club* and *Sweet Valley High*, always dreading the moment when one of my friends would say, "you've never had a manicure? That's so *weird*."[4] I sought out cozy stories about big families like Sydney Taylor's Jewish American *All-of-a-Kind Family*, or the ode to maple syrup that was *Miracles on Maple Hill* by Virginia Sorensen, so I could figure out the correct way to celebrate Thanksgiving. As it turns out, the turkey is *not* supposed to be stuffed with glutinous rice, shiitake mushrooms, and pork belly. I modeled myself after plucky, bookish types, experimenting with feminism via Anne Shirley and Hermione Granger. And, I read and reread *Grimms' Fairy Tales*, relishing in gruesome stories about maidens made wealthy as a reward for their goodness. Be kind, work hard, find a slipper, leave your poverty behind.

Just as I could feel myself falling deep into a story, though, my mom would nudge me. "How do you say this word?" she'd ask, holding open a junior novelization about Harriet Tubman, and "what is *abolitionist*?"

"Just sound it out," I'd snap, "it's not that hard. Why do you have to bother me?" I know, I'm cringing at how awful I was, too.

"I'm sorry I'm not smart like the other moms," she would say. Or, in an argument, "I know you weren't born into the family you wanted. Maybe you'll be luckier in the next life." Seeing the hurt in my mom's eyes, I'd set aside my own book to listen to her labored reading, fighting back irritation to prove my love for her. Still, she wasn't wrong about me. My mom is the love of my life, but I still can't silence the part of me that wants her to travel to new cities with me, gripe about the assessment culture in higher education, and challenge the limitations of my reading of *Middlemarch* in my senior thesis. Thanks to the power of assimilation, I didn't need to wait for reincarnation to live a life separate from my mother. Every degree earned, my week at theater camp, and the first time I used oregano in a pasta sauce all sent me further away from her. Then I wore red underwear for the Lunar New Year because she told me to, made tea with the ginger she insisted on mailing to me to stoke my internal fire, and asked her to explain Taiwanese politics during the boring parts of a Korean drama—and I'm right back again.

A few years ago, my brother and I accompanied my mom on her annual trip to Taiwan; our last visit was fifteen years ago for our grandmother's funeral. The last time I saw my grandfather he was doing tai chi at dawn. Now, he's bedridden with occasional moments of lucidity. Looking at our family pictures, my uncle comments on how much my mom looks like my grandmother. Later that day, my mom has a realization. "I think that your grandfather thinks that I'm your grandmother," she says, "and that you are me. That's why he won't let go of my hand, and why he grins whenever he sees you." My grandfather is not wrong about me, either. I am turning into my mother. I worry like it's a competitive sport. I anthropomorphize the appliances. If the tin foil looks clean enough to use again, I fold it into a neat square and tuck it back into the drawer. It is reassuring, knowing I can't shake off my mom.

There was also this strange thing where each day, some quirk or unusual preference of mine would be exposed as the default standard in Taipei. All beverages were served at my favorite temperature (slightly warm), with a straw. I could reach the straps on the train! Shopping for blush was easy because all the shades were designed to flatter my skin tone, and they all came in dinosaur- or cake-shaped packaging (I love dinosaurs and cake!). I felt an intense, liberating sense of ease. I was also lost a lot and had no idea how to answer the most basic questions about whether I had a loyalty card or if I wanted a bag. Due to miscommunication, I accidentally got a perm instead of a conditioning treatment. One afternoon, as I was trying on Hello Kitty sweaters, the shop girl asked, "where are you from?"

"The United States," I replied, laughing inside at the unavoidability of that question.

"Oh, that's so weird," she said, "your Mandarin is really good, and you don't have an American accent. But you don't sound Taiwanese, either." Which, of course, sums up my problem.

* * *

After Yoshino's talk, I committed to uncovering as much of myself as possible. I wanted to dismantle decades of self-loathing and inauthentic identities. Some efforts came easily, like the class I co-taught with a Chinese librarian around my age, with a similar haircut. In the past, I would have been consumed with worries about whether students could tell us apart, and whether any department could have more than one of us. As it turns out, students could tell us apart because we were two different people (duh), and though there were five Asian librarians at my institution, the time-space continuum remained stable. More important, teaching with Hong was incredibly fun, and her perspective as a non-American was illuminating on numerous topics, including net neutrality and active learning. This semester, I put together a display celebrating Asian Pacific Heritage Month, full of all the Asian and Asian American authors I've sought out in the last few years, ignoring the small voice that still whispers, "maybe if you stay away from Asian things, everyone will forget that you are different." I talked to my first-generation and immigrant students about maintaining boundaries when assimilating. I spoke up more.

Other efforts were more complicated. I applied, for example, for one of two open spots on a national committee with a feminist agenda; every member of the committee was a White woman. "Feminism without intersectionality is just white supremacy," I whispered to myself while writing an application that uncovered all the parts of my identity I would normally conceal. Despite a stated commitment to diversity, and though their lack of diversity was attributed to the (non-diverse) individuals who previously applied, the committee chose two more White women to fill the open seats. In an e-mail encouraging me to reapply next year, the chair wrote, "we currently have three academics on the committee and we try to balance types of librarians." We. Try. To. Balance. Types. Of. Librarians. I took a deep breath, and moved on. It's complicated.

It has been seven years since my MLIS, which means I can officially call myself a mid-career librarian. I don't think it's a coincidence that my decision to stop covering coincided with an emerging sense of competence and professional confidence (and I doubt I could have stopped covering without feeling competent), but I do wonder what else I could have done with those early years. I may never catch up to my library school friends, but today I volunteer as a clinic escort for Planned Parenthood, and I have a second master's degree. As the first year experience and reference librarian at LaGuardia Community College, a CUNY institution, I teach semester-long credit courses. With the support of my department, I went up for an early promotion. As of fall 2017, I will be an associate professor, which bodes well for tenure (CUNY separates promotion and tenure). I'm an Adult Person and a real librarian, all toes intact, no thanks to any magic slippers.

"The thing is," I said to my friend and frequent collaborator, Lori, "by the time I was applying for jobs, I had no rough POC edges. The rift between my actual personality and my work personality was already there. Every choice I made has been on the side of assimilation and compromise and making White people feel comfortable around me. The way I talk and the way I teach and my whole personality is based on meeting expectations of fit. I fit in."

"That's all of us, though," Lori replied. "If you're a librarian and a person of color, you already proved you're one of the 'good ones' who won't make trouble."

"Is it too late to stop?" I asked.

NOTES

1. This is not a thing. Only three states have laws setting a minimum age for children left at home alone; California is definitely not one of them. Taiwanese aunties are a complicated information source. See https://www.childwelfare.gov/pubPDFs/homealone.pdf.

2. Free People is a sister store to Anthropologie and Urban Outfitters.

3. This is also not a (legal) thing. My father threatened to send us overseas to be raised by our aunt in Hong Kong.

4. My first real manicure didn't happen until college.

Part Four

Leading by Reflection

LEADING
— BY —
REFLECTION
REFLECTION

Chapter Eleven

"While I Have the Floor . . ."

Mark D. Winston

The title of this chapter has two meanings (at least) related to opportunity and responsibility. First, as the idiom of "having the floor" (or the turn to speak) suggests, the title refers to my sense of the importance of thinking carefully about and making the most of any opportunity to address an audience. In the context of this chapter, there are things that are important for me to say, as I have the opportunity to write about my career, opportunities, and my decisions. In addition, the title refers to my wanting to accomplish all that I can from where I sit professionally. While I "have the floor" (meaning I am in a position allowing the potential to exert some influence and to have some impact), I want to do so thoughtfully and to maximize that impact.

When I developed my chapter, "The Minority Librarian: Why Your Role Is Different," for *IOOV* 1996, I was a doctoral student, studying full time, and thinking and writing about both my most recent position in libraries and about where I would go next (Winston 1996). Ultimately, my dissertation research focused on recruitment theory and the decision-making factors (reflecting decisions of individuals to enter the profession) correlated with the extent to which individuals become leaders (broadly defined) in the profession (Winston 1997). Coincidentally, as I prepared to meet the due date for the selection of a draft title for the chapter in this current volume, I was in discussion with a university colleague—a writing instructor. As a part of my responsibilities as engagement officer for the University Library at Widener University, I had been invited to present to a group of high school students who were participating in a summer program at the university. The focus of the program was that of preparation for college-level coursework. I was asked to introduce the young people to the library and to the research process, using library databases, to support their classwork in the program. While the program focuses on writing, reading, science, math, and "success skills," there is limited discussion of professional options for the students. In addition to preparing to talk with them about subject research, I wanted to spend a few minutes discussing how they can conduct research on careers. As I introduced this topic, I asked each of them to tell the group what he or she would like to do professionally. The responses ran the gamut, but, as the instructor jokingly referred to the relevance of this question for herself, she indicated that her goal has been and is to become a librarian.

Subsequently, I met with her to encourage her to pursue a second master's degree in library and information science. (I considered titling this chapter "My Profession: I Recommend It Highly.") In fact, my career path, in the positions of academic librarian, assistant director and director in academic libraries, assistant chancellor for academic affairs, teaching faculty member, and, now, public library director, has been very rewarding and provided the opportunity to further goals that are important to me. The core goal that guides me and defines my leadership ethos is that of working toward the professional principle of ensuring access to information.

LEADERSHIP

In my scholarship and my professional activity, leadership has likely been the primary, broad, overarching focus. This has been the case when I have written explicitly not only about leadership but also about access to information, diversity and organizational success, and economic inequality, for example. In this regard, my writing and scholarship have operated in tandem with my professional positions. This has been conscious, pragmatically making the decision to write about issues that were of interest to me and directly relevant to my day-to-day work. In addition, engaging in the reading, research, and writing enhances my work and makes for more informed practice as a librarian, as an administrator, and as a teaching faculty member. The research helps provide a frame of reference and reduces the impact of our own biases and potential lack of objectivity in our work. The research also reduces the lure of thinking that our individual institutions are so unique that we cannot learn from the perspectives and experiences of others and their institutions. I have valued the opportunity to contribute to the academic and scholarly discussion, as informed by my perspective, my analysis, and my vantage point, by engaging in scholarship.

Of the hundreds of definitions of the term *leadership*, at its heart, *leadership* has been defined in relation to the issue of influence—the potential for individuals, in particular, to have influence. As an administrator, I have been most gratified, and have most enjoyed, the opportunity to influence the direction of the organizations of which I have been a part. From a management perspective, enhancing the effectiveness and efficiency of an organization is challenging and rewarding, whether we are refining processes, making hiring decisions that benefit the organization in a substantive way, or more closely aligning our work and our spending with the articulated mission of the organization.

In libraries, our mission, at its heart, relates to fostering access to information, in order to enhance the ability of individuals to make informed decisions and to be full participants in society. Clearly, this is a goal that requires leadership because of the factors that work against it. For example, unlike the case with some other academic units in universities (such as business or medical schools) and other public organizations, the genuine importance and role of libraries are not fully understood by many of those outside of the discipline and the profession, including those who make funding decisions for libraries. Our role as leaders, then, relates to articulating a compelling case for the value and importance of libraries. In the academic context, we have the responsibility to make the case to university administrators and to teaching faculty, often in a context in which the pervasiveness of information available online causes there to be questions about the need for and the future of academic libraries. Similarly, in public libraries, there is the need to make the compelling case with boards of directors and political officials, who may value books and literacy, for example, but possibly not the broader issue of access to information and high-quality and high-level information services, in an information literate society.

In addition, aspects of racial, ethnic, and economic diversity have been correlated with documented efforts to limit individuals' personal and professional opportunities on many levels. Unfortunately, it is also the case that there are even recent examples of political leaders and other policy makers who have acknowledged the importance of access to information and who have worked proactively to limit access for certain segments of the population, including recent cases involving the poor, in relation to Obamacare and the Medicaid expansion at the state level (Novack 2014; Killough 2014).

After having been a teaching faculty member for ten years (and working in library administration prior to that), I began my first position as library director for Rutgers University's Newark (New Jersey) campus in August 2008. The timing was noteworthy, in general, because of the start of the major economic downturn and the related organizational budgetary issues facing the university and the library. However, the timing was also noteworthy because the presidential election campaign was well underway. In terms of diversity, few milestones have been as monumental as those election results. On the morning after the historic election, I was walking through the lobby of the library toward the elevator for a meeting on the fourth floor. One of the staff members, who had completed a graduate program at the university not too long before, entered the building and was walking toward the elevator as well. We said hello. And, he showed me the election headline on the newspaper that he had just purchased, I assumed, at the student center, just one building away from the library. I said, "The world changed yesterday." He agreed and told me about the gathering of friends he had had at his apartment to watch the election returns. We both left the elevator on the fourth floor and wished each other a good day, as I recall.

A short time later, he cc'd me on a message that he sent to his friends, summarizing the events of the prior day and that morning. He quoted my statement about the world having changed and said that after we spoke, he went went on about his day. At the time when I read his message, I was put off by it. The suggestion seemed to be that I had been somewhat dismissive. In retrospect, I have come to think of his statement very differently. I think he intended to indicate that the world had changed. And, I fully acknowledged that fact and realized the need to be fully conscious of the enormity of the change but to not be distracted from the task at hand—my leadership of the library and my next meeting, in particular.

THE CASE FOR DIVERSITY IN RESEARCH AND COMMUNITY

An anecdote about awareness and having the floor figures prominently in describing my thinking related to my work with diversity. In a totally different context and on a totally different scale, as Michelle Obama said to her husband just prior to his first major speech on the national stage at the Democratic National Convention in 2004, "Just don't screw it up, buddy" (Obama 2007, 185). Given my own life experiences, my own group membership as African American, and the examples of leaders who have been an influence on me, I have worked actively to make diversity a high priority in recruitment and hiring. While many might assume, and have assumed, that my emphasizing diversity is based on my group membership and is simply a personal agenda, that is a limited view.

In much of my published scholarship related to diversity, I have emphasized the empirical research, which indicates the direct correlation between the representation of diverse perspectives in organizations (in organizational decision making and in targeting and engaging with segments of the market) and organizational success. Making a compelling case for diversity as a high priority is important, given the pervasive misperceptions that "qualified" minorities are in short supply. Having seen the "pipeline" from the vantage point of the undergraduate and graduate classroom as a faculty member, from academic administration and library administration on the college campus, I have worked to foster diversity with an informed perspective.

In addition, in my positions in two urban universities in Newark, New Jersey, and in Chester, Pennsylvania (Widener University), and the J. Lewis Crozer (Public) Library (also in Chester), I have had the opportunity to promote access to information when issues of economic inequality (and race and ethnicity) are front and center.

Here, in fostering access to information, leadership is key, whether we are working with campus security or law enforcement to ensure a "presence" that balances safety with inclusion; making decisions regarding policies that prioritize primary user populations, while supporting secondary user populations; or fostering a tone and tenor of respect for the prominent member of the community, who uses the library, as well as the person in tattered clothes. Leadership, in the urban context, requires the ability to influence those with competing concerns, about the emphasis on the underlying and bedrock principle of access in the most real world of circumstances.

WHILE I HAVE THE FLOOR . . .

"But the one who does not know and does things deserving punishment will be beaten with few blows. From everyone who has been given much, much will be demanded; and from the one who has been entrusted with much, much more will be asked."—Luke 12:48

In my first position after college, with the federal government, I had an experience that, to a large extent, epitomized the idea of being underestimated and, subsequently, motivated. As a part of a training program for the thirty or so newly hired professionals in all the locations of the federal agency for which I was working, we spent a period of extended training at the headquarters. As is typical in such facilitated training, sessions included work in groups and individually. And, we were asked to "report out" to the larger group at times. After having interacted with the other participants for a few days, I presented, based on some activity or another. A little later that day I was in the men's room when two of the other participants came in. Because of where I was standing, they could not see me. They began talking about me. (They described me in a way that was specific and definitive—demographically and what I had presented.) One of the individuals said the following about "that Black guy"—"He did really well. I was surprised." When I walked into their view (up to them at the sink), his facial expression reflected genuine surprise, and guilt, it appeared. I thought of my reporting out as effective, but not necessarily unusual for myself or someone who looked like me. The fact that one may be underestimated is somewhat unfortunate. To be privy to the thinking when those who do the underestimating articulate the sentiment so boldly is also somewhat surprising. However, his statement represented both a back-handed compliment and a great motivator to maintain high standards and to not "screw it up, buddy," when one is the first in a given context or the only one in the room (of whichever underrepresented group).

Those who doubted me, work(ed) against me, and, particularly those who have said that they simply did (do) not like me, their impact on me has been better than good. Certainly, it has been used for my good. In the most direct way, I learned. And, I am pleased to be more conscious, focused, and to never doubt the value of keeping at it, in pursuit of goals, when there is opposition.

I am fortunate. Being a part of a profession that exists in large measure to support the full engagement and participation of individuals in society is an opportunity. And, I am particularly fortunate to have been able to devote my professional energy to this worthy cause in support of both the mission of institutions of higher learning and in the community-based organization of the public library.

In this regard, I have always loved the idea that annual performance evaluations, particularly in the academic community, require our summarizing activities and accomplishments for the past year. My enthusiasm for this aspect of the process is consistent with my longer term thinking about the value of ensuring that we leave organizations a little different and a little better than was the case before we arrived. It is also the case that the process of documenting one's activities and accomplishments, as well as areas for further development, represents a valuable and ongoing opportunity to enhance one's level of self-awareness, which is so key to success as a leader. Accurately identifying one's strengths and weaknesses is so important in determining how one works most effectively and targets one's time and talents, consciously compensates for and addresses areas in need of development, and assembles a team that provides a counterbalance and support.

If at the end of my career, there are those who underestimated me, who say, "He did really well. I was surprised," some progress will have been made. The key will be having done well for a good cause—that of libraries and fostering greater access to information.

Chapter Twelve

What Have I Learned from the Past, Present, and Future?

José A. Aguiñaga

It is hard to imagine that over twenty years ago, I wrote a chapter (Aguiñaga 1996) for *IOOV* 1996. Since the book was published, many other experiences and events have taken place in my personal and professional life. I began my academic librarian career at the University of Houston Libraries (UHL) in 1994, as a social sciences librarian, and eventually had a dual role in public services and as the libraries personnel coordinator. The combination of these two roles served as a solid foundation for what I would experience over the next two plus decades as a member of the academy. While still working at the UHL, I attended my first Association of College and Research Libraries (ACRL) conference in Nashville, Tennessee, in 1997. This conference served as a catalyst for me to consider moving back home to San Diego, California. A short while later, I became aware of a reference and electronic resources librarian position at my undergraduate alma mater, the University of San Diego (USD). I applied, interviewed, and was selected for this position. As we all know, the cost of living in San Diego is considerably higher than most other places. After moving to San Diego, my wife, April, also a librarian, was unable to obtain full-time employment. I am grateful to her for allowing me to return home, but after twelve months it became obvious to the both of us that we needed to do something to be more financially stable. So we began our job searches, this time, looking beyond Southern California. We decided to focus our search in Phoenix, Arizona, where April has roots. We met in library school at the University of Arizona (UA); April earned her undergraduate degree from Arizona State University (ASU), and has family members who still reside in Phoenix.

In the fall of 1998, I applied for and accepted a social sciences librarian position at Arizona State University, West Campus (ASU West). Simultaneously, April began applying for opportunities in public libraries in the Phoenix area. Eventually, she landed a position as a children's librarian with the Glendale Public Library. It was a difficult decision to relocate from my hometown, leaving friends and family, but for both of us, being financially stable, and active in our professional associations (for example, the American Library Association), was paramount to continuing with our early careers as librarians. In early 1999, we relocated to Glendale, Arizona. I literally lived across the street from the ASU West campus. This would be my third job as an academic librarian since receiving my MLS in the fall of 1994. Reflecting on these early experiences demonstrated to me that other library professionals may wonder about my short-term library experiences, and I needed to be cognizant of the perception of my actions. I owe many for refining and reenergizing my work ethic, whether it was my mom, dad, April, or other professional librarians impacting and informing my career path and choices. Without conversing and hearing out their suggestions and then making the final decision and taking a chance with the new location, I would not have learned as much. I truly believe that to experience life, you have to live life. Plain and simple, learn from the good and bad and, most certainly, don't repeat the mistakes you've made in the past.

ASU West provided me with another level of expertise and awareness of my development as a person. As I reflect now about my two-and-half years at ASU West, I learned that sometimes working environments might not be the right fit for me. The librarians I worked with made me aware of my deficiencies (lack of leadership, engagement, participation). These elements were truly missing from my daily contributions.

ARIZONA

In transitioning from California to Phoenix, it took some time for me to acclimate. Adjusting to the idea of not having a visible view of the coastline and realizing that I was beginning my third academic librarian job in five years made me pause to wonder if I could continue as an academic librarian. Should I remain in this professional field? I contemplated pursuing another career, but after various lengthy conversations with other well-seasoned librarians and, of course, talking with April, I decided to remain in the field. Analyzing what you are doing in the given moment and applying the appropriate steps to improve is not a simple process. You have to be honest in your own assessment and then apply the corrective steps to expand your future opportunities. With that in mind, I began to dig into my social sciences librarian work duties at ASU West and continue my professional development as an academic librarian. This occurred in different ways, whether it was by being mentored, demonstrating my teaching skills to colleagues, or working on library, university, and even national projects.

My mentoring experiences at ASU West were multifaceted, and initially I had more experienced librarians offering their suggestions and advice on how I should continue with my career development. Second, I also had ASU West faculty and even administrators who offered their counsel on my contributions and helped me focus on what I wanted to do in the immediate future. These mentoring experiences made me rediscover my raison d'être for being an academic librarian. I had chosen this career path to help others, people who were trying to enhance their own personal and professional lives. I recalled that, when I went to school, I was able to succeed because, during my undergraduate and graduate years, many individuals, whether they were family or faculty, had encouraged and guided me. Now it was time for me to pay my community back. Additionally, one mentor with whom I remain in contact from my ASU West days is Dr. Alberto Pulido. While we were still at ASU West, he and I connected in a harmonious way that made me understand what I needed to achieve and continue working on in order to continue my contributions as a member of the academy. His strategic suggestions have proven to be very relevant throughout my career. He was able to make me understand how my professional demeanor could be improved, for example, by asking clarifying questions in order to contribute during meetings. This little recommendation would open up other opportunities for me to be actively engaged during topics of discussion. On a side note, Dr. Pulido and I literally have deep roots from the same neighborhood. His family owned the local grocery store where I grew up in San Ysidro (a suburb of San Diego), California. In an interesting way, this made me feel comfortable having conversations with him about topics that went beyond the academy. Our frank discussions made me realize the opportunities that existed, when one is candid and can confide in others, while still maintaining a professional decorum. What I learned from my ASU West days: continue thinking about the future and ask myself what my passion is for being in this profession.

LONG BEACH, CA

I began rediscovering my passion for helping others while at ASU West, and then another career opportunity developed. In early spring 2001, I applied for a social sciences librarian position at California State University, Long Beach (CSULB) and was successful in securing it. During the on-campus interview, one question that stood out was the path of my academic librarian career and how long I planned to stay at Long Beach. Of course, this question implied that I had moved too often with regard to my past library jobs. I answered the question with a frank response. I realized that my short-term employment history may give the perception that I moved too often, but I then added the rich experiences that I had acquired from the three varied higher education institutions, which had prepared me to seek this opportunity with CSULB.

I was enjoying the work that I was contributing to the everyday operations of the library. Whether it was through instruction, research, or committee initiatives, my work week flew by quickly. I owe much to Roman Kochan, CSULB library dean, and Susan Luévano, CSULB librarian, who inspired my ongoing development as an academic librarian in different ways. Mr. Kochan's no-nonsense attitude refined my skills, in that I discovered how to be focused in getting the job done and, of course, doing it well. My discussions with Ms. Luévano about academic librarianship, the academy, and society made me reflect deeper into who I was and what was I doing that would contribute to the success of others and myself. Conversations with both individuals during my tenure at CSULB opened my eyes to different kinds of mentoring and led to other academic adventures within my future career decisions, for example, whether I should I pursue another master's or delve into a doctoral program.

I tremendously enjoyed working with undergraduate and graduate nontraditional students at CSULB. By nontraditional, I mean students who have returned to college, are working part time or full time, have family obligations, and, of course, are no longer in the eighteen to twenty-two age range. Additionally, most of these students were minority students, which encouraged me about the future in higher education. Each type of student possessed a desire for completing their studies, and in my experience, students of color had an extra drive in achieving their academic goals. It was great to be a member of this academic community, and I made sure these students knew they had another ally on their side who would assist them in their academic tasks. Teaching and conversing with students about their goals and dreams in relation to their studies was uplifting, and it was during this time that I finally started to understand that I, too, could influence others in the pursuit of their educational goals. That in itself was an aha! moment for me. By this time, I had been an academic librarian for more than seven years, and I was finally realizing and living out why I decided to become a librarian—to help others.

My academic librarian position at CSULB was full of adventures, and, adding another element in my career path, I became a faculty-in-residence. Each year, the university had an annual call for applications for faculty members who wanted to participate in a program that provided mentoring and tutoring services to students living in the dormitories. In exchange, the selected faculty member and their significant other could reside in the dorms with free room and board. Twice during my time at CSULB I applied, and after submitting my second application, I was selected. My wife and I both looked forward to living on campus and enjoying and absorbing all we could from this new learning adventure. Ten faculty members were selected for this program as well. Within a short period of time, we established a new community of colleagues and became highly engaged with students who lived on campus in the dorms. Living on campus provided me the opportunity to reflect deeper on my own development and how I could contribute and influence future students and library staff. Of course, another positive of this experience was saving money for other aspects of our lives. Overall the faculty-in-residence program was a very positive experience for my wife and me.

MASTER OF PUBLIC ADMINISTRATION

In 2002, I decided to apply for the master of public administration program (MPA) at the CSULB. One of the benefits as an employee was the ability to take two courses per semester at a very low tuition rate. Besides this wonderful benefit, the reason why I decided to pursue the MPA was due to the curriculum, which would give me the theoretical and, at times, practical knowledge base regarding personnel, budget, policy, and organizations. Acquiring this field of expertise would hopefully assist me in my future librarian career opportunities. During the day, I was focused on my librarian duties, and in the evenings and on weekends, I was a graduate student. I definitely enjoyed the courses as well as the faculty and new colleagues I met during my program of study. Working on this degree at that stage of my life was the right thing for me. My maturity as a student and person, and as an adult, assisted me in successfully completing the challenging and, at times, daunting assignments. After graduating with my MPA from CSULB in August 2004, I began to wonder if I should pursue a doctorate in public administration. I had thoroughly enjoyed the academic rigor and discovery of new knowledge, and I began my review of universities that offered such programs. There were two that got my attention—the University of Southern California (USC) and ASU. After a bit more research, I decided to apply to both programs. While preparing my application's statement of purpose, I realized that I enjoyed being an academic and had a passion to pursue my personal, ultimate goal of getting a doctorate. In early 2005, I received notification of my admission status from each university: one said yes, and the other no. This became a pivotal moment in my academic career. Should I say yes to Arizona State University's admissions offer, and leave Long Beach and my family and our friends again? My wife and I discussed this possibility, and ultimately decided to return to the Phoenix area.

THE DOCTORATE

Before commencing the relocation back to Arizona, a job posting appeared for Glendale Community College (a suburb of Phoenix) in Arizona. They were looking for a reference librarian with opportunities to delve into other aspects of librarianship, which I had not experienced before. Additionally, I had worked part time for one semester at this community college during our initial time in Arizona. I decided to apply for the job, got an interview, and then was selected for the position. I wholeheartedly believe in the saying "everything happens for a reason." My transition back to Arizona provided me with vast opportunities beyond work and influenced my choices in life. During the summer of 2005, I relocated back to the house we bought in 2000, in our earlier years, and I was grateful we still had our house in Glendale, Arizona. If you recall, the housing market eventually crashed shortly thereafter. As I began my tenure with Glendale Community College and initial doctoral courses at ASU, I was pushing the envelope on two fronts—and not very well, to say the least. My job was going fine, but my doctoral classes were challenging beyond what I expected. I survived the first semester of classes just barely hanging in there with my grades. During the spring semester, I was just not in tune with what the professors were expecting from me. I took some time to reflect deeply on what my next move would be, and before the spring semester ended, I decided to stop my pursuit of the doctorate at ASU. At the time, I was devastated, but looking back now, I am relieved and grateful that I made that decision.

NOT GIVING UP

Beginning my second year (2006) at Glendale Community College got my creative and intellectual juices flowing as a librarian and faculty member. Work was keeping me occupied with many one-shot instruction sessions, reference desk duty, small library projects, and eventually, committee work. The combination of these varied experiences made my days go by fast but also gave me the ability to see the end results of my contributions in different ways. In 2007, I was assigned to oversee the acquisition, development, and maintenance of the library's online resources. My experience at the University of San Diego assisted in my development of this area for the community college. That same year, I became aware of an e-mail that had been widely shared and disseminated about the Northern Arizona University master's and doctoral programs. The e-mail got my attention, and I decided to attend the informational forum about the doctoral programs. More specifically, the educational leadership doctoral program got my attention. Based on the description of the courses and objectives for this program, it was a better fit for my academic interests, and I submitted my application for this program. In early 2008, I received notice that I had been accepted into the program, and during that summer, I began coursework. In four plus years, I completed and defended my dissertation in fall 2012, and graduated. What I experienced as a full-time academic librarian at Glendale Community College while simultaneously pursuing the doctorate degree changed the way I looked at things in life and expanded my intellectual horizons and awareness of the academy and society. Reading scholars from the education, higher education, public administration, and even political science disciplines gave me greater insights into how individuals and leaders make decisions and truly inspire others to achieve great things in life. When I walked across the stage and was hooded by my dissertation advisor at Northern Arizona University, I felt in awe of achieving this academic milestone. Sitting back down and watching the graduate and undergraduate students made me truly understand that success is not accomplished by one, but is supported by many individuals in your life. The only regret that I have of this achievement was that my mom was not there with me to see this proud moment. She passed away earlier in the year, but I truly felt her presence there with me. Life is always interesting to look back at and be able to express gratitude to and for those who assisted and guided you on your journey to become who you are. Never forget where you came from.

After earning my doctorate of education in educational leadership from Northern Arizona University, what was my next move? By early 2014, I had an answer. I recall the day like yesterday. I have always enjoyed politics and diplomacy; from 2007 to 2014, I was a faculty senator at Glendale Community College. Participating and representing my colleagues in the formal shared-governance process was my way to give back to my academic community. In early 2014, the faculty senate president approached me, and he wanted to talk about an issue. We set up a time, and to my surprise, he wanted to encourage me to run for faculty senate president. He had been involved with the faculty senate for more than ten years and had recognized my level of engagement and participation regarding a multitude of faculty-related issues. I thanked him for making me think of this opportunity. After discussing this opportunity with library and nonlibrary colleagues and, of course, April, I said yes. The election was held, and I won by a slim margin; the other candidate was a very worthy opponent. Applying what I learned from the MPA and EdD programs would assist me in the next two years, 2014 to 2016. The one thing I learned about being faculty senate president, you're always on call, 24/7. Developing a greater understanding of shared governance and making sure due process is followed by the college administration were my primary objectives as faculty senate president.

PRESENT AND FUTURE

After completing my term as faculty senate president, I thought I was going to just focus on a new responsibility as the archivist for the library. I was looking forward to expanding my library knowledge base, and in late summer 2016, I received an e-mail from the chair of the Association of College and Research Libraries (ACRL) Leadership Recruitment & Nomination Committee inquiring to speak with me via telephone. We agreed on a date, and when she called me, we exchanged pleasantries. What happened next astonished me. She wanted to know if I would accept standing for election as vice president/president-elect of ACRL in 2017. As you might imagine, I was just in a daze; I am sure she picked up on my response. This committee must vet members of ACRL before they are asked to stand for election. We spoke for more than thirty minutes about what this opportunity would entail if I were elected. At the end of our discussion, she mentioned that I should consider this opportunity and that she would give me a week to make my decision. I was still in shock. Why would I be asked to stand for election? Guess what? I certainly *reflected* on what I was being asked to do. Since joining the library profession in 1994, I had been involved as a member of various library associations. I had been fortunate enough to be involved as a member and chair on many ACRL committees. I believe my level of participation and involvement had been noted by higher ups. So those of you considering if you should be an active participant in any library association, you know my answer: most definitely YES! Twenty plus years of membership with ACRL provided me with this shot to be the next elected leader. Even though I was not elected, I was grateful to stand for election, and to get to know the opposing candidate, Ms. Lauren Pressley, from the University of Washington in Tacoma. Once we both were announced as candidates, we reached out to each other and maintained an open dialogue about the campaign and future of the association. I do not regret not being elected, and I am truly humbled that I was asked to be one of two candidates for this election.

Besides standing for election, I recently had a personal and emotional moment at the 2017 ACRL conference in Baltimore. While volunteering at the ACRL booth, an individual started to approach me. She looked familiar, and as I was trying to remember where I had met her, she shook my hand and introduced herself. She wanted to thank me for the advice I had given her during a presentation I gave in April 2015 at the Texas Library Association, regarding her pursuit of an additional master's degree. I thanked her for the kind words and was happy that she was moving forward. After she left, it dawned on me that I had a concrete example of how I had influenced someone's pursuit of their goal that contributed to furthering their professional development. This tiny moment made my day, month, and year.

My ACRL candidacy and conference attendance would not be my only major events in 2017. You ask again, what was I planning to do with my doctorate since 2012? Part of the answer was being faculty senate president, then ACRL approached me, and finally I decided to consider applying for library dean positions with community colleges. My twelve years at Glendale Community College provided me with rich experiences that would prepare me for a future leadership position. Around the same time of the election, I had applied for a library dean position at Rio Hondo College in Whittier, California (a suburb of Los Angeles). Yes, folks, if this was meant to be, I would be relocating back to my home state. The Rio Hondo College student body is more than 70 percent Hispanic, and the library had been without a dean for three years. Working at a minority-serving institution would be another way for me to give back to my community. I had two interviews, first with the search committee and then with the vice presidents and president. Each interview was challenging and welcoming. During the entire process, I researched the institution but also examined what I had experienced in my library career and how these experiences would prepare me for the interview and leadership position. To make a long story short, I was offered the position as dean of the library and instructional support, effective July 2017.

Acknowledging my past failures and triumphs has enhanced my present and future development as a person and academic librarian. This comes from self-introspection, reflecting, learning, and contributing to the well-being of those I work with and aiding in their pursuit of academic endeavors. During my twenty-three years as an academic librarian, I have never regretted what I experienced as a member of the academy. The vast number of experiences I have had provided me with different lenses with which to view the inner workings of each institution's organizational culture where I have been a student, librarian, and faculty member. With the national, and to some extent, the international political landscape changes, the advocacy and relevancy for the future of librarians and libraries appears to be in question by individuals who don't believe in facts. We as information professionals provide access and guidance to sorting out the alternative facts that are being disseminated for our present and future students.

Part Five

Family

Family

Chapter Thirteen

Like Our Lives Depended on It

Reflections on Embodied Librarianship, Counterspaces, and Throwing Down

Nicholae Cline, Jorge R. López-McKnight, and Madelyn Shackelford Washington

"Diversity is being invited to the party. Inclusion is being asked to dance."—Vernā Myers

On Friday, March 24, 2017, a few hundred librarians attended the Chair's Choice program at the Association of College and Research Libraries (ACRL) national conference in Baltimore, Maryland. Harvard-trained lawyer, entrepreneur, and author Vernā Myers's program, titled "What If I Say the Wrong Thing? Interrupting Bias in Ourselves and Others," was intended to help the audience learn not only how to address the verbal and written missteps and negative actions of others but also what to do if one finds themselves doing or saying things that may cause great pain, confusion, and disengagement to others (2017b). Myers, a cultural innovator, activist, and self-described recovering lawyer, challenged a sea of academic librarians to be thoughtful about their cultural lenses and not to feel guilty, but instead be vigilant about taking responsibility for the mistakes made in social situations regarding race, ethnicity, diversity, and inclusion, "so that all cultures, all people, all voices can thrive" in the workplace, in educational situations, and in their lives (Myers 2017a).

We, the authors of this chapter, had to survive before we could thrive. As embodied librarians, reflecting on the process of becoming academic librarians only came about after creating personalized plans that serendipitously placed us alongside each other "in the stacks" in which we called upon each

113

other for motivation and to sustain professional growth. We were in the same library graduate program at the School of Library and Information Science (SLIS) at Indiana University (IU) at the same time, between the years 2010 through 2012. Bloomington, a city where accidental discoveries spurred into friendships, informed the development of a community. It was an unexpected private entry into the relative counterspaces organically emerging from our self-determination and shared experiences. Though wary of using statistics and demographics to define our setting because of the limitations and its historical and continued use to erase marginalized peoples, we provide data to illustrate just one aspect of the environment in which we found ourselves. A reported 825 underrepresented people of color (less than 9 percent), sought graduate and professional degrees at IU in fall 2010.[1] Although unable to locate specific demographics of the library science graduate program at that time, we collectively recall it was more of the same, if not more. That was our memory, our feeling, our reality of being and moving through that particular space at that specific time.

Throughout the process of creating this chapter, it became clear that our individual and shared experiences during our time at IU seemed to omit what Myers mentioned in her presentation. We had been invited (sort of) to the party, but we were definitely not asked to dance. Even there, in a sea of Whiteness, we defined our community, autonomously, that centered our bodies—along with their implicit/explicit social expectations—on our journey to becoming librarians.

It was essential that we created counterspaces—in homes, hallways, bars, cafés—for the selves we were and would become. Those spaces were sites of resistance and solidarity; our togetherness made us stronger, allowed us to hold one another, while celebrating ourselves. It was community; it was love.

SPEAKING (AND LISTENING) TOGETHER

When faced with the task of creating an organic chapter for the twentieth anniversary of *IOOV* 1996, each of us readily agreed when Nicholae encouraged the creation of something that resonated with our experiences as individuals of color at SLIS. Currently residing in different states, this journey took each of us through multiple phases of writing, virtual and face-to-face conversations, introspection, and reflection.

After several e-mails and completing Dinty W. Moore's memoir exercise from *The Truth of the Matter: Art and Craft in Creative Nonfiction* (2006), collectively we generated questions probing our SLIS experience. A set of questions emerged from our conversations and personal reflections on shared and individual experiences at IU. These questions served as a guide for the conversation we would record and transcribe for this chapter. The recorded conversation was hosted on the WebEx platform, an electronic roundtable; each of us took turns moderating the discussion, using the questions we generated as prompts. The conversation ran two hours and included one musical/dance interlude.[2] We spent weeks creating a written transcript based on the recorded conversation. Out of the thirteen questions generated, eight correlated with the most intriguing conversations relevant to Nicholae's initial encouragement. As a result, references are made to points made previously within the overall conversation; however, all point(s) may or may not be fleshed out in the text selected for this chapter.[3]

Can you talk a little bit about how you met each of your coauthors? Describe each of your coauthors, and the first impressions you had of them.

NC. I remember in that S401 (Computer Based Information Tools) class we had together, Madelyn, you said we never interacted, but I do remember we had to write a series of responses in our online course forum. And I remember being aware very immediately of your intelligence. Because it seemed to me that I had approached librarianship as a professional possibility on a whim, and so I didn't have any background knowledge and didn't have a sense for the theoretical underpinnings of the field, but you seemed to be really on top of it and I was impressed by that.

My first impression of Madelyn was that she was, in that class in particular, intelligent and eloquent, but also that she exhibited such huge, positive energy, and I was very drawn to that in an immediate way. Especially in, as Jorge has already referenced, the sea of whiteness that was our class and cohort for sure. Whether or not that was an accurate assessment of the program's demographics, I think your memory of it is legitimate because that's how it felt and seemed for us and is something that has been noted by other people in the program, then and now. I think Madelyn stood out to me for that reason in a really good way, and for me it was so positive just because I didn't know a lot of Brown folks; I never really had, at least relative to how many White people I was surrounded by. I mean, being in Bloomington it's not as easy as it might seem once you've connected with a group of Brown and Black folks. So that was really significant for me, and I think that was one of my first experiences of feeling community and solidarity with other people of color. The town in which I grew up, there were so few folks of color, and I was one of them along with the few Latinx individuals . . . and Jorge, I'm trying to remember how we first interacted. Because I don't think we met at that party, right?

JRLM. I didn't really have impressions of Madelyn and Nicholae from the classroom. I do remember seeing you move through Wells,[4] and that was important for me to see, visually, you in that space moving through, with your body. Most of my understandings of both of you are outside of the academic space.

A good friend connected me to Madelyn. Some of the same stuff that Nicholae said. Very smart, very open, down-to-earth. Very welcoming and like "come on, let's go, let's stick together, let's do this." Nicholae, the first time I met you, I think Madelyn organized a group get-together at the Vid.⁵ And you were there, and we were talking about your creative writing background prior to coming to libraries. Nicholae was really down to earth, and super smart, really thoughtful, and listening. I just remembered feeling as though I was being heard and understood.

MSW. You smolder Nicholae—a smoldering of constant thought—a kind of smolder that doesn't burn hard and fast. In class, I remember you wore a neat, homie hat. I was always interested in how you dressed. Always very comfortable, but I always thought you were smoldering with thoughtfulness. I remember when we did a panel together in August of 2011 that I could see the effervescence of your contemplation. A member of the growing community introduced me to Jorge, I thought, "his tattoos are hot" and your intoxicating warmth was magnetic. Here, our bond began to grow.

How were our identities represented, expressed, celebrated in the various spaces we moved in and out of? How were questions and discussions related to race, gender, sexuality, and class incorporated in your program, in your classes, in your work?

JRLM. For the most part, I just remember in class once it being talked about in library management, like diverse populations and the understanding that there were all these White folks in the class just wanting to help. There was a [I believe White] woman that sat across from me, and she kept looking at me. My understanding of her looking at me was that she was pretty disgusted with the conversation and looking at me, thinking "how are we dealing with this?" The conversation was around wanting to help and that to me felt so off base. It wasn't about helping; it wasn't about this feeling good thing—it's some of that—but it's more of understanding these structures that are in place and being in solidarity. It was painful. I just remember leaving that class feeling really hurt.

MSW. Library management? **JRLM.** That was library management, dealing primarily with race and gender. Maybe a little bit of class but more in terms of efforts libraries were involved in that [were] supporting diverse populations, at least that's how I remember it. I really liked how Nicholae phrased it—of thinking about it in that space, at that particular time but not being expressed. That's what I remember—the absence of it, really.

NC. That seems important to me, because my memory of that time is also centered around an absence rather than a presence. I think that, discussing in one of our preliminary conversations [for this chapter], how it felt to move through certain spaces, to be a part of this program, to feel—I mean, "othered" is how we usually express this experience—othered, but also feel like our bodies were taking up and creating space where there was otherwise a vacuum of sorts, and standing out in specific ways. That's how I often felt, and I mean I say that as someone who is usually seen as being ethnically ambiguous or "safely mixed." I've certainly never had anyone guess at my Native heritage; usually people assume I'm Latinx, so I try to acknowledge that I have a certain amount of privilege in this regard, in that I stand out but not necessarily in a particular (or threatening) way or as part of a defined, racialized category.

What kinds of resistance did folks engage in that challenged dominant norms? In what ways did you feel (un)comfortable in the spaces you inhabited and traversed during your time in Bloomington and in the SLIS program? Did you always feel safe—physically/mentally/emotionally/spiritually? How did you work to create counterspaces with people who could hold you?

MSW. In general, that occurred outside of academic sites, and, if I may quote Nicholae from previous conversations, the locations in which we "threw down"—Emilie's home, the Vid, Atlas, Uncle E's, the Back Door, my house—were all sites of resistance. I just remember alcohol, voguing, and emerging conversations that would be deemed subversive, I think, by the dominant culture. Normalizing things the dominant culture freaked out about occurred in those locations away from the academic arena. But I also remember limitations of those expressions and celebrations of our identity. One very specifically, close to graduation 2012, when the crew went to that nasty bar—Dunkirk.[6] I remember someone saying "Girl . . . I can't dance here. I am too queeny for these people." The safe spaces in Bloomington where we could express [ourselves] were limited.

NC. You know, I agree completely, but I think sometimes the limitations were present even when, occasionally, we were too drunk, too "feelin' ourselves," too getting down together to notice. I don't know about Madelyn, but I find myself spending a lot of time feeling apart even when I'm a part of something, whether a group or an experience. Which means I'm often preoccupied with observing and perhaps hypervigilant of the spaces I inhabit. In doing so, I noticed, even when we were at the Atlas or at the Vid, we had our own little Brown corner and people were aware of us, people watched us. I think this necessarily limited what was possible; even when we didn't feel the need to push back against those potential restrictions at all times. Because we could still have what we needed in that space, even if there were limitations. I'm also thinking about, and this isn't entirely relevant, but going back to what you said—and I know Jorge probably doesn't want this chapter to be about who he kissed in these spaces—but I'm going back there. I'm going back to it because it's illustrative of, and a really important part of, the creation of counterspaces, which we created necessarily because we needed to find places to be—both ourselves and with one another—and to create that kind of community. And so you're exactly right, some of those rules were suspended, even if there were limitations, some of those normative mores were suspended when we got together. We were able to be and become differently in those spaces. The point being, that, for me, was an important and fundamental part of being and becoming non-monogamous and realizing that non-monogamy is an important structuring framework for how I want to do, and be, in relationships. It was in those spaces, in other words, that not only did we get to be ourselves but we got to become and explore new selves and new ways of being as well. For me, that wasn't just about being Brown or being queer, it was about many different ways of being and of being differently.

JRLM. Seeing you folks walking to class, or walking to the digital library space on the fifth floor. Just seeing you move physically through that space, for me, I think of that as resistance because it encouraged me, supported me, and pushed me to be fully present. To actually come into the space and engage in some type of effort. I think we can unpack it more, looking at Nicholae's question, "Did you always feel safe—physically/mentally/emotionally/spiritually?" That's a super challenging, hard question because there, I didn't, but in these other "counterspaces," I did to some extent, to the extent that it was possible—in people's homes typically.

Do you feel like you stood out in town and in the program? Did you ever feel like you, or the identities you performed and expressed, were "too much"?

MSW. Was my version of femininity too much for Indiana? I worked feverishly to create a counterspace at home. I was not safe or comfortable in class. I was obsessed with the "outer gaze." Always thinking about it. Always knowing my hair needed to be done a certain way. Always feeling strange covering my hair. Because I knew it might be "too much" for some people. I remember at home, how I really wanted people to feel free to be themselves. There was a manic-ness I felt inside about making certain people feel normal. I did not ever want anyone to feel, not normal—in my home. **JRLM.** This gets at Nicholae and Madelyn's questions about the stare/gaze. I felt, for me at least, I was under this professional White gaze, and I was also happily practicing it [Whiteness], to a certain degree [with the way I dressed and groomed], performing this sort of safe, ambiguous, multicultural body, there to put people at ease, but also to show how great this space [academic libraries] is for everybody, in this post-racial world. **MSW.** We met each other in the Obama era.

JRLM. I was very aware of that. This gets back to safety and moving through that space. I remember moving down in a U-Haul, coming down from Indianapolis, and this cop pulls up right beside me; I'm like "damn, this is not good." Coming from Michigan, from Ann Arbor, and not having spent much time anywhere south of Michigan, it felt different. I'm hearing folks with accents, there's religious stuff in my face, Confederate flags. I didn't feel particularly safe.

I wish we could have had more of these conversations there. This is what I really needed; I was struggling with depression and trying to figure that out. Also being hit with *this* is what we're up against. You're in this program that is producing White heteronormative practices and values. I knew that all along, but it felt more clear for some reason, at that particular moment.

NC. Well, all of that is really resonant, in that it all feels really true for me as well. The only difference is, I'm *from* Indiana, and I'm from a pretty tiny town at the southern tip of the state near Louisville, Kentucky, so I was moving from a space . . . suffice it to say, I've never felt safe, in this way, and still don't. If I leave my house, or those few other spaces in which I've come to find comfort, I often feel unsafe. Obviously, we live intersectional lives, so my gender and my queerness are not separable from my racial identity. The ways in which my body is racialized, especially, considering my formative experiences as a child during which I was much Browner and much more obviously mixed (there was no mistaking my Brownness for anything other than what it was) than I'm often perceived in the present—it was as I got older, as an older child and teenager, that my gender became less legible in binaristic terms and, thus, more clearly gender nonconforming and femme. The point is I've mostly felt unsafe, less as a Brown person and more as a queer and nonbinary individual. So it's my gender expression and my sexuality that structure my experiences of comfort and safety in most public (and other) spaces. Which is why, you know, coming from a small town, finally getting to Bloomington, and on my first night here I see two men walking downtown holding hands, and I thought, "Maybe this is my home, maybe this is the kind of space I've been looking and waiting for." But then I eventually realized, safety might just not be real for someone like me or people like us. Our lives are always precarious, we're always potentially vulnerable, and we can create these spaces of relative safety and comfort and resilience and solidarity and community, but my experiences taught me to resist the precarity my body and identity create in the world and recognize that those experiences, whether it's as a result of my gender or my queerness or my race or my anxiety/disability, structure my engagement with the world and how I'm received, or not, by it, and also how they structure the needs I have for and within what we've been calling counterspaces. It's also why my relationships with all of you were so important and continue to be so meaningful.

What did we need/want from one another, and what called us to invest in the relationships we had together? What was it that we created, among ourselves and with others who were willing to do justice to our identities?

MSW. The reaction to the circumstance. I always wondered why I felt so compelled to work *so* hard at school or at creating a safe counterspace, because if I didn't, my mind would move into this very uncomfortable space. There was so much discomfort in other spaces, but I had control over my school, work, and my professional work. Everything I did was so intense. When we threw down it was like *DAYUM*, and we outdid ourselves each time. **NC.** It seems like some of the manic energy you described is a function of the necessity thereof. We needed that; it was part of our survival. **MSW.** Remember, Nicholae said, people watched our Brown bubble; they envied, loathed, and lusted our Brown bubble. **NC.** And some people felt all three simultaneously. **MSW.** Each time we got together, I felt stronger. **NC.** You know what I keep thinking of, as you were speaking, is how it seemed like we partied "like our lives depended on it." And that's a metaphor, but there's also a realness to it. **MSW.** To balance things out I had to overcompensate.

JRLM. Part of how I read that question was thinking about it as, what would I have liked/needed now that we've experienced this and now that we know what we know. It's something I've been thinking about and wondering: What that would look like for folks now? **NC.** It doesn't really answer your question, but I think what I realized through the relationships we had and the spaces we created together was at least in part a new awareness of the fact that I needed this, and they were necessary. And it wasn't until we went to Minnesota,[7] Jorge, that I realized how thoroughly I had forgotten this fact and this need. I had allowed myself to forget that I needed these kinds of relationships with people of color, I needed this form of sustenance: the community aspect of the relationship we had and the spaces we occupied; forcibly sometimes. I was speaking to a member of our administration, here, and she was asking me about my experience at Minnesota, and I told her, "you know, I have much less to say about what I learned about leadership or being a librarian, at least in any coherent way, but [what] I definitely realized was that I need to be around people of color." I just can't do without it. That was very important to me, and a lesson, I suppose, that I had forgotten I already knew or had felt from the time when the four of us all still lived in Bloomington. **MSW.** Just how important developing a sense of community is needed, and shouldn't be understated in this chapter.

What are some of the terminology (slang) we communicate with (e.g., hair whip, stunt, gagging, thirsty)?

MSW. Vocabulary?? You talking about vocabulary . . . you want some tea, hunty?[8] The Tea?[9] **NC.** Yes! I was just thinking about *Paris Is Burning* (Livingston 1990). **MSW.** I never realized how much of the vocabulary of that movie I had usurped until my roommate brought the film home in the summer of 2011. The vocabulary. . . . "Tea" the "Shade" the counterspaces in the film . . . were influential. Helped me understand the community in which I feel comfortable. The vocabulary [was] private entry into those relative counterspaces. We had our own way of communicating. Do you remember how I said *Muy cracker* or *todo cracker*? Spanglish is fluid in my life, and I enjoyed imparting a little bit of *cholita* to the folks wanting to be a part of the crew in Indiana. Spanglish mixed with Drag Speak[10] learned from *RuPaul's*

Drag Race (RuPaul 2009), . . . in Hoosierlandia . . . that's how we communicated.

JRLM. Even in our conversations, and this was my experience, in Bloomington with our group, was the fluidity with using different pronouns to talk about and address people in a very loose way, which I thought was interesting and a sweet connection we had among us.

NC. I think that was very important about the space we had, but also very valuable to me now as I've gotten older and more willing to be open and vulnerable and affectionate with people. There's a way in which the figurative language we had, the gestures, as Madelyn mentioned, originated very clearly from vogue culture, from ballroom culture, and from sources like *Paris Is Burning*, but for me one of the important things was, of course, gaining a new vocabulary for racial being and racial becoming but also the affection we were willing to show one another, the ways in which we were willing to be physically intimate with one another, in both platonic and sometimes romantic ways as well. The intimacy mattered, and it wasn't only the way we talked, it was also how we interacted and demonstrated affection with one another. That, to me, was very significant and memorable.

REFLECTIONS

As new(ish) academic librarians, in the profession five years or less, we are all involved in the process of becoming practitioners, researchers, and scholars in the academy. Like McLeod and Badenhorst (2014), we, too, believe gathering, reflecting, sharing, and producing knowledge are important parts of constructing strong identities as academic librarians. It is equally important that we produce and own that knowledge, rather than have it be produced by the prevailing academic discourse and hegemonic structures of power. In this chapter, we decentered research as a product, and provided an autoethnographic set of optics, in order to bring into focus how we, as researchers, understand ourselves, our work, and our processes. We hope our contribution will be useful for members of outgroups inside the walls of academia. We hope our stories interweave with the stories of others who are also new(ish) to academic librarianship. We hope all *In Our Own Voices, Redux* readers can identify with our embodied dispositions and social knowledge practices. Our experiences have transcended our academic world, and we hope the narratives presented in this chapter may help many others make informed decisions about defining and sustaining a substantive sense of community.

122 *Cline, López-McKnight, and Washington*

NOTES

1. University Institutional Research and Reporting, Indiana University (2016).
2. Ondatropica (2012).
3. There were four individuals in these conversations, but due to unforeseen circumstances, this written dialogue only includes recollections of three of them.
4. Wells is short for the Herman B. Wells Library at Indiana University.
5. Short for the Video Saloon, the Vid is a bar in Bloomington, Indiana.
6. Dunkirk is a bar in Bloomington, Indiana. See http://kilroys-dunnkirk.com.
7. In July 2016, Nicholae and Jorge had the privilege of attending the Minnesota Institute for Early Career Librarians (MIECL) for traditionally underrepresented groups.
8. See UrbanDictionary.com. http://www.urbandictionary.com/define.php?term=Hunty.
9. See UrbanDictionary.com. http://www.urbandictionary.com/define.php?term=tea.
10. See http://rupaulsdragrace.wikia.com/wiki/RuPaul%27s_Drag_Race_Dictionary.

Part Six

Disrupting the System

DISRUPTING THE SYSTEM

Chapter Fourteen

Una De Solamente Cuatro

Overcoming Barriers to Minority Recruitment in Appalachia

Monica García Brooks

More than twenty years ago I had an opportunity to be included in the inaugural edition of *IOOV* 1996. The chapter I wrote described several experiences that helped shape my commitment to infusing diversity topics into lesson plans, library collections, programming opportunities, and campus service opportunities such as committees and/or task forces (Brooks 1996). At the time when I entered the field, I reported on several instances in which I felt compelled to study, share, and insert multiculturalism or matters relating to Latinos in my everyday activities. It was a rewarding experience imparting these issues to a wider audience at a time in my life when I was finding my place in the profession and in the library network in my home state. In ensuing years, I moved on from my first professional position at West Virginia State University, eventually joining the library faculty at Marshall University (Marshall) in Huntington, West Virginia. With some rapid changes that took place soon after I arrived, I went into library administration at Marshall in 1996 and held several increasingly more responsible positions, culminating in the position I have today of associate vice president for both the libraries and our online learning programs. In my current role at the university and throughout my tenure, I have had supportive colleagues and managers who have made it possible for the libraries I oversee to attract, retain, and cultivate talent committed to their users, students, peers, and the campus at large. Job satisfaction and a sincere love for the region and its people have all contributed to my decision to remain at Marshall.

Love for the area does not mean I am blind to its flaws. West Virginia has its issues. Poverty, low educational attainment, lack of industry, and rough terrain all contribute to some of the problems the locals experience; yet, like me, they choose to live in practically untouched rural beauty and natural bliss. This seemingly idyllic life among the warm embrace of my West Virginia hills and the academy did not prepare me for several challenges that emerged of late. While the focus of my chapter pertains primarily to issues facing Hispanic librarians and the hope to attract more diverse individuals to the profession and Appalachia, I cannot explore these concepts without providing readers with some information about how recent challenges have nearly shattered the community in which I live.

Over the period of two decades, West Virginia did not change that dramatically around me. The overall population in the state has remained constant while some aspects of its ethnic composition have changed. Wild and wonderful West Virginia[1] is indeed becoming more diverse while also becoming older. Like nearby depressed regions lacking industry to keep or attract younger generations or upwardly mobile young professionals, the brain trust tends to leave the comforts of home while others return to the nest after retirement to be close to family and enjoy a slower pace. Educational attainment has improved during this time, rising from 12 percent of the population to 18 percent; however, West Virginia is still ranked fiftieth in the percentage of residents with bachelor's degrees when compared to other states (U.S. Census Bureau, American FactFinder 2010). Aside from being fiftieth, we share a lot in common with five or six other southern states competing for this rank that deal with similar problems.

Another constant is the ethnicity of the state overall. In 1990, West Virginia's population was 96 percent White—today 94 percent. Changes in the Black, Asian, American Indian, and Other categories were very minor; but when reviewing the Hispanic population, this group did actually improve its numbers. Originally[2] boasting a little under 9,000 Hispanics, by 2015, this number grew in concert with national trends now comprising 1.5 percent of the population (U.S. Census Bureau, QuickFacts 2017). One might assume that this growth would result in more Hispanics entering various professions in the state—namely, the library profession. Lamentably, there is still a significant lack of diversity in our field. Nevertheless, this Latina has remained here and thrived. Active in many facets of my university, I have enjoyed the camaraderie and fellowship among peers as an avid member of our state library association, serving in several leadership positions through the years. At various times, my fellow Latina librarians have joined me in providing programs at annual conferences that expose our friends to Mexican, Cuban, or Puerto Rican music, customs, and culture. Efforts have always been welcomed warmly and with much enthusiasm or kind curiosity. When I entered the profession in 1990, a grand total of four Hispanic women (including myself) worked in libraries as professional librarians across the state. Over the years, there have been some new faces replacing old ones; however, *hay solamente cuatro. No más.* Still, this doesn't faze me. In addition to enjoying the act of sharing information about my culture, heritage, and ethnic family ties, I also enjoy being unique and having an opportunity to make positive change to help attract a more diverse library workforce in this region.

The passing of time has also helped me expand my academic role at the university, branching out into mentoring opportunities with future graduate students in library science or colleagues interested in administration. I have partnered with faculty here and beyond to start new programs; created and taught new courses; and provided continuing education opportunities for library workers at all levels. While I continue to work on these important projects and remain committed to developing or fostering programming that attracts and retains talent to this region, some of the gusto is hard to muster when the campus, community, and region are in such extreme crisis. Punishing economic, social, and political dramas have unfolded in the last two decades to form the perfect storm of dysfunction in our region. To fully understand how my multicultural mission fits into the current landscape, it is crucial to share what has transpired in our city in recent years that still desperately requires a resolution.

From about 1850 to 2010, West Virginia enjoyed a robust coal economy and thousands of high-paying jobs that fueled the creation, growth, and purpose of most of the cities and towns in the state. Still among one of the least populated states in the country with difficult mountainous terrain, towns of 700–1,000 residents with no cellular service, cable television, or broadband access remain. Sometime during 2011 due to a variety of economic reasons at the national level, the oil and gas industry began to flourish in neighboring states as a cheaper, safer alternative to coal extraction; international coal exports declined sharply; and environmental regulations increased, making it more difficult for smaller mines to comply and continue to function. Many West Virginia mines went bankrupt while others consolidated, moved, or reduced production. The result was a loss of over 35 percent of the jobs available to coal miners at a time when these jobs were essential to not only the workers' families but also the economies of the cities or towns in which they resided (Bomey 2016). For those miners who were already retired, mine closures had an instant impact on their pensions and access to health care. Without skills, training, or education to provide more opportunities for employment or personal well-being, these workers and their families did not have many options. In a state that has steadily lost population over the years, those who did have the ability to retool themselves did so and found work elsewhere. Those who stayed could not revise career options and made do with what was available to them, such as taking minimum wage positions in retail establishments like Walmart, the largest employer in West Virginia from 1998 to 2016. Retail and service industry jobs tend to be the largest employers unless workers are able to acquire the skills needed to enter the health care industry—the second largest private employer in West Virginia (WorkForce West Virginia LMI 2016). With a per capita income of a little over $23,000, it is not surprising the West Virginia Department of Education recently reported that 18 percent of West Virginia residents live in poverty and 60 percent of school-aged children are eligible for free or reduced meals (West Virginia Department of Education 2015). Imagine thousands of people—often over the age of forty or fifty—having to seek employment after twenty to thirty years of steady work in the one field they knew best. In many instances, they may even have been the second or third generation to work in the mines. With solid research showing a nexus at which education and employment impact the potential for substance abuse and aggression (Patrick et al. 2012), West Virginia became the personification of this predicative model. The residents are the perfect targets for pharmaceutical pill-mill operators or out-of-state drug dealers who have successfully infiltrated the state at all levels of its social strata, giving us unwanted national attention. Featured in *Vice*, the *Washington Post*, CNN, and several other national news outlets, as well as the Netflix documentary *Heroin(e)*, Huntington, West Virginia, became notorious for experiencing close to thirty heroin overdoses in less than five hours on August 15, 2016 (Drash and Blau 2016). Serving as the model for the opioid epidemic, Huntington city leaders have worked hard to combat this image by partnering with higher education, local health agencies and hospitals, and faith-based groups to bring solutions to the community despite substantial funding difficulties. Knowing that prevention and education are some of the methods we can use to help keep students out of harm's way, our institution works tirelessly to make essential services available to everyone, ensure campus safety, and provide support. While Huntington might be the city holding the record for the most overdoses in one day, we share some new social problems with many other regions desperate for jobs and opportunities.

In addition to the drug epidemic, events at the national level shed new light on hate groups operating throughout the country and online. In West Virginia, two of these organizations are located within a hundred-mile radius of Huntington in cities that I visit, work in, or travel through frequently. If one lives in any state situated in the Southeast, there's literally no way to avoid being within a hundred miles of a Ku Klux Klan chapter or similar hate group (Southern Poverty Law Center 2017). When considering the current state of affairs, I am more determined to combat politically incorrect behavior in an area in which I know I can affect change. Attracting and retaining qualified professionals has become harder and harder to do in recent years, but it still can be done. When a candidate comes to campus, we are honest about the various neighborhoods when giving the city tour of prospective rental properties or family homes. When we discuss salaries, we share the issues relating to the local economy that help to drive down wages for all professions for K–12 and higher education but allow for lower cost of living expenses and no taxes on food. When providing the snapshot for the state, we ensure that prospective employees see how beautiful the state can be, how tourism is still a draw, and how so much of our region remains green and untouched. In some instances, the opportunity to help city leaders resolve the drug epidemic while providing students with real-life clinical experiences is attractive to prospective faculty in public health, sociology, political science, medicine, and others. With the current state of affairs, everyone at the university has been challenged to participate in the solution in some way. This has influenced how I look at everything today—including minority recruitment to help bring diverse voices and experiences to librarianship in Appalachia.

A method of formulating quality experiences and programming for minorities at the start or mid-point of their professional careers emerged from my experience as a member of a recent dissertation committee. A colleague opened my eyes to another series of issues that help us empathize, anticipate, and empower mentees in a more comprehensive fashion. As a member of a dissertation committee, I found myself engrossed in a study compiled by my colleague Kelli Johnson, titled "Minority Librarians in Higher Education: A Critical Race Theory Analysis." Exploring the tenets of critical race theory (CRT), she interviewed several minority librarians from a variety of institution types at various points in their careers (Johnson 2016). I pored through her results comparing my own experience to the CRT matrix as I critiqued her paper. Several impactful trends emerged from her study that I hope to see in the literature soon, but a few are worth previewing here as they seem to tie into the challenges that may hinder our ability to cultivate opportunities for Hispanic and minority librarians locally.

The first major outcome of her study provided a sobering commentary about our own profession. Dr. Johnson noticed that despite minority population growth at the national level, the number of minority librarians has not grown commensurately (Johnson 2016). This is a curious detail that demands further study and possible action at the national level. Google the word *librarian*, and explore hundreds of memes and images that represent fun, hip, tattooed, and pierced multiethnic and heroic television, movie, and comic book representations of librarians, archivists, and curators. They aren't stereotypes. Instead they are slaying dragons, fighting ghosts, dancing in the stacks, traveling through time, or solving crimes. Librarianship is still a thriving career that may even be cool thanks to a growing need for digitally savvy information professionals who are connected to social media and understand the importance of preserving and providing all types of information to all types of users. After an influx of men in the profession during a period of rapid technology change in the 1990s, the male-to-female ratio has become lopsided again. Data from the American Library Association from 2010 show that the field remains dominated by white women. Female librarians comprise 83 percent of the workforce and 67 percent of the paraprofessional workforce overall. Among research libraries, women make up over 60 percent of the workforce and administration; yet, similar to K–12 principals and superintendents, male university librarians comprise 17 percent of the workforce but hold 40 percent of the university library administrative positions (Godfrey and Tordella 2006).

These media images portray a multiethnic library workforce of male and female hipsters while the statistics for minority college-going and completion rates present a different picture. When applied to Hispanic populations, the Pew Research Center (Pew) reported that 35 percent of Hispanics between the ages of 18 to 24 were enrolled in school. Only 12 percent ultimately succeed in obtaining a bachelor's degree. Compared to graduate education, this number drops to less than 2 percent (Pew Research Center 2017). Despite major improvements to the dropout rates among this population, post-secondary educational attainment rates are not improving at the same rate. Pew studied the economic conditions and showed that Hispanics still tend to hover at the national poverty rate with respondents reporting that joining the military or seeking employment soon after high school was necessary to help support the family. Hispanics, even those among the third generation of U.S.-born people of traditional college-going age, tend to pursue two-year college programs in technical education at higher rates than four-year liberal arts or professional programs (Pew Research Center 2017). Some of these issues explain the lack of Hispanics in the profession even though this tendency is still unacceptable for a career that attracts socially conscious advocates for a myriad of important causes that benefit the community.

Critical race theory emerged in the 1970s and challenged the institutionalized oppression of minority populations in the justice system and society at large. Incorporating several tenets such as endemic racism experienced by a person of color; the use of storytelling to counter assumptions; the intersectionality of race, class, and gender; and a true commitment to social justice (Haskins and Singh 2015), CRT provides a structure from which to challenge the dominant power structure in the United States that favors Whites (Adams et al. 2013) and marginalizes any other racial or ethnic group. As I shared in my original chapter for this project, I believed at one time that most of my Appalachian neighbors' somewhat racist questions or comments simply emerged from ignorance or a lack of education or exposure to people of color and not nefarious origins (Brooks 1996). Now I know these were actually microaggressions, but this term was not part of the lexicon at that time. Reflecting on the appointments made to public offices by President Trump, the ethnic makeup of the West Virginia state legislature, the university administration, or the city government loudly reinforces some of the more provocative arguments made about institutionalized racism by CRT scholars. Studying where power, race, and the legal system intersect to subjugate certain groups and retain the status quo of those in power may oversimplify CRT but provides a context for the lay person. Stemming from CRT, Dr. Tara Yosso's "cultural wealth model" in *Race, Ethnicity, and Education* in 2005 seems especially relevant to our ability to address Hispanic student and faculty needs at Marshall. By the time a Hispanic person has chosen to accept a position or attend Marshall University far away from home, we can assume he or she may already possess some aspects of "aspirational," "linguistic," and "familial" capital from which we can build. The "cultural wealth model" provides an arsenal from which Latinx[3] students or professors may draw upon in all facets of life (Yosso 2005). It can be applied to their growth to ensure that they will be successful in the campus community or once they leave the university's bosom. The remaining tenets of her model are requirements for a successful mentoring experience while a minority person studies and lives in this Appalachian environment. Helping a Latinx person become aware of the "social" and "navigational" capital (Yosso 2005) needed to maneuver a college campus, a majority White classroom, homogenous colleagues, and a predominantly Protestant Anglo community may help better prepare them for what life has in store outside the campus borders. Likewise, a successful mentoring experience can build on the "social capital" needed to forge their own community relationships to ultimately acquire "resistant capital" to stand up for themselves and combat racism or discrimination in their educational lives and beyond (Yosso 2005). When I apply the CRT model Yosso developed to the Latinx experience a student may have at Marshall University, I'm struck by a few unique characteristics that emerge. The confluence of an opioid epidemic hitting the White community at a greater rate than any other group and the vitriol at the national level targeting minorities and other minority groups can serve as an opportunity to attract ambitious outsiders of color who can develop their "social," "navigational," and "resistant" capital while helping others rise from the ashes (Yosso 2005). Academic librarians have a golden opportunity to use the university's influence to our advantage by developing minority mentoring programs that serve both the student and the community using this framework to reach the Hispanic population.

Dr. Johnson's research indicated that mentoring was cited as one of the most significant factors that brought most of the respondents to the library profession. Their mentors did not have to share their ethnicity, gender, or race (Johnson 2016). The sheer act of concern and demonstration of proactive support for their growth and well-being as a potential new member of the profession helped instill confidence and perseverance (Johnson 2016; Crisp, Taggart, and Nora 2015). We know from our own experiences and the literature that mentoring students of color as faculty of color creates a safe space atmosphere in which they can thrive. Academe is largely built upon a hierarchy that rewards research, scholarship, and publication. This predominantly White meritocracy that perpetuates its own power base may be out of reach for most Hispanics who come from immigrant and working-class families (Figueroa and Rodriguez 2015). Mentoring is especially crucial to Latinos who comprise a fraction of the student populations in most colleges and universities. Put the university in a state with the fewest number of Hispanics per capita and mentoring not only becomes a necessity but also a critical mission for those who wish to help their minority students be successful.

Applying some aspects of the "cultural wealth model" may help shed light on minority student needs—especially Latinx students who may benefit most from edifying and fostering their cultural wealth arsenal (Yosso 2005). West Virginia has the lowest percentage of Hispanics in the country even though statewide numbers have increased with each census. Migration trends in the United States show us that Latinx immigrants tend to migrate to geographic areas in which farming or factory jobs are available within the Sunbelt and border areas. West Virginia is the third most forested state but still has over twenty thousand farms and close to one hundred farmers' markets. While agriculture brings in over $800 million annually, the state is still ranked forty-third in cash receipts when compared to the rest of the country (United States Department of Agriculture Economic Research Service 2017). Despite these barriers, Marshall University can happily boast that the Hispanic student population has almost tripled in a decade (from eighty-seven students in 2004 to over 250 in 2015), similar to the state's Hispanic population growth. Oddly, Marshall's faculty-staff population of a dozen or so Hispanics has not grown accordingly. Latinos come and Latinos go, with the number of faculty consistently hovering at twelve or thirteen (Marshall University 2017). Unfortunately, the university has not had success in attracting and retaining certain ethnic groups. Once we lure them to this valley and overcome its current problems, unless they have a familial tie to the region or find satisfaction in their research and teaching, they do not stay longer than a few years. Huntington is not close enough to major metropolitan areas to appeal to Hispanic faculty and staff on its own merit.

While it is not my primary role at the university, I enjoy meeting new people and helping to make them feel welcome. Each fall, I obtain the list of new faculty members and reach out to incoming Hispanic colleagues by connecting them with individuals from their respective countries or metropolitan areas with whom they may want to forge new relationships. For the faculty, I provide Guatemalan-crafted stoles that they are permitted to wear with academic regalia for the winter and spring commencement exercises. Turning heads each time we don our *astolas*, this small gesture has created a sense of camaraderie surrounding our ethnic roots and pride as we showcase the craftsmanship of the handmade stoles and rainbow of colors mirroring the Latinx experience of a group of people from over a dozen countries and three continents.

As a faculty advisor for more than one student organization, I do the same with the incoming student list to ensure that everyone can connect with each other should they desire to do so. On campus, we have several student clubs that include a Latinx culture society and Spanish language students. With our dubious ranking of fiftieth for most good things and first for most bad things, West Virginians of all colors, ages, and origins need to rely on each other for affirmation. Nevertheless, students of color tend to gravitate to individuals who resemble themselves so providing an initial contact has helped some of our newbies get acclimated. These small gestures help create an inclusive climate in which we hope our students may thrive. We also hope these gestures impact retention. In a recent study produced by the IZA Institute of Labor Economics, the presence of one Black teacher in an elementary school reduced the probability that a Black student in the same school would drop out by almost 30 percent. When considering Black boys specifically, the probability that they would drop out was reduced by almost 40 percent (Gershenson et al. 2017). Understanding that an elementary school is significantly different from a college campus, I believe that some of this logic could still be applied to the university classroom. As recently as fall 2016, a new Chicana faculty member and I laughed uncontrollably when we realized our speech pattern had changed dramatically as we inserted Spanglish into a funny story when nobody else was around. It's not often that I "code switch" into a *Tejana* inflection in West Virginia . . . but put me in San Antonio, Texas, and most people cannot tell I am not a native San Antonian. Hearing her inflection at work sounded like home, like when cousins and I might lapse into a funny story with much inflection and Spanglish interjection. A Hispanic student worker from the Washington, DC, area overheard us and joined the conversation while plucking spicy Mexican candies from a bowl on my desk. Until that moment, I had not met the student and didn't even know she was Mexican American! She was missing chili-covered watermelon pops from home, so I made sure she left with a dozen or more *rebanaditas* from my personal stash.

Another theme common among the minority librarians Dr. Johnson interviewed helped validate my personal experiences. Each person described one or more situations in which he or she was deemed the de facto responsible representative of his/her ethnic group during campus committee discussions, departmental plans for programming, or even during conflicts that related to civil discourse (Johnson 2016). This is still the case at my institution and in the library profession in our state. I embrace the role but have to admit being a little resentful that all eyes turn to me when certain topics arise, as if I alone hold the power to speak for an entire culture or ethnic group. Even though I may not always be in the mood to "represent," I still rise to the occasion knowing that I have an opportunity to steer the conversation toward a positive outcome—especially when it involves students. Often using research on my family's Mexican circus as a catalyst, I have been able to propel a personal interest into an educational opportunity that is both interesting and unique enough to hold most people's attention. Using my position at the university, I have been able to support and sponsor joint ventures with Latinx faculty to bring guest speakers, art installations, film screenings, dramatic readings, displays, and other opportunities showcasing diverse topics to the libraries and to the campus. I have also had the ability to encourage the recruitment of a variety of qualified ethnic and cultural minorities in both paraprofessional and professional positions in my organization. National numbers may show that librarianship is still a female-dominated profession, but while at Marshall there are almost as many men as there are women on the library faculty (10:9), the leadership roles in our organization are equally divided between men and women (2:2). Reflecting on the last twenty years in context and through the critical race theory matrix Dr. Johnson introduced to me, I am gratified that I have been able to promote Hispanic culture in some small way; attract people of color to jobs in a largely homogenous state; and mentor young librarians of all races, ethnicities, creeds, and backgrounds to appreciate their role in a vital profession that has the ability to shape young minds at the collegiate level. I am proud of what I have been able to accomplish with my colleagues in my beloved home of West Virginia and am anxious to apply ever-changing concepts to mentoring experiences and recruitment strategies. At the same time, I am duly anxious knowing that there's still a lot of work to be done before my Hispanic colleagues and I can boast *¡más de solamente cuatro!*

NOTES

1. "Wild and Wonderful West Virginia" is a former official slogan for the state.
2. For 1990 U.S. Census data, see U.S. Department of Commerce (1990).
3. Latinx is a gender-neutral term to represent all Latin people. For a standard definition, see the Oxford dictionary entry: https://en.oxforddictionaries.com/definition/Latinx.

Chapter Fifteen

How Does It Feel to Be a Problem?

The School-to-Prison Pipeline

Sheree D. White

Twenty years ago in *IOOV* 1996, I was writing from the perspective of an independent school educator (White 1996). I enjoyed that career route; I had my first taste of school librarianship as a library intern at the Ellis School in Pittsburgh, Pennsylvania. From Ellis, I began my professional career in Marin County, California, at Marin Country Day School, as a K–8 librarian. Under the tutelage of Tessa Gaddis, the head librarian, I learned how to not just be a librarian, but an activist. I like to call myself the subversive librarian. Tessa taught how to infuse activism in my teaching and collection development. After leaving Marin, I was pulled to the Midwest where I found myself at one of the most diverse independent schools I had ever seen. Maumee Valley Country Day School (K–12) was the best experience I could ask for in the city of Toledo, Ohio. The students pushed me beyond my boundaries, and parent interactions were amazing.

In 2003, I relocated to the Washington, DC, area to care for my mother. I became the Upper School head librarian for the Maret School; but in 2007, as I was looking out the window of my office on top of Woodley (a historic building that has been a summer home to two presidents and a U.S. secretary of war) at the Maret School, I realized that these students would be fine with or without me. As some of you may know, working in an independent school can take up a lot of your time, your life, your soul. Once I realized this was happening, I thought to myself, "If I'm going to give up my soul then I might as well do so for my community."

I parted ways with Maret, and in 2012, I began working with the Maryland State Department of Education at Cheltenham Youth Facility (CYF). Originally opening in 1870 as the Cheltenham School for Boys, currently, it is an all-boys detention facility that has gone through multiple renovations and name changes; the latest in November of 2016, came with a new building with seventy-two beds, and a new name, Cheltenham Youth Detention Center (CYDC). The boys who are remanded to this facility range in age from twelve to nineteen and come with a record of a variety of infractions, from violation of parole, to rape and murder. Often we see youth more than once. Recidivism is high. This new setting is settling into my soul and causing me to question aspects of our education system and society that I seldom critiqued before. Remember that I started out in private schools, and now I am with some of our most disadvantaged and vulnerable populations. Some of the questions I want to address here are "How do these youth get to a facility like mine?" "What will become of many of these youth?" and "What can a library media specialist do for them?"

Enacted in 1975, the Individuals with Disabilities Education Act (IDEA), formerly known as the Education for All Handicapped Children Act (EAHCA), mandates the provision of a free and appropriate public-school education for eligible students ages three through twenty-one. IDEA was meant to provide eligible students with the resources and opportunities needed to advance educationally. Eligible students are those identified by a team of professionals as having a disability that adversely affects academic performance and as being in need of special education and related services. According to the National Center for Educational Statistics (2016), both the number and percentage of students served under IDEA declined from 2004–2005 through 2011–2012. There was evidence that the number and percentage of students served leveled off in 2012–2013 and 2014–2015, but by 2014–2015 the number of students served was 6.6 million, or 13 percent of total public-school enrollment (NCES 2016).

At CYDC, we receive young men from Maryland and a few from the District of Columbia (DC) who have allegedly committed a crime or have been picked up with warrants for their arrest. Once the police have determined they are juveniles, they are sent to us until a decision about their fate is made by the courts. Some of these young men will be found innocent or will be released due to a lack of evidence. Some may be put on parole with electronic monitoring (i.e., ankle bracelet) or be remanded to juvenile placement, a group home, or drug treatment facility. Some may eventually be tried as adults (depending on their age at the commission of the crime) and sent to an adult correctional facility. A number of students have been arrested and detained on school property. Within our facility at any given time, more than 35 percent of our students are considered special education students. Some of these students require so many accommodations and modifications in their learning plans, one wonders how well they will adjust after high school.

As our technology- and information-driven economy becomes more specialized, how do our struggling students make it? The answer is that a sizeable number will *not*. Therefore, to the critical mind, one wonders if the school-to-prison pipeline is a conscious effort to find a solution to that problem. To put this in context, in the early 1990s, schools began adopting "zero tolerance" policies as a means to discipline with the application of predetermined consequences, often severe and punitive in nature, that are intended to be applied regardless of the gravity of behavior, mitigating circumstances, or situational context.

The tension produced by these policies is tenuous as more students are going to school under increased policed conditions. Infractions that were previously handled by school detention, the principal, or parents are now in many cases shuttled straight from school to a police station, courtroom, or detention center. "Zero tolerance policies assume that removing students who engage in disruptive behavior will deter others from disruption (Ewing 2000), and create an improved climate for those students who remain" (American Psychological Association 2008).

As suspensions and expulsions increase, so does the disparity of those affected, widened by race and economic level. In other words, these policies are disproportionately used against students of color and poor students. A trip to the police station has become a badge of honor for some of these students, followed by a trip to the detention center, jail, and ultimately, prison. This is evident whenever you overhear conversations, and the young men with the most experience within the system seem to get listened to more among their peers.

I love being a librarian because I can be quietly subversive. Most of the time, the young men will be led in a single-file line with a resident advisor (RA) in front of the line and another at the end. The students generally arrive calmly. They may try to run and grab a magazine or get on a computer, prompting me to announce that we will read first and use the computers after the lesson. They sit at small round tables in groups of four to six; some will choose to sit by themselves. I love it when I hear a student say, "So what are we doing today, Ms. White?" In my class, I have a series of lessons on what happens when a person does not find a situation or system to their liking or advantage. The students all agree that there are essentially three choices: leave it, conform to it, or confront and change it. Unfortunately, too many of our young people are choosing to leave an educational system that they feel does not address their needs. Once they leave, many will not systematically continue to develop their literacy or academic skills.

In 2015, the Schott Foundation for Public Education released *Black Lives Matter: The Schott 50 State Report on Public Education and Black Boys*. The report "is intended to again alert the nation to the serious reality of a quieter danger that does not instantly end young lives, but creates an all but insurmountable chasm of denied opportunities" (2015). Many of these opportunities are reduced because of the correlation between literacy levels, suspension rates, and graduation rates. *Black Lives Matter* analyzed data from the National Association of Educational Progress (NAEP) for reading and math proficiency in grades three and eight. In 2013, less than 20 percent of Black males in Maryland (12 percent nationally) scored at or above proficient in reading in grade eight; 28 percent of Latino males (17 percent nationally) scored at or above proficient, versus 49 percent of White males (38 percent nationally) (2015). In the state of Maryland, the disparity in reading proficiency between Black and White males was nearly 30 percent versus the 21 percent disparity between Latino and White males (2015).

The authors also analyzed suspension rates for the same time period. Although the rates are low, suspension rates for Black males (8 percent) in Maryland are nearly twice that for White males (5 percent) and Latino males (4 percent). Nationally, the rates for Black males are double at nearly 16 percent, 7 percent for Latino males, and remains steady for White males at 5 percent (2015). Ultimately, we see how these lead to a disproportionate amount of Black and Latino youths not graduating.

Few people would argue that literacy is a human right. Think of Cuba and its grand efforts circa 1961 to turn itself into a country with one of the highest percentage of literacy rates of any population in the world. Think what is required in America today to secure basic needs—food, clothing, and housing—and hopefully a job that pays a wage to afford this. More sophisticated levels of literacy are being required of our young people to pass standardized tests; for example, in Maryland, we have the Maryland High School Assessment (HSA) exam, the Partnership for Assessment of Readiness for College and Careers (PARCC) exam, and the revamped General Education Development (GED) test.[1] I have administered these tests, along with the Practice GED test in preparing our students for the GED. The Maryland HSA is a series of tests that measure school and individual student progress toward Maryland's High School Core Learning Goals in English, algebra/data analysis, government, and biology. Passing the HSA is a graduation requirement. Students take each test whenever they complete the course. These tests may present the first hurdle or sifter for selecting which students will be passed on and which ones may not be. All these tests are predicated on a certain level of literacy competency. For example, I wanted to get a sample of how the young men in my classes were reading. They are primarily African American (approximately 75 percent) and Hispanic (15 to 20 percent), with a small number of White males (5 to 10 percent). I teach grades eight through twelve, and a handful of GED students (who did not participate in this exercise). I gave them all a portion of a practice PARRC Reading exam for their respective grade levels. Only one student out of twenty-six test takers scored a 100 percent (grade eleven); four students scored 75 percent; three tenth graders scored 70 percent; and eighteen students scored 60 percent or lower. Some received their score because of their skill level, while others simply refused to do work or take assignments seriously, so it's hard to gauge their true academic skill set. More frequently than not you will have students who will refuse to do class work for an assortment of reasons, such as receiving bad news from home, visiting a parole officer or court, not liking the teacher, not attending school when they were detained so why do work now, or not believing their school work with us will count.

The cogs of an efficiently running capitalist machine must find a way to keep the system intact. What happens, then, when you have members of your society who don't appear to fit into that smoothly running machine? Even in our facility, there is a unit called Intensive Services Unit (ISU) in which these students are kept in their own group because of their behavior (aggressive, harmful, or instigating a fight) in the general population. This is the only group that may not physically come to the library or participate in other social activities.

> The U.S. Department of Education conducted a five year $14 million study of U.S. adult literacy involving lengthy interviews of U.S. adults. . . . The government study showed that 21% to 23% of adult Americans were not "able to locate information in text," could not "make low level inferences using print materials and were unable "to integrate easily identifiable pieces of information." (Schott Foundation 2013)

This finding is important to me as a library media specialist because part of our job is to help our students develop these very skills (i.e., locating, analyzing, and integrating information). Therefore, if adults are lacking these skills, then what does it say about the work that needs to be done with our youth? I also worry because of the trends of social media, including fake news, live streaming, and augmented reality, which may change the landscape of how we report and see news.

What do you do with these individuals whose lack of education and perceived aggressive ways disturb the temperament of the community? In any given class I teach, easily 60 to 75 percent of the boys in attendance grew up without their biological father, and some foster anger and resentment about this. Some will say, "I wouldn't be in CYDC if my father was with me." Some students have experienced trauma, both physical and emotional. We have male prostitutes, assault victims, and those who have abused drugs. All these things, along with limited employment opportunities, have contributed to many of these young men winding up out of school or on the other side of the law.

Despite such a dismal forecast for many of my students, I believe the library is one of their favorite places in the school. I wish I could say it's because of my sunny disposition, but it's actually because the youth can come, be comfortable in a well-lit environment, and read what they want. It's safe because the youth can all see each other, so there is no sneaking up on someone; they know that they are free to ask questions and get help with their reading without having much attention called to themselves; and it genuinely feels peaceful. Though we have been working on expanding our collection, you still hear "there's nothing good to read in here" (translation, not enough street stories with drugs, guns, or sex). Nevertheless, that doesn't seem to diminish their enthusiasm for coming back to the library.

Now let's look at another regular group that visits the library with their respective classes. They come in, and many make a beeline to the magazines as well as to books like *Guinness World Records* or the oversized animal books (anything with pictures in them). They tend to ignore the lesson and seldom do written work; depending on their mood, they may verbally participate in class discussion. What does this tell me? Either I have students with very low reading and writing skills or they have become too cynical of school. The latter students can be difficult to deal with because they don't think you have anything to offer them. Some of these students are so jaded or possess such institutionalized mentalities that one cringes thinking about where they may likely end up. These students are a little tougher around the edges. They will often ask for street fiction with gangs and guns in them. They will ask you to order urban and erotic fiction like *Boujee with a Lil Hood in Her* by Lady Lisse and Kia Meche' (2017); Princess Diamonds's Cartel Love Story series (2016); and Sister Souljah's *The Coldest Winter Ever* (2006).

PEN OR PENCIL

There is nothing wrong with reading this genre of literature; however, I want my students to understand the following: Literacy is a human right, the world will require critical literacy skills of you, you won't like everything you have to read, and literacy is essential to defining yourself and transforming oppressive social structures. This last lesson has been essential to the curriculum I have been blessed to teach through a program called Pen or Pencil (POP).[2] Pen or Pencil, a program of the National Alliance of Faith and Justice (NAFJ), a national United We Serve partner, is a social action and educational movement designed to influence the lives of youth at greatest risk of academic failure and potential incarceration. "Pen" is short for *penitentiary*; "Pencil" refers to education. POP is a trademarked cultural-based mentoring curriculum approach, endorsed by the National Council for the Social Studies, which utilizes African American history as a priority in enhancing academic achievement and as an intervention in reducing delinquency and transforming behavior. POP is designed around the struggles and victories of human and civil rights made parallel to the complicated matrix of issues relevant to young lives today. This program is meant to help participating young men by providing them with mentors they can talk to in the facility and contact once they are released. Our two mentors, Carl Dunn and Richard Beckwith, both African American men and former military servicemen, have been faithfully coming to the facility on a weekly basis for five years now. Unfortunately, state laws prohibit the mentors from initiating contact with juveniles; however, the juveniles or their parents can, and must, initiate contact. Another dimension of the POP curriculum is getting the young men to read and write about African American history and themselves, which is not always easy; however, we try to start each class with a five-minute journaling exercise that is meant to get them thinking about themselves or an issue we are discussing. The fact that I have other colleagues who believe in literacy as a human right and in the importance of activist education is encouraging. This lends to a different set of priorities in collaborative meetings. It becomes more than, "Is this student behaving and doing his work?"; it becomes, "Why is this student acting the way he is, and how can we help him advocate and empower himself?" These teachers have consciously offered students multiple opportunities to express themselves (i.e., literary journals) and included guest speakers in their classrooms to enhance the cultural exposure of our students. These occasions are important because they afford our youth the opportunity to interact with professionals from all walks of life.

MY WORK

As the facility's only library media specialist, I have had the opportunity to work with both formal GED prep classes and one-on-one test prep. I found the structured self-contained GED prep classes to be most effective in getting our students focused on reading and truly preparing themselves for the exam. In 2012–2013, our class produced a 100 percent pass rate. To this day, the dismantling of this program within our facility is a mystery to most of us. The offering of Apex (credit recovery program) and tests for credit are also incentives for our students to take their academics more seriously. When they realize they can actually do something that they can see immediately benefiting their progress, they are more inclined to persist in completing these tests. Unfortunately, not all our students are so intrinsically or extrinsically motivated. Their cynicism and history of failure within the education system has diminished their desires to even attempt academic challenges. This connection goes to the emotional state of students who feel (warranted or not) that many of the schools they attend are not catered to their success.

As mentioned earlier, the library also offers a less stressful opportunity for our students to read and explore literature. They are given library and research instruction, but Internet instruction is limited since they cannot access the Internet. Students are exposed to different genres, the steps of information literacy, the history of graphic novels, and bibliographic instruction. Providing effective instruction can be challenging because, as in any classroom setting, you have a diversity of skill levels. Some students will say that the assignment is too easy, but when you give them something more challenging, they may or may not do it. There have been numerous times that I have had students who simply refused to do the class work, even though we were there to work with them. Those instances often leave me wondering, "When is the student held accountable for their learning or lack thereof?"

I am still pleased to say that the library is a valuable part of the school and the facility. More than sixty-five of the youth have books checked out at any given time. When they are in the library, the most popular book is the *Guinness World Records* (according to reading logs and time seen on tables); and the most requested book is the Holy Qur'an.

Despite the importance we put on literacy, the fact remains that daily life is harder for people with low literacy skills. This reality manifests as low communication skills, resulting in poor conflict resolution skills, and an inability to fully articulate oneself, resulting in frustration and dissatisfaction. I wish our students took these facts to heart. It is as if many of them find themselves in an ill-suited educational system, and instead of conforming or trying to change it, they choose to shut down and drop out. Therefore, what becomes of this problem?

NOTES

1. For more information on PARCC, see https://parcc.pearson.com/. For more information on the Maryland High School Assessment (HAS), see http://www.marylandpublicschools.org/programs/Pages/Testing/hsa.aspx. For more information on the state of Maryland revamped GED, see Lasko (2014) and McCartney (2014).

2. For more information on the Pen or Pencil program, see http://www.penorpencilmovement.org/about.php.

Chapter Sixteen

"I Shall Become a Collector of Me"

Kimberly Black

Sonia Sanchez's invocation "I shall become, I shall become a collector of me. And put meat on my soul" (Sanchez 1997) adroitly describes the last twenty years of my journey in the profession and in the world. Twenty years ago, I was at a crossroads in life, and today I find myself in a similar place, meeting again with Papa Legba[1] at the intersection of race, education, information, and, of course, power.

ACT 1: THE SETUP

Papa Legba has been my constant companion over the last twenty years (probably longer, but that is a story for another day). Twenty years ago, I had finished my master's degree and was embarking on a PhD degree in library and information science (LIS) at Florida State University (FSU). I was ambivalent at that time (and even now) about a career in library science. I wasn't sure that the field was scholarly enough—that it didn't engage in a sustained or critical dialogue about the politics of knowledge, its production, and its effects on people, especially the underrepresented, nor its ability to liberate.

I completed the terminal degree in fits and starts. For a long while, I was uncertain whether I would finish at all. I dropped out for a while and gained professional experience working in the academic library environment. I found working in the profession to be far more satisfying than studying it. My first professional experience was in an academic setting that served nontraditional students in an urban environment in the south. I enjoyed serving older, working students. I found a greater appreciation for learning among these students whose hopes for upward economic and social mobility hinged on gaining a degree. This population had significant life experience, which made the substance of their formal education more meaningful and real. They had purpose in the academy. Despite being overworked and underpaid and whose labor and effort often went unacknowledged and unappreciated in the workplace, they pursued their degrees with a singular tenacity. Some of the students were younger and worked without the benefit of adequate preparation for college work. However conflicted I felt about the scholarly side of the profession, I was (and am) profoundly impressed with its practice, especially in the lives of people who live in the margins.

One of the important lessons that I learned at this stage of my life is that power, in this information age, is exercised through the access to, and deployment of, information. I learned that poverty and disenfranchisement that is manifested in the physical world is often the by-product of information asymmetries deliberately maintained by the powerful.

I reached another crossroads. I moved several times during this period, eventually landing in a suburb of Philadelphia. I was making no progress on my degree, and I knew I needed to move back to Tallahassee, Florida, in order to finish. However, the move would require a large sacrifice—selling a home and leaving a stable employment situation for the uncertainties of student life with no guarantee of success. I did not know whether it was worth it. Eventually I did choose to return and to finish. As most decisions in life, making a choice requires risk. Making a choice does not guarantee any particular outcome.

I had three dissertation chairpersons. I can't describe how important a dissertation chairperson is for a person of color to complete a terminal degree. There is absolutely no way I could have finished if it was not for my chairperson Ronald Blazek. There is a saying that "not everyone who is my color is my kind, and not everyone who is my kind is my color." Dr. Blazek was a perfect personification of this quote. My first chairperson, Doris Clack, provided insight and encouragement at critical times early on in my journey. She took a personal interest in me, she encouraged my desire to study issues related to African Americans, and she mentored me. She died right before I sat for my qualifying exams. I took my exams and passed, but it took several years for me to deal with her loss. I was assigned a second dissertation chair who was supportive but who eventually left the university. The program had changed significantly during these years, eventually becoming an iSchool. I hadn't worked with many of the newer faculty, but Dr. Blazek was still there and agreed to take me on. He diligently worked with me, encouraged me, and somehow kept me motivated until I was able to finish—all this despite having made plans for retirement. I may have been his last doctoral student. The dean, Jane Robbins, was also an instrumental figure who provided assistance, support, and encouragement. She, too, retired soon after I finished my degree.

In writing my dissertation, I had the opportunity to explore the relationship between knowledge and power and how it intersected with race and gender. My dissertation was about U.S. research libraries' patterns of collecting literature (poetry and prose) written by African American women (Black-Parker 2003). I used the case of African American women's writing to explore the Foucauldian concept of power/knowledge: "if we seek to ascertain what knowledge is . . . we need to understand what the relations of struggle and power are. One can understand what knowledge consists of only by examining these relations of struggle and power, the manner in which things and men hate one another, and try to dominate one another, to exercise power relations over one another" (Foucault 1994, 12).

I wanted to call attention to the practice of collection development in academic research libraries—libraries that have a mandate to preserve knowledge for posterity. Literature and poetry encapsulate the culture and wisdom of the race, and its preservation by libraries was the site of social resistance that I wanted to understand. The bringing together that is collecting is where I wanted to explore power. I also wanted to explore the power of African American writers, to name and to call forth understanding through their words. I was able to explore these things, and more, in completing my dissertation.

ACT 2: RISING ACTION

I spent my early career as an academic in LIS working at two library schools at public flagship universities in the south. At both places I experienced varying levels of racism and sexism, as well as the random weirdness that individuals who didn't grow up in the south experience upon living there as an adult. Some of the racism and sexism that I experienced was (sadly) anticipated, and some of it actually caught me off guard. I worked at institutions that were racially segregated only a few decades before, including one that was, at the time, still operating under a consent decree to eliminate a long legacy of past discrimination in higher education in the state. I believe there is a lot of unfinished business when it comes to race and the preparation of practitioners. Neither the profession nor LIS educators have adequately dealt with the fact that many LIS programs are located at institutions with long histories of segregation—of racism without any truly meaningful reconciliation. The structure of consent decrees and court rulings increase the presence of Brown and Black bodies by numbers, but they do nothing to change habits of mind or ways of being in the world among those deeply embedded in academia. There has never been a truth and reconciliation within this profession about its history with race.

Consequently, LIS faculties seem to need a token Black or Brown faculty member in order to prove to themselves, and to the profession, that discrimination is safely a relic of the past. The Hurstonesque "Pet Negro System" (Hurston 1979) is alive and well in library and information science education programs. A number of my colleagues assumed that African American faculty members were offered jobs simply because of race—not because of capability—and that the presence of non-majority race and capability were mutually exclusive traits.

I believe that I was the second person of African descent to serve on either faculty in the history of both programs (one of which was quite a lengthy period). Both of these universities' LIS faculties included senior members who came of age at a time when segregation was legal and sexism was a prerogative. The times changed, but most of these individuals did not, and deeply entrenched institutional structures enabled all kinds of subtle and overt malfeasance. All too often, these individuals were aided and abetted by their more progressive peers who nonetheless looked the other way in exchange for whatever perk they wanted, and by younger academics who were eager and willing to do things that contradicted their espoused beliefs in order to curry favor and get ahead. At one institution in particular, I was outright persecuted. One good thing about persecution is that you quickly find out who your friends are. I developed deep and enduring friendships during that difficult time.

Serving on these faculties was an education! I was aware of, and to an extent, expected racism, but I didn't anticipate the high level of sexism. It also seemed that there were deep wells of insecurity and feelings of inadequacy among many of my former colleagues. Those demons were excised through grandiose and brutish behaviors to colleagues and general mistreatment of students and staff. I was truly surprised at the prevalence of alcohol abuse (and what appeared to me to be untreated or uncontrolled mental illness) with all the concomitant deep denial and enabling behaviors that follow in these situations. At my current institution, I share laughs with a colleague who had similar experiences at other institutions, including one where faculty members were reportedly trading antidepressants with each other before going to faculty meetings. At any rate, the confluence of character flaws, racism, sexism, and abuse of substances made for a very difficult working environment.

I reached another crossroads, and Papa Legba was there to greet me. I guess I came to a slow acknowledgment that library schools are going to reproduce what is already in superabundance in the profession. That is how institutions work—they are constituted to perpetuate themselves and their cultures from one generation to the next. For a while, I was somewhat angry and frustrated about this. Then I became determined to help develop alternatives. Somewhere along my journey in life, I gave up on the idea that a library school located in a majority institution was ever going to be able to do any more than nibble away at the edges of the problem of entrenched racism and sexism in the academy and the profession. The presence of a diverse faculty member or two, or a minority student scholarship program, or the adoption of a diversity course was not going to cause any kind of meaningful transformation of the profession.

ACT 3: THE RESOLUTION

Part of the problem of racism and lack of diversity in many library schools is the location of the schools themselves. Many of them are tucked away from the major metropolitan centers that tend to be progressive and heterogeneous. An opportunity arose for me to take a faculty position at Chicago State University (Chicago State), a predominantly Black institution located on the South Side of Chicago. Chicago State serves a nontraditional student body of older, working students. This was the same type of student body that I enjoyed working with at the start of my career as an academic librarian. I was very excited at the prospect of moving back to a large city and living in the Midwest where I grew up. Chicago State has a very old library science program that historically produced school librarians for the city of Chicago. The program was in the process of seeking initial accreditation from the American Library Association (ALA). I knew the state of Illinois was facing financial challenges and that it was hard work to be in a program seeking initial accreditation; still the prospect of living in a city of nearly nine hundred thousand African Americans was too much of an opportunity to pass up.

I hadn't fully appreciated the importance of Black Chicago until I lived in the city. It was not a coincidence that Barack Obama rose to the highest public office in the land from a base located in the South Side of Chicago. The political machinery and financial and intellectual capital needed to place an African American in such a high office was possible only in a place like Chicago. It is very hard for me to describe in words the power of the institutions and of the people of Chicago's South Side. There are overwhelming problems confronting the African American community on the South Side, yet the strength and power of the Black institutions in the city are as astonishing, as are all the problems.

At Chicago State, I worked as a faculty member in LIS and then (and currently) as an academic chairperson responsible for two distinct academic departments: library science and educational leadership. Seeing the profession of librarianship through the lens of an administrator within the field, and from outside the field, has been an interesting experience. This dual viewpoint allows me to simultaneously see the field as the profession does and as

other disciplines do. The departments are in distinct fields within the same college so, in a sense, they are in competition for resources with each other.

LIS is not well understood as an academic discipline within the academy. In the current climate of higher education, this is not a good thing. As an administrator, I find that I am always making the case to upper-level administration for the significance of the profession, and I engage in a low-level, yet constant, battle with other disciplines over ownership of intellectual territory. There have been some particularly nasty fights with the computer science department and some uneasy alliances with the management information systems department. I believe the traditionalist practitioners in the profession have not done a good job positioning the field to persist as an academic endeavor. Upper-level administrators realize that librarianship is a profession; however, they are perplexed as to why the program isn't more like pharmacy or nursing (two professional programs to which LIS is often compared). I am not convinced that the profession has protected the wages of individuals working in the profession—the field is consistently rated as one of the lowest paying occupations that requires a master's degree (Pfeuffer n.d.; Dhillon 2014; Dill 2016; Dishman 2016). Over the past year, prospective applicants have asked me if the LIS field can assure them stable and secure employment—master's degrees are increasingly an investment in which individuals will only make if there is absolute certainty in its return. The expected return is salary (a frequent question) and job security. The questions prospective students asked about the profession used to be different. The ALA, and the profession, do not provide program administrators much ammunition to work with—the world of information has assumed strategic importance in contemporary life and yet the profession most concerned with it is rated poorly. I believe that there is a disconnect between the profession and the current political economy of higher education. The profession has not preserved the number of professional positions (full-time professional positions are often replaced with part-time positions), nor has the profession maintained the nature of the work in a way that makes the profession attractive to the kinds of people who can provide the innovative services and knowledge that society needs to move the profession forward in the twenty-first century (a lack of cultural responsiveness reflecting a diverse society and broader thinking about the information worlds that people inhabit that get manifested in innovative services). So much of the justification for public spending on higher education is now focused on the quality of the jobs for which academic programs prepared students.

A few years after I arrived in Chicago, real challenges emerged that have had dire consequences for Chicago State and all public postsecondary education in Illinois. What has come to be known as the state of Illinois "budget impasse" has been calamitous to higher education in Illinois (Bosman and Davey 2017; Brown 2017; Masterson 2017). The epic clash between the governor and the Illinois General Assembly has resulted in the failure of the state of Illinois to produce a complete budget since mid-2015. Despite the lack of a budget, spending has continued through court orders and consent decrees except for spending in higher education and social services. There have been no state appropriations for higher education since 2015. The state has made some limited stopgap funding available to higher education, but there have been no regular appropriations made. Essentially, higher education and social services have become the pawns in a fight between political parties in the state.[2]

Chicago State University was hit particularly hard by these events, receiving the largest percentage of budget cuts of all public higher education institutions in the state (Center for Tax and Budget Accountability 2017). These budget cuts were catastrophic. The Chicago State University Board of Trustees made a declaration of financial exigency and the creation of a committee to oversee a mass layoff (Curtin 2016). At one point, all employees received a layoff notice (Eltagouri 2016). The exigency declaration then triggered a sanction from the regional accrediting body (Higher Learning Commission 2016). The declaration of exigency also made it easier for Chicago State to qualify for some of the stopgap funding from the state that, from my perspective, wanted all the state institutions to become weakened and completely exhaust their reserves before receiving public funding from the state. The situation is very complicated—there is corruption at the university, as is present in most Chicago institutions (the local euphemism to describe this is "the Chicago way"). Nevertheless, a report by the Chicago-based Center for Tax and Budget Accountability (CTBA) noted that "the cuts imposed on Chicago State University constitute particularly questionable public policy, because Chicago State University serves predominantly low-income students of color, and hence is crucial in helping those students, many of whom are first-generation college students, move into middle class and self-sufficiency" (Center for Tax and Budget Accountability 2017). I still struggle with finding the vocabulary to describe what it is like to be an administrator under these conditions.

Chicago State is now at a crossroads (and Papa Legba is waving at me). The institution's survival is precarious, and I am fearful of the imminent compromises that will have to be made to endure in the future. I am also gravely concerned about the future of higher education as a whole in this country. I am convinced that Illinois is on the bleeding edge of a new, meaner era for higher education. The old social contract that saw the investment in higher education as a public good has fallen away. What happens in Illinois and to Chicago State is highly consequential and is a harbinger for what will happen elsewhere in the country. The type and price of educational access is being threatened. The value of the traditional four-year university credential and of universities in general is no longer self-evident. Federal level education policy is favoring cheaper and shorter periods of education (non-credit-bearing certificates and "micro-credentials") over traditional, four-year college education. There is an instrumental rationality applied to learning with an emphasis on the attainment of narrowly scoped workforce skills over the development of deep analysis, dispositions toward critical inquiry, and effective communication competences that result from a traditional liberal arts education. The liberal arts tradition is increasingly becoming the purview of the rich and training programs the purview of the poor. The liberty, empowerment, and self-determination that comes from an authentic education at an institution embedded in its community is of incalculable value. What has been happening in higher education in Illinois is not an accident—it is an assault on people of color and on people experiencing poverty.

I am also convinced that we need institutions embedded in communities of color to produce information professionals who can deeply serve communities of color. In the current political milieu in the United States, replete with "alternative" facts and the mass circulation of specious truth-claims, information professionals will need to serve society well by educating it about the politics and power of information.

So, here it is, twenty years later. What have I collected over the years? It is still difficult for me to assess this. Changes related to race in the profession and in a post-Obama America are very slow to realize—there is a durable inertia to change, which is dangerous in this world that moves so fast and is infinitely changeable. The potential for the profession is still as boundless as I believed it was twenty years ago, but I feel we are no closer to realizing it today than then. Maybe the idea of progress is illusory or, perhaps, it is imperceptibly slow. Time seems to move faster now than it did when I was younger—I guess that is a peculiar trick of age. So for now, I will reserve coming to a conclusion about matters, and I will take my wisdom from Jean Toomer (1999, 6):

> We must not expect one act of liberation, one note of transformation, to produce a whole new being./It takes a well-spent lifetime, and perhaps more, to crystalize in us that for which we exist./The growth of a human being is a dynamic symphony of forces playing in this field of force that is ourselves./We start with gifts. Merit comes from what we make of them.

NOTES

1. Legba is "A Yoruban god associated with the crossroads (the junction between the physical and the spiritual worlds; the point where a person has to make decisions that may affect his or her life)" (Ervin 2004).

2. The Illinois budget impasse ended on August 31, 2017, when a budget was approved for FY2018.

Part Seven

They Persisted

THEY PERSISTED

Chapter Seventeen

Serving the Sons and Daughters of Mechanics and Farmers at the Crossroads of America

Madelyn Shackelford Washington

Developing an empathetic practice is essential to becoming a harbinger for intellectual freedom in a highly homogenous and insular community. Crucial to living up to this professional commitment is the capacity to self-reflect while in the throes of (other people's and your own) emotional and irrational behavior. I spent the first five years of my professional life as an academic librarian in south central Indiana. Rife with awkwardly hilarious, painful, and powerful interactions, I captured my experience as an Obama-era academic librarian of color in daily journals. In this chapter, I hope to share a selection of primary source material—unpublished daily journal entries, e-mails, and social media posts—written between August 29, 2011, and June 17, 2017, and reflect upon some of my own social missteps. This material reveals times I found myself doing and saying things that caused pain, confusion, and disengagement with my service population; success stories; and turning points leading to the transformation from musician to librarian to musical activist.

THE METHOD

I used narrative stream of consciousness in my home and work journals to depict thoughts, feelings, and reactions to my surroundings in southern Indiana. I separated home, travel, and work journals by geographic location of each entry written (e.g., my home journal entries were written at my home address, my travel journal entries were written in a variety of locations, and my work journal entries were mostly written in my office in Columbus, Indiana). The original journal entries were handwritten in two 144-page gold-tooled and polychromatic books and two 366-page leather-bound books. All entries included in this chapter have been abbreviated and edited for clarity. At the top of each page is a header with the title for the entry along with the location, date, and time (military).[1] A probing question or culminating statement follows each entry. All pages were numbered, and entries are cited in endnotes.

As an information professional, gaining the interpersonal communication savvy necessary to love and serve a population that does not share one's own political or social ideologies may (not) sound liberating. It was for me. Bored by the traps of confirmation bias, working in Columbus, Indiana, the home-town of then governor of Indiana, Mike Pence—our forty-eighth (current) vice president of the United States—for close to five years shook me away from my cozy corners of comfort. In southern Indiana, I learned that no matter how politically or socially permeable you think you are, there is always another perspective to acknowledge; taking a genuine interest in dis-courses of difference was empowering. This is especially important to em-phasize as we find ourselves in what many are calling a "post-truth" era. Armed with the ability to filter information ingestibles with ease, librarians of many colors feel quite affirmed by the National Public Radio (NPR), Remezcla, and AfroPunk publishing echo chambers and forget that some of our (rural) patrons may not quite understand (or wish to celebrate) our Brown, Black, queer, gynocentric pride. Especially if it is perceived that one has—at least in their eyes—(unfairly) benefited in some way from their gender assignment or their ethnic identity. According to the United States Census, approximately one-third of Bartholomew County's population holds a bachelor's degree or higher and are 88 percent white[2] (mostly conservative Christians). Some of my colleagues and patrons opposed affirmative action and resented diversity initiatives. During these years, I learned how little the word *diversity*, as it is used in the academic industrial complex, captured the variety of the human condition.

Teaching a semester-long first year experience seminar was my platform of connection to the inner-thinkings of southern *Hoosiers*.[3] At the helm of a class full of mainly White first-generation students from Decatur, Bartholo-mew, Shelby, and Jackson counties, I realized that I was the first Black person with whom many of my students developed a personal relationship. The opportunity to hone this gift of teaching[4] helped me broaden my own definition of diversity.

Spread Too Thin—21:18—August 20, 2013—Home Journal
Today was my 1st day teaching my own [semester-long] class . . . a first year seminar . . . and my class was so extremely open on the first day. I was

amazed. Two girls revealed histories of domestic abuse and one lady has four foster children and 4 of her own. More than one person, has a disabled child and I have three musicians in the house. Quite the diverse crowd I have and I hope the best for them all.

Just keep enjoying . . . (love it)[5]

During a conversation about financial literacy and student success, I was forced to reckon with my own position of power as a librarian of color in the Obama era, a third-generation educator among a family of Black(ish) giants in the Los Angeles Unified School District, the daughter of a speech and language pathologist and an engineer. Growing up hearing the self-affirmations of librarians and educational administrators, early on I was inspired by a sense of satisfaction knowing my ancestors held noble posts: farmer, engineer, nurse, lawyer, law enforcement official, dance ethnologist. Accustomed to a mix of progressive and old-world family values, conversations about learning were common at the dinner table. My family encouraged me to focus on studying rather than hurrying to get a job.

My students looked at me in shock and disbelief when I suggested they "quit working and live off of financial aid and scholarships." After two years of serving a community largely made up of first-generation students, this embarrassing moment proved significant. These students gave me the inside track on a particular southern Indiana socioeconomic experience. Before this, I thought everyone's family could pitch in to help the next generation get an education. Not the case.

One of my patrons told me her husband of twenty years thought she was selfish for going back to school. Another told me her mother wouldn't babysit so she could attend her classes or do her homework. Some of my student assistants worked several jobs to help take care of their families with health or substance abuse issues. This was my reality check. Raised (for the most part) in Simi Valley, California, I was accustomed to always being "othered" by well-to-do conservative White Christians and hyperaware of the outer gaze; but until I started working in the heartland of America, I was plenty ignorant to the daily struggles of the *poor White man* (Earle 1894).

Aside from the casual flying of Confederate flags that I passed during my daily commute from Bloomington to Columbus, it took me some time to start questioning the state's reputation for "Hoosier Hospitality."[6] It came under intense public scrutiny after Governor Pence signed an additional bill as an amendment to the Religious Freedom Restoration Act intended to protect LGBTQ (lesbian, gay, bisexual, transgender, queer) citizens.[7] During this time, I began to wonder how librarians of color in the state could live up to the standard of fostering inclusivity in locations where homophobic, xenophobic, and Islamophobic citizenry are social norms. How can one librarian of color positively influence a service population that, in my opinion, largely subscribes to rhetoric of social apathy? To answer, I analyze and describe my transformation from a constrained, controlled librarian into an independent yet dialogical agent, as narrated in my personal journals.

Looking in the Mirror—21:06—January 28, 2015—Home Journal

While chatting with [a colleague] in my office, I complained of the distance that I feel from straight white men here. "They stare," I told him . . . "and stare." I wonder what they are thinking all the time. He responded, "they're probably thinking, well. . . she's light enough that maybe my parents won't get mad at me." I laughed but it was a shame that shocked me, I didn't expect to hear that kind of guffaw. But I quickly realized that my guffaws were covering up the pain of his honesty.

Time to unpack your social ills[8]

Mapping an individual librarian's process of professional transformation is a significant act. Often, tenure-line librarians exist in an isolated teaching culture, making the transparency of the process of educational change essential. Understanding educational change requires examination of the experiences of an individual educator. Identification of the contexts a librarian may have to consider when transforming their professional practice may provide new(ish) librarians insight into the complex nature of educational transformation. This chapter is intended to pique the interest of those wishing to serve in rural America, looking to adopt a tool to help "focus on the personal, emotional, and dialogical processes" (Lanas and Kiilakoski, 2013) enabling personal and professional change.

Positively impacting a population that does not reflect your cultural or political ideologies requires a heightened sensitivity to a variety of patron learning needs. I endorse daily journal writing practice as an effective means of self-evaluation. Key to helping me develop an empathetic professional practice, daily journaling applications in academia are used widely in language teaching, teacher training, and student learning assessment (Lakshmi 2014). Despite its reported advantages in both teaching and research, journal/diary studies available based on the writings of academic librarians are most often focused on producing qualitative evidence to improve library services, rather than highlighting its role as a reflective agent in the process of professional transformation. The explorative properties of journaling have been cited as "useful in exploring one's thoughts and feelings about work challenges and work decisions" by veteran reference librarian Katherine Murphy Dickson (2002). A common challenge with academic librarians is that often campus-level service (committee work via shared governance) can impede everyday librarian work. Writing through this challenge, I realized a skill of being able to identify "manipulators, and followers . . . quickly,"[9] and I learned to especially give people in the workplace the benefit of the doubt when the going gets tough. Key to developing an empathetic practice is to remain radically hopeful in the face of deceit, ignorance, and manipulation.

"Keeping a work journal can help bring about greater fulfillment in one's work life by facilitating self-renewal, change, and a search for new meaning" (Dickson 2002, 687). Since taking an interdisciplinary approach to my education, I turn to my journal to reflect on my next educational and professional goals. This keeps me forward thinking and fills me with a great deal of confidence. This is evident in the entry written on the evening of my thirty-seventh birthday.

> **37—20:43—May 10, 2015—Home Journal**
> I still want to be a politician. I still do think that the JD is the next step. Then (maybe at the same time) a DM or DMA. Then later . . . the PhD. I have such lofty goals. Keep 'em. I have muted my personality too long. Raise those expectations and live Madelyn! Bless up yourself.
> Dang, I need some companionship :)[10]

When discussing professional transformation, one must place the discussion in a specific context. This chapter's specific context, in which the need for transformation arose and was carried out, was southern Indiana. I struggled with questions of identity and (re)discovery of self during this five-year period. After arriving to librarianship with thirteen years of experience as a professional musician, dancer, and choreographer, my artistic self conflicted with life as a generalist librarian. Filled with roadblocks to satisfaction in my work and life, my personal, travel, and work journal[11] entries expressing a longing for more engagement with music or dance read as lamentations and are plentiful: "I miss music/I miss dancing." Uncovered in several entries were unexplored feelings, wishes, and dreams (of performing), sabotaging my satisfaction at work.

> **We All Die Sometimes—21:06—August 29, 2012—Home Journal**
> I will dance, sing and publish. . . . I will make others cry, copulate, and cut up with my passions.
> Self-affirmations[12]

> **Always Expect Change—20:19—August 24, 2014—Home Journal**
> I am a musician first, dancer second and librarian third. I wonder what interesting somethings are going to present themselves to me this academic year.
> What will I learn?[13]

> **Moving On—20:36—May 15, 2015—Home Journal**
> I must go. Today's meeting at IUPUI[14] confirmed it. All of these "into it" collection development librarians were full of passion and little ol' disgruntled me lacks it. I gotta get out . . . started considering music librarian gigs and foundation gigs.

I strive to be wicked bad—like my Mom [15]

These entries outline some of the reflections of a developing (proud) interdisciplinarian. Through the process of keeping a journal, I was able to gain the focus to identify my strengths and the activities that bring me the greatest joy as an information professional.

> **Enrichment Programming—23:36—May 16, 2015—Home Journal**
> Since accepting the duty of co-chair of the Programs and Social Committee of the Indiana University Librarians Association, I have had a great time planning facilitating events for IU Libraries. I love seeing people have a good time and it is quite satisfying to see people enjoy my hard work.
> I do this event planning thing well [16]

Others cite keeping a work journal as a great planning tool. After three years of library instruction and teaching a first-year experience class, evidence of professional burnout and stagnation became apparent in my writing. I longed to make a meaningful difference pedagogically, and I sought to "challenge presuppositions, explore alternative perspectives, transform old ways of understanding, and act on new perspectives" (Mezirow 1990) in a dialogue with the generalized Midwestern Anglo other.

> **Being Anxious Is Not Helpful—21:25—March 3, 2015—Home Journal**
> I worry so much about every little thing I do professionally: my artistry, my service, my teaching. Worry/agonizing about things is not healthy. . . . Did a much better job teaching tonight, but realized I have a long way to go. I think these readings about critical/radical library instruction are going to be right up my alley and hopefully transform how my instruction looks and is ingested.
> Learn to relax a bit more. [17]

Several authors in various fields recognize in various ways the pain involved in such a pedagogical transformation. Lanas and Kiilakoski (2013) note Gert Biesta's (2006) discussion on the difficulty and painfulness of coming into the world, taking awaiting responsibility and exposing ourselves to that which is other and different, and Zembylas's (2015) views on the ethics of discomfort. My professional transformation to music activist was prompted by several converging factors: my expressed commitment to music as well as personal and professional turning points. Transformation was enabled by the availability of the necessary space, support, and emotional resources for personal and professional reflection and small, concrete changes in the surrounding environment.

TURNING POINT #1

Indiana University's diversity initiatives gave rise to the office of Intergroup Dialogue, which provided me with a stellar opportunity to engage with a promising approach to encourage understanding, explore social and cultural differences, identify common ground, and communicate honestly. Intergroup dialogues (a product of the University of Michigan[18]) encourage direct encounters and exchanges about contentious issues, especially those associated with issues of social identity and social stratification. They invite participants to actively explore the meanings of singular (as men or as women) or intersecting (as men of color or as White women) social identities and to examine the dynamics of privilege and oppression shaping relationships between social groups in our society. These dialogues build dispositions and skills for developing and maintaining relationships across differences and for taking action for equity and social justice (Zúñiga 2003).

Exhausted—20:28—March 31, 2015—Home Journal
Today's intergroup dialogue on race at IUPUI was wonderful. Thoroughly enjoyed myself but had to suffer through a bit of pain. . . . I told a story about my grandpa, there were lots of tears in the room, mostly from weeping White women and one Black woman. I do like this method and am inspired to see what more I can do to rock social justice.
It is a refreshing exhausted . . . you know?[19]

One must pick and choose battles wisely working as a generalist librarian of color in the crossroads of America. People (thankfully) mind their manners in Columbus and social anonymity isn't a priority, so personality is important. I learned to value (a kind of) neutrality that seduced me. I used that neutral space to feel safe (and to make my patrons feel safe), build social capital, and find crucial teaching moments about social identity, social stratification, and race with patrons who are largely different from me—White, conservative Christian, first generation, daughters and sons of mechanics and farmers.

TURNING POINT #2

In April 2015, I was afforded the opportunity to involve myself with the campus's first ever drag show. Lending my voice to the cause of the Trevor Project,[20] a youth LGBTQ suicide prevention organization, was a public demonstration of my commitment to equality and my dedication to music as a discipline: I opened the show with a Cuban bolero.[21] This act was also crucial to placing me at the center of the cultural hub of the city and institution. Singing for my colleagues in this event featuring gender performance was significant in my shift from generalist librarian to music librarian.

OK . . . So I'm Sick—21:13—April 26, 2015—Home Journal
IUPUC's[22] 1st drag show was wonderful. Guests Mocha Debutante and Richard Cranium were the best! . . . The show was (very) well attended and the performers received a [lengthy] standing ovation. Faculty members and staff alike were in drag. It was truly a night of Kings and Queens . . . we raised $611.00 for the Trevor Project.
 I need to have a clear head before traveling again next weekend.[23]

TURNING POINT #3

Addressing shifting social climates and bias identification should be issues of potential interest to new(ish) career librarians of color. Self-analyzing the process of personal transformation requires situating yourself in personal, local, national, global, and cultural settings. In my sheltered existence, growing up in Simi Valley, California, I had little experience socializing with othered-White(r) populations: poor Whites. In Columbus, I realized not all White folk were rich. In my work journal entries, I explored the shadows of my workplace—my disappointments and anger—which led me to catharsis and great insight. Exploring your resistance to your biases may help develop empathy, which is necessary to positively impact and love a service population subscribing to a rhetoric of social apathy.

Feeling Too Many Things—09:39—June 29, 2016—Work Journal
Dr. Finance and I started off the conversation sweetly enough, talking about clairvoyance and ethnic origins. He told me his son was one-quarter Native American, I said to "make sure he checks that box" for scholarship opportunities, then all hell broke loose. He told me affirmative action increased the problems of our racial inequities. It seems as though he does not see his white privilege. I understood, but reacted with intense emotion.
 We went back and forth, in a very animated fashion, trying to one-up each other's racial and [socioeconomic] inequality experiences [he told me to "get over" slavery, I called him "white-y" and made a Klan reference]. The conversation was so many things: frustrating, invigorating, scary, real. And I loved it. . . . I am proud we could both provide each other with a safe space to talk about uncomfortable issues. [Fortunately] [t]here was no love lost in the intense talk. We gave each other a nice squeeze before departing.
 I am confused and need rest.[24]

Achieving such a transformation in personal and professional thinking and practice may require thorough and deep changes in oneself. Using ethnic slurs[25] in unexpected ways sometimes provokes people and can cause a great deal of discomfort and disengagement. In the aftermath of Turning Point #3, evidence of regret in my pursuit of a transformation that, in my conversation with a dear colleague, appeared to deviate from the local norm—the use of the term *redneck* with reference to my own White heritage—appears in several work and travel journal entries. This use brought the entire norm (slur) into question and caused a momentary conflict, resolving itself through adopting a new form of collective identity (how a mixed-race person may or may not claim the term *redneck*).

Still Unpacking Things—10:30—June 30, 2016—Work Journal

I have been isolated too long and the use of the word "redneck" is becoming much too easy for me to be comfortable with. I told Mom how Dr. Finance checked me on my use of the word and I was thankful, as it is something I am uncomfortable with. Mom said, it's great we had a breakthrough and can feel open/comfortable enough with each other to talk. When one can't talk openly, one cannot grow.

I never want people to feel as though I am a bigot. [26]

MY TWO CENTS

As mentioned earlier, this chapter is intended to be of interest of those wishing to serve in rural America and those interested in writing a memoir. Nonfiction writing is rewarding, and the process of making sense of my own personal thoughts has been transformative. The necessity to deeply self-reflect during and after emotional, and sometimes irrational, interactions is crucial to developing an empathetic professional practice. Spending the first five years of my professional life as a librarian building a reputation as a sincere consensus builder with colleagues I largely did not identify with is something I am proud of. The entries shared here are the most revealing look at the risks taken to engage in open dialogues with trusted colleagues in an attempt to understand social difference, and assert myself as an interdisciplinarian and musical activist.

For methods on keeping intensive work journals, I highly recommend Katherine Dickson's (2002) guiding questions to consider:

How do you interact with your coworkers? What kinds of feedback/help do you need and get at work? How do you feel when doing your work? After completing the intensive journal, look it over a while later and see what it tells you. What do you want to change in your work? What feels right as is? Are you in the right job? The right type of work? (700–701)

If you are on the tenure line and wish to venture into journaling, I understand that your time is precious and the thought of taking time to write in leisure may seem far too luxurious. If this is the case, you may wish to start down the nonfiction path by writing conference diaries/reviews. Professional organizations such as the International Association of Music Libraries, Archives, and Documentation Centres publish conference diaries, and many other associations need librarians to write conference reviews.[27] Turning your life's work into tangible outcomes for your tenure dossier may also be possible by approaching your journal writing as an ethnographer. To gather information in my travel journals (which often become travel/conference reviews), I use the guiding questions for observations in *Doing Case Study Research* (Hancock and Algozzine 2011, 49), adopted from John Creswell's 1998 book, *Educational Research: Planning, Conducting and Evaluating Quantitative and Qualitative Research*:

> Participant and setting? Individual Conducting observation? Role of the observer (participant, nonparticipant, other)? Time, place and length of the observation? Descriptive observations (individuals, setting descriptors)? Reflections (experience, hypothesis, guidance)?

If you aren't on the tenure line but are thinking about writing nonfiction, publishing travelogues, graphic memoirs, and zines might be appropriate options for you to explore.

In response to a Facebook post by Jenn Riley, the associate dean of digital initiatives at McGill University, figure 17.1 illustrates my two cents for keeping journals.

NOTES

1. Header suggestion from Emeritus Professor Johnie Scott, http://www.csun.edu/~hcpas003/home.html.
2. United States Census Bureau, "Bartholomew County, Indiana, 2016."
3. For a definition of the word *Hoosier*, see Graf (2016).
4. Madelyn Shackelford Washington, "So Pleased," Home Journal entry, September 8, 2011, 79–80. Written at the end of my first day teaching library instruction.
5. Washington, "Spread Too Thin," Home Journal entry, August 20, 2013, 295.
6. For more on "Hoosier Hospitality," see Mack (2016).
7. Indiana State Assembly (2015).
8. Washington, "Looking in the Mirror," Home Journal entry, January 28, 2015, 14.
9. Washington, "Rude Awakening," Home journal entry, 6. After serving as chair of the faculty affairs committee, I became disillusioned about working with some of my colleagues.
10. Washington, "37," Home Journal entry, May 10, 2015, 66.
11. I've been writing in daily journals since I was fourteen years old. Around twelve years ago, I started keeping separate journals in different writing locations. When I am on vacation or on the road to a conference, I write in a travel journal (a 144-page book). I started keeping a separate work journal in my office in 2014 (a 144-page book). I also maintain home journals in two locations, my mother's house in California and my current permanent address.
12. Washington, "We All Die Sometimes," Home Journal entry, August 29, 2012, 217.
13. Washington, "Always Expect Change," Home Journal entry, August 24, 2014, 363.
14. Indiana University–Purdue University, Indianapolis.
15. Washington, "Moving On," Home Journal entry, May 15, 2015, 71–72.
16. Washington, "Enrichment Programming," Home Journal entry, May 16, 2015, 73.
17. Washington, "Being Anxious Is Not Helpful," Home Journal entry, March 3, 2015, 25.

Figure 17.1. MSW's response to Facebook post from Jenn Riley on June 16, 2017, regarding keeping a journal. Courtesy of Samax Amen.

18. National Intergroup Dialogue Institute, https://igr.umich.edu/article/national-intergroup-dialogue-institute.

19. Washington, "Exhausted," Home Journal entry, March 31, 2015, 42.

20. The Trevor Project, http://www.thetrevorproject.org/.

21. A bolero is a slow-tempo Latin ballad.

22. Indiana University–Purdue University, Columbus.

23. Washington, "OK . . . So I'm Sick," Home Journal entry, April 26, 2015, 57.

24. Washington, "Feeling Too Many Things," Work Journal entry, June 29, 2016, 60–61.

25. Racial slur database, http://www.rsdb.org.

26. Washington, "Still Unpacking Things," Work Journal entry, June 30, 2016, 62.

27. Conference Diaries, International Association of Music Libraries, Archives and Documentation Centres, http://www.iaml.info/fr/tags/congress-diary-kongresstagebuch-journal-de-bord-du-congres.

Chapter Eighteen

Grief in Five Stages

Postgraduate Librarian Degree

Leni Matthews

Prior to entering librarianship, I was teaching and fed up with the classroom. I worked for Chicago Public Schools for about ten years. There was no support from the system to help teachers or students succeed. My frustration with the school system was the beginning stages of deciding to become a librarian. I thought that becoming a librarian would be an easy transition: I had experience with students of all ages, I loved literature, and I had a master's degree; however, preparing for a librarian position became a grieving process. My background and experience were not enough to land a position. I had no idea it would be so difficult. It took me about three years to be hired as a librarian after my master's degree. My story tells how I coped through the five stages of grief while trying to find a librarian position.

Dr. Kübler-Ross's five stages of grief are denial, anger, bargaining, depression, and acceptance (Kübler-Ross 2005; Bretherton 1992). I went through these backwards while looking for a librarian position. My grief was for the "loss" of a librarian job I never had from being rejected repeatedly for positions. Just like any griever, you do not know the grief stages until reflecting or until someone else experiences them. I had no idea I was grieving until reflecting for this chapter. Dr. Kübler-Ross's stages are not prescriptive. So, use my story as a guide for contextualization, not a prescriptive process of what to expect. The tips in this chapter are to motivate you, and hopefully, you may also be able to help others in their job search.

I had little experience in librarianship, and I knew I would have to work harder than those with experience. I was not fully aware that being a Black woman was part of this struggle. I soon learned that many women of color have issues when looking for work in librarianship, coupled with the fact that our representation in this profession is low. I knew that gaining experience was important, but I was a full-time teacher. Time was scarce. The school I worked in had a library and my class went there for research, but there was no librarian, just a room that housed books. Books were unorganized, but I tried to learn as much as I could to help me better understand a library's structure. As a full-time teacher, I completed my degree in library and information science and looked forward to reflecting on my teaching career. Unfortunately, my search would take longer than I could ever imagine.

I attended the University of Illinois, Urbana Champaign (UIUC),[1] the top school for library and information science in the country, thinking it would give me an advantage in the job search while giving me a great education. When I attended UIUC, there were only three other Black women in my cohort of over fifty. I noticed this immediately on the first day of class. I also found out that many people in my cohort already had librarian or librarian-like positions. After library school, I wondered, *How could they have had those library positions without a degree?* And for those who did not have librarian status, I also wondered, *How were they able to make a living on a non-librarian salary?* They were already ahead. I submitted applications before graduating so that I would have a smooth transition. I even put in applications to volunteer on the weekends and school breaks. Unfortunately, most internships and volunteer work were offered during the school semester. In library school, I did not have library experience, but I had many years of experience working with students of all ages. That should have provided an equal playing field.

Between 2010 and 2015, I applied to approximately two hundred librarian and librarian-like (roles not needing an LIS degree or not in a traditional library) positions at various institutions. I was keeping an open mind. I was not sure where I wanted to be, and I hoped that my first position would help me envision my future role in librarianship. *If only I could get hired . . .* After library school, I went through the grieving phases over and over again: looking for work, being rejected, being invited to interviews, never hearing back from the committee, and working internships that did not grant me the amount of experience expected in many positions for which I applied. I visited libraries and had conversations with librarians and learned that some did not have their degree: they were in school. It bothered me to know that there were people in positions who did not have a degree, but I had the degree with no job. *How can this person who was still "learning" have the job before me and I can't even land a volunteer position?* I was crushed. Before I knew it, years passed, and I still had no position.

I was tired of applying, mostly tired of being rejected and not knowing how to "fix" my problem. *Is something wrong with me?* I read countless blogs and articles, and I attended workshops about the application process:

- Résumé versus curriculum vitae
- Résumé length
- Résumés through data and art
- Online résumés

I have many styles to my résumé, from listing the institution's requirements on the résumé, then highlighting them in white (so it is not visible) so the algorithm will place the résumé at the top of the list, to creating the résumé as a visual work of art. I did Google searches about job hunting and subscribed to organizations like LAC Group, ALA on LinkedIn, IL Network, The Ladders, Beyond.com, and The Career News[2] to get the latest information about job openings and job preparation skills. I also kept current with my Spectrum Scholars[3] cohort to learn about job openings and ways to get involved. It hardly worked. . . . *I can't be part of this! I have over seven years of teaching experience. I could at least land a public or school librarian position. This would be a guaranteed career, right?*

NOPE! That was not enough. I even took a part-time job after teaching during the day. I was able to be part of the library environment as a tutor for students. I became familiar with a librarian's role. What I saw the librarians do, I could do. I knew it was well overdue for me to have a position. I worked this second job for a year. I believed that I was "almost there" in my Princess Tiana[4] voice. I was gaining firsthand experience.

I have been on so many interviews that I became brave. This either meant that I had become a skilled interviewee or I was just numb to this process. I still came to the interviews enthusiastic, with hopes of being offered the position. *I am the one, a great fit for their library.* Eventually, I was able to intern at beautiful places most people dream of working like the Art Institute of Chicago and Argonne National Laboratory. These were short but rich internships. I was the only Black woman working in those departments, but I was optimistic but worried about job prospects when the internship ended. I would be back at square one, looking for a job. I was traumatized.

My feelings were all over the place: Am I good enough? I have a degree. I have experience with students. Just be patient; someone will hire me. I should complete at least seven applications a week. My résumé looks good. Maybe I should continue teaching. Is my résumé fine? It should be; I have four versions of it. There are no jobs in Chicago. I need to start looking out of state. Didn't I apply to this position? I should start calling some of the committee members. No one ever contacted me from that on-campus interview. Was it my hair? I need to redo my cover letter and résumé.

I was trying to reconcile putting in many applications with the rejections. I knew that sacrifice was imminent. I was raising two children, teaching full time and part time, glad and willing to give up my weekends, holidays, and breaks to be a librarian. My confidence was very low. My grieving process is nontraditional because it is not in order, or concerning the loss of a loved one, but, instead, the loss of opportunity.

ACCEPTANCE

I accepted that switching careers would be hard work. Entering any profession comes with its pains, and this was not an exception. I looked forward to the transition and its challenges. I accepted:

- Being new to the field and possibly struggling to find a position
- Taking a pay cut
- Having a lot to learn
- Giving free time for the "cause"

I was not prepared to be rejected repeatedly for positions I qualified for. Some of the public librarian positions wanted engagement with students as well as reference experience. I had this. A teacher engages more deeply and more often with students than public librarians by conducting constant assessment, creating activities, and interacting extensively one-on-one and with groups. Librarians do not lack this ability. It is just not their daily interaction with students.

Tip: Do not forget that people start somewhere, and at the bottom, unfortunately, *is* a start. Keep applying. Ask librarians about how you can enhance your chances of being hired.

ANGER

I am pissed. Months passed. I received e-mails noting that I was such a great candidate, but they had chosen someone more qualified. One snail-mail letter read, "We have offered this position to another candidate, and are pleased she has accepted." That was rude and weird. I wondered, *Why can't I find a position? What do they want from me?* For my public library applications, I believed my experience with students of all ages was beyond the requirements. As a teacher, I taught and planned every day, multiple times a day. Some academic librarians teach courses (one-shot courses), but never as often as K–12 teachers. Now that I am an academic librarian and teach one-shot courses, I know it is something that I could have done years ago. I was qualified then, as I am qualified now.

I also felt uncomfortable when I interviewed at libraries and there were few to no people who represented my ethnicity. I wondered if there was something I lacked when I was not offered a position. I wondered if a White woman was what they really wanted in a candidate. *I work hard. This is*

Bull#@%$! I don't deserve this. I have a lot of experience, a degree, and a teaching certificate. WTF?! People who look like me love to engage others in learning, lead instruction and storytelling, and be creative. I checked my e-mail again . . . another rejection letter.

Tip: Give your sanity priority. Do not take rejections personally. They are missing out on a great candidate. Respect the people in the profession. Their accomplishment is not your weakness.

DEPRESSION

I'll never find work. I fell into a somber mood, thinking about "sticking it out" with teaching. I thought I would have to stay in the classroom whether I liked it or not. *Maybe teaching is my calling, staying here, feeling miserable every day.* As I searched for librarian positions, I continued to teach full time. One year after receiving my library degree, I was laid off because of an "economic action." I began to substitute teach at various Chicago schools (that's another book). I had to continue to earn money. I figured that being laid off got me one step closer to a librarian position. I was wrong. I did not find a librarian position until approximately two years later.

Months later, still no librarian position. I looked every day. I did not want to miss a thing. Eventually, looking each day was not helpful; it was, in fact, stressful, especially when there were no new positions available. Subbing depended on the openings available. When I could not find a substitute teaching opening, I stayed home, thinking that if I went outdoors, people would somehow sense that I was laid off, that I was not "good enough." I was embarrassed and ashamed. It was very odd and uncomfortable not working every day. I had two school-aged children, and they had never seen me not working. My children began to ask why I was at home. I felt like I failed them as a parent. This was a huge emotional and mental change for us. I then started to look for teaching positions in other school districts. *If all else fails, I'll go back to the classroom.* I thought that this LIS degree would open doors, but it seemed that I could not find work for the life of me. Then, I dragged myself to the laptop to find more positions. *I will take anything.* I looked at all librarian jobs imaginable, all over the United States. On a positive note about being laid off: I volunteered at my daughter's school library. I was proud to be able to invest time with her and her school. Again, I saw the daily activities of a school librarian, confirmation that I should have had a position.

I remember receiving two rejection letters in one day. That was heart-breaking. My confidence was already low. *I feel horrible. I must share this with someone.* I relied on family and friends. They gave me job leads, advice, and motivation.

Tip: Do not forget who you are and how hard you've worked. Take a break from the search. It is frustrating to look every day, and new openings will not appear that quickly. Talk with supportive people so that they may help you—mentally, or to find work.

BARGAINING

Of nearly two hundred applications, I was granted interviews for twenty of them. Most were face-to-face, via Skype, and others over the phone. I began to reflect on the many reasons why I did not get to the interview in the first place, and when I did, why I was not offered the position. After so many rejection letters, I began to change my résumé and cover letter: the style, font, and tone of my language. I thought that if I submitted a different kind of résumé, I would get noticed. I incorporated the "résumé art" style layout, highlighting my skills with vibrant colors and graphics. *My* résumé *isn't cool enough. I need to make it look more attractive. They need to see me as enthusiastic; then I may get a call.* I told myself that if I only added information here, and took out information there (no matter if I thought the information was necessary or not), it would make me a stronger candidate. For example, on some of my résumés I left out the various schools I taught at and just put in Chicago Public Schools, combining my years of teaching because I figured that library committees would only care about the fact that I taught. However, my diversity of teaching experience is very important because it shows my desire and ability to work with various populations.

Hair change? I thought about the different styles I could wear my hair. My hair is very thick and naturally curly. If I get it straightened/flat ironed, it is halfway down my back. Some people would ask if I were mixed. A Black person definitely could not have hair like mine. Wrong! I am Black. No Indian in my family . . . at least not that I am aware of. People are amazed when my hair is straightened. "Your hair is beautiful." "How long have you been growing your hair?" "What do you put in your hair?" "You can't be all the way Black?" My hair is part of my identity as a Black woman. To consider changing it somehow changes the way I want to look or be represented. I thought that I had to look different to get the job. To choose between looking the way I wanted and what I thought the people who interviewed me preferred should never be an issue.

Our society prefers White features, and this includes straight hair. This is a global issue in communities of color. It is a shame to think of bargaining this way, or even succumbing to this racist concept, but I wanted to be a librarian.

I knew that not finding a position could also have been because I applied only in the Chicagoland area. I eventually applied for jobs out of state. I bargained: *This may be the key. Why didn't I think of this sooner?* I was not sure if I wanted to leave Chicago. I had never lived away from home. I began to regret not looking hard enough during library school. However, I bargained, noting that it is very rare that full-time, decent paying positions are available before you receive the master's degree. I began to tell myself that I should not have to repay the school loan since I was not able to find a job to help pay it off.

Tip: Make sure that when you bargain with yourself that you do not cheat yourself. Be realistic about your options and the consequences. Believe that you can make good decisions. Also, be yourself. Not to sound cliché, but confidence is important, as well as the determination and prowess to back it up. Once we start thinking about changing who we are to fit in, we become slaves to "colonial mentality"[5] and ill representations of who we are.

DENIAL

The rejection letters are spot on. I don't qualify for these positions. Then I realized that some of the rejection letters were automated responses reading, "Thank you for applying to ___ Library. We regret to inform you that ___." I wondered what I was missing. What was I doing wrong in the interview, on my résumés, on my cover letters? I was dumbfounded. *Me, with two degrees, can't find a job. HAHA! Who am I? What was college for if I can't land a job?* I always felt that I should look for more jobs with an improved résumé and cover letter. And I thought I always did this. I believed that my degrees would take me just about anywhere. I believed that my teaching experience was a huge asset to librarianship.

I did not want to believe that my experience was not enough, that I needed more experience in a "real" library, that most librarians had more knowledge about teaching and learning than I had.

I received a call for an interview. Given the number of positions I had applied for, a call was a huge accomplishment. I was even in denial about the interview offer: *Was I the last option? Am I just another candidate to fill their interview quota? Do I deserve this interview?*

Tip: Practice telling yourself positive self-affirmations. You are smart, lovely, and a great librarian. Surround yourself with people who think so as well.

ACCEPTANCE

I arrived back at this stage because I was offered an interview. I was happy. I felt that I was on the right track, that my hard work was finally paying off. Someone noticed my skills and passion. I accepted all my strengths and weaknesses, and I was ready to give this interview my all. When job prospects seem dire, accept who you are, your ethnicity, culture, skills, and experiences. Sometimes, it is easy to place emphasis on the negative aspects of a situation. So, accept and respect the positive aspects of yourself.

Almost three years later . . . I did not get the job I interviewed for. But, months later, I received a call for another position, and now I am working as a full-time academic librarian. Finally! *Will there be another five stages while I'm on the job? I welcome this new challenge, an opportunity to grow.* I know that this is the beginning stage of my career and I have much to learn. It is hard working in a place with few people who look like you. This fact hovers over all the stages. You must learn the new environment, the people, and their communication style. *Who can I trust to talk about work-related issues?*

Tip: While grieving, find a person to confide in for support. Accept who you are, your level in the profession, your skills, and experience. Anger is natural. Turn it into positive thoughts and actions. Depression should be temporary. Stay in close contact with people who are encouraging. They will help you feel better. Bargaining is a natural way of reconciling your thoughts and the real circumstance. Denial is a result of not accurately weighing the situation. Be honest with yourself and keep in mind that you have room to grow.

The fear of not finding work still haunts me. Call it lack of confidence, learning from experience, or PTSD.[6]

Let's share tips on getting through the library experience. I will coin it LibEx.

Thanks to everyone who have helped me along this journey with advice, words of wisdom, and listening.

NOTES

1. According to U.S. News and World Report, the University of Illinois–Urbana-Champaign was ranked number one in 2017. See https://www.usnews.com/best-graduate-schools/top-library-information-science-programs/library-information-science-rankings.
2. Online resources for library professionals and prospective librarians.
3. American Library Association, Spectrum Scholarship Program. http://www.ala.org/advocacy/spectrum.
4. Tiana, the first African American princess. A fictional character in Disney's *The Princess and the Frog*, released in 2009. https://en.wikipedia.org/wiki/Tiana_(Disney).
5. *Colonial mentality* (internalized oppression) is a term coined by E. J. R. David in his book *Brown Skin, White Minds: Filipino -/ American Postcolonial Psychology* (2013).
6. Posttraumatic stress disorder is defined by the American Psychiatric Association (2017) as "a psychiatric disorder that can occur in people who have experienced or witnessed a traumatic event such as a natural disaster, a serious accident, or a terrorist act, war/combat, rape or other violent personal assault." See also Centers for Disease Control (2017).

Chapter Nineteen

Confessions of a Retired Librarian

Lisa Burwell

FROM THE BEGINNING

In a lot of ways, I'm one of the fortunate ones; I knew fairly early that I would be a librarian. I was meant to be in this field, and I always joked that I would do this job for free or they could pay me in chocolate—either way, I'm all in!

Whenever we went on family vacations, I always wanted to visit the library wherever we traveled. My love of books and libraries didn't just happen; it was a gift given to me by my parents, and particularly my mother. Chicago public schools implemented a new way of teaching children to read—using pictures. My mother was outraged. Not all words have pictures associated with them. Mom wanted me to be taught the old-fashioned way, sounding out words; so, she took it upon herself to go to our local library and talk to the children's librarian. She borrowed books on how to teach a child to read. Armed with all her tools, she set about her task, and I took to it like a duck to water.

When the time was right, she signed me up for a "book of the month club" membership. Every month I got a piece of mail addressed to me alone; I felt so grown up and important! Each book was age appropriate, and as I grew up the books changed—it was wonderful! When I was older, I volunteered at a public library so that I could be near the books, but doing that led me to finding a job in an academic library at Chicago State University, which gave me exposure to a different kind of library. Now I had experience in public and academic libraries, and I found that I loved both.

The biggest push in deciding the type of library on which to focus my efforts came when I was hired at Carol Berger and Associates and I got to work at academic, public, and special (business) libraries. Being exposed to these different libraries helped me decide which direction to move in. Actually, I could have gone into public or academic librarianship and would have been perfectly happy with either one.

So, how did someone go from loving libraries so much that she would happily agree to be paid in chocolate, to a point that she couldn't stand to walk through any library door or read a book?

NEWLY MINTED LIBRARIAN! NICE!

I loved being a librarian. I was looking forward to exploring different areas of my field, and I had a ball. Chicago Public Library has two regional libraries, one on the north side and one on the south side. I was working at the south side, locally known as the 'hood. The south regional library provided support for twenty to thirty branches on the south side; plus, we supported high schools, grade schools, and colleges and universities in the area. The patrons were varied and interesting.

One time I got a reference call from a young man who developed a shoe; Nike was interested in backing it, but they needed to see a mock-up first. He wanted to know where he could have one manufactured in Illinois. I gave him the name, address, and phone numbers of several companies. He called me back about fifteen minutes later, all excited, and told me he was going to share some of his first million dollars with me. I never did hear from him again!

In the meantime, life got really interesting when my department head had an idea for a class she wanted me to develop. She wanted to teach senior citizens how to use the Internet. I thought it was a bad idea and tried to talk her out of it. But she insisted. Since I had to build a class out of thin air, I decided to figure out what I wanted them to walk away knowing. Turns out, I was wrong about the class. It has been more than ten years since I was asked to develop that class, and I'm very proud to say that even though I have moved on, the class is still going strong! I think that is the thing I am most proud of. I wrote an article highlighting the class for *American Libraries* (Burwell 2001). I had never written an article before, so I thought I'd try it. I had always been interested in trying new things. A few years earlier, I had written a chapter (Burwell 1996) for *IOOV* 1996. Again, I had never written anything for a book before and wanted to try it for the first time. Another first in my career was the opportunity to teach a seminar at the Black Caucus of the American Library Association's conference in Ft. Lauderdale, Florida, in 2002.

I was spreading my wings and trying new things and exploring many avenues of librarianship. I loved the library then, and I wanted to see what else was out there for me to see and experience. I'm not sure when it happened or even how it happened, but somehow, I progressed from all that interest and excitement to reaching a point where I had to get out of the library. Fast. I couldn't step into a library, and I even stopped reading! If it was associated with a book or library, I was not interested in it at all.

BRANCH MANAGER

It took me awhile to sort it out. In fact, it's been a year since I retired in 2016. I finally figured out that there were several things at play. Number #1: I never should have gone for the position of branch manager; it was decidedly *not* for me.

As a branch manager, you are in charge of not only the staff but also the physical building, the patrons, and of course, community users. Slowly I realized what was involved in managing a library, and it was more than a notion. It was exciting and challenging at first, but then, my elderly parents' health began to decline, especially my dad, and it got to be too much.

Another issue was that my particular branch was located in kind of a rough neighborhood. The community really wasn't into reading much; circulation numbers were low, and the library was primarily used for the computers. Patrons would come in to update their résumés, write cover letters for jobs, or play computer games.

The first thing I noticed when I became manager of the Jeffrey Manor branch library was that the library was empty in the morning. I often felt like shouting, "HELLO! IS ANYONE THERE?! THE LIBRARY IS OPEN; DOES ANYONE CARE?!" My old branch, South Shore, had people standing outside waiting for the library to open in the morning. I was fortunate enough to have one of my closest friends, and one of the best library associates, Loretta, assigned to the branch. She came up with the best and most interesting programs. Together, she and I would learn some things we didn't know.

Your library location has a huge impact on who and how many will come to your programs. We offered programs that people were interested in attending right up until they realized where the branch was. Very often, we had zero people at our programs. Sometimes, if we were exceedingly lucky, we would have two to three people in attendance. I wasn't used to failure at that level, and I now recognize that my joy about my profession was being snuffed out. It was practically gone by the time I saw it for what it was.

I now understand that staffing is a huge issue in a library. People were retiring but were not being replaced. Every time a position was not filled, it put pressure on the rest of the staff. Each staff member was being asked to do more and more things. As the manager, I felt that this extra responsibility was wearing me down. We were still being asked to prepare and submit reports, do monthly calendars, mentor staff, and handle whatever else popped up in the day-to-day activities of the branch.

Things were piling up on my shoulders from the job *and* my private life. Eventually, it got to be too much; my health began to suffer as well. When I retired, all my friends and family agreed that if I hadn't left under my own steam, I would have been carried out. It's funny, you normally can't get two people to agree on lunch, but in this case, there was upward of about ten people (friends and family) who all agreed that I was being depleted physically.

May 2016 was when it all hit the fan. We brought Dad home from the hospice on his birthday, May 6. He died on May 9. I retired on Monday, May 16; Dad's funeral was on Tuesday, May 17; and we buried him on May 18— my parents' anniversary. They were married for over sixty years and had known each other since they were ten years old. I managed just about everything, and by that time, I was practically bedridden. I had nothing else to give. It has been a year, and I am still recovering. I'm better than I was last year, but I still have a long way to go. At least I finally understand what happened. I'm getting my love of books and the library back, and boy, did I miss it.

I think that you have to know yourself; and you need to honor that truth. Know your strengths and weaknesses. I believe that I could have saved myself that whole nightmare by just remembering and honoring the fact that I am a very good second in command. I can run things, but only on a short-term basis. I was the second in command at South Shore. And in hindsight, I should have stayed there.

Chapter Twenty

Being a Super Token at the American Heritage Center–University of Wyoming

Irlanda Estelí Jacinto

I arrived at the American Heritage Center (AHC) in April 2015 to begin my first professional archivist position. I felt so proud that I had been selected to join the AHC and had become a member of the very competitive archival profession. I had made the decision to come to Laramie, Wyoming, with a bit of reluctance because the town was very small, but I figured I could make the best of it. I was an optimist.

The day of my interview, I did not bother asking my coworkers if I was the first faculty member of color. The thought didn't even cross my mind. In retrospect, I realize I did not ask this question because we, as a society, have been sold on the idea that race should not be discussed. During library school at the University of Arizona (UA), I took a cultural competence class, but racism and its effects on our society was not taught from a critical perspective. The miniscule systems that exist and that make systemic oppression possible were not analyzed. Naïveté, I suppose, is the reason that discussing race didn't cross my mind. On the flip side, the people responsible for hiring me also did not bother to discuss race and the way that it would affect my coworkers and me. I wonder if they also think of themselves as naive.

I do not regret taking the position of university archivist at the AHC at the University of Wyoming (UW). Professionally, it has been an honor to work at an archive of such caliber. Personally, coming to Laramie has allowed me to experience structural elements that are at the root of my oppression. My experience as an archivist of color makes me think that all diversity initiatives are falsies enacted only with the intent of soothing, not eradicating, the concerns of professionals of color. My narrative seeks to illustrate what it feels like to be a person of color in a predominantly White, rural environment. This is written with the intent of illustrating a particular system and a particular experience.

UNDERSTANDING THE SYSTEM: TOKENISM, INTERSECTIONALITY, AND THE SELF

Tokenism Is a Thing

The term *token* causes people to cringe. People do not like to think of themselves as tokens and do not like to be called a token (I learned that the hard way), and White professionals, in my experience, do not like to think there is such a thing as a token. Acknowledgment of a token, and its status, forces us to see differences that traditionally have not been outlined in our society. This refusal to see ourselves as different from each other, by both White professionals and professionals of color, has caused us to neglect the very real psychological effects of tokenism.

The first time that I referred to myself as a token was at my first-year review. The attendees to the meeting were eight White faculty members, myself, and our White male associate director. It was here that my White coworkers first addressed their issue with my use of the term. They were worried about the title that I had chosen for my presentation at the 2016 joint conference of the Art Libraries Society of North America and the Visual Resources Association, "Being a Super Token at the American Heritage Center," on which this chapter is based (Jacinto 2016). One colleague's response was to note, in a very maternal tone, "We do not see you as a token." She said this, I believe, hoping to reassure me that my race had nothing to do with my experience at work. I responded, "It does not matter how you see it. Tokenism and its effects on people are individualized and are relative to our experiences. This is how I feel, and you have to acknowledge it." She did not respond to my comments.

The term *token* has traditionally been used to describe women who make up the minority in male-dominated professions. Sociologists and psychologists have since moved from a gender-oriented definition and have applied the term to any marginalized group within a dominant working environment. "Tokenism is likely to be found wherever a dominant group is under pressure to share privilege, power, or other desirable commodities with a group which is excluded" (Laws 1975).

According to Laws (1975), tokenism is the manner by which the dominant group promises mobility to marginalized groups. A reciprocal, yet controlled, relationship between token and sponsor (the dominant group) delineate the structure of tokenism. This relationship is beneficial to both entities just as long as the two defining constraints of the relationship are maintained and respected. First, the flow of outsiders (tokens) into the dominant group is continuously restricted numerically, keeping tokens at a constant low percentage. Second, tokens are allowed in the system by members of the dominant culture (sponsors), and because they are operating under sponsorship, they are conditioned, as well as expected, to not alter the system they have been allowed to enter. The inability to change the system restricts the quality of life for tokens. Tokenism allows for permanent marginality to occur (Laws 1975).

Kanter (1993) theorized that the significant numerical discrepancies between members of the dominant culture and tokens would cause tokens to experience higher rates of stress and psychological symptoms than members of the dominant workforce community. She argues that tokens would experience three sources of stress: performance pressure, boundary heightening, and role entrapment (1993). These three are delineated by other scholars including Laws (1975) and Yoder (1994) as visibility, contrast, and role encapsulation.

Performance pressure or visibility occurs because tokens are highly visible in the workplace due to their low numbers. This might make the token feel like they are being constantly scrutinized; or it might cause them to feel like a symbolic representation of their socioeconomical or racial type. This representation may cause tokens to feel as if they have added pressure to perform well, because they see themselves as a symbol that might determine future opportunities for people of their same type.

Boundary heightening or contrast occurs because of the harsh differences between members of the dominant culture and tokens. Both Jackson, Thoits, and Taylor (1995) and Yoder (1994) note that this contrast can lead tokens to isolate themselves. Contrast can also lead tokens to alter their personality traits to show that they are the exception to whatever stereotype is being inflicted on them. Tokens alter themselves with the hope of becoming more socially accepted by their peers in the dominant group.

Role entrapment, also known as role encapsulation, is caused by the dominant population's perception of token subgroups. Role encapsulation emerges from the constant application of stereotypes by dominant group members. This application can happen consciously through genuine prejudice attributes or unconsciously through predisposed bias. Role encapsulation can cause constraints in the token's ability to work because it limits them to socially attributed stereotypes and traits. Further, role encapsulation, like contrast, may cause tokens to alter themselves in hopes of being accepted by their coworkers (Laws 1975; Yoder 1994; Jackson, Thoits, and Taylor 1995).

I refer to myself as a super token because I am one! At the AHC, I am the first, and only, faculty member of color. As the lone Mexican American, I represent 11 percent of the AHC faculty, which places me below Kanter's (1993) 15 percent mark that defines token status, regardless of the way my coworkers see me. I feel the psychological effects of tokenism on both my personal and professional life.

Intersectionality and the Self

Kimberlé Crenshaw (1989) popularized the term *intersectionality* when she sought to put forth a theoretical feminist framework that showed the multidimensionality of the discrimination experienced by Black women. Derived from the legal theoretical literature, intersectionality emerged as a framework from critical race theory. Intersectionality proposes that oppression should be analyzed through multifaceted dimensions—ones that look at the whole of an individual's identity, not just fragments of it (Crenshaw 1989, 1991). Intersectionality allows us to see the many ways that oppression is sustained in our society.

Individuals whose actions, language, values, and norms perpetuate notions of superiority help sustain systems of oppression within society. Areas of our identity that are used to preserve this notion of superiority include race, ethnicity, gender, sexual orientation, social class, ability/disability, religion, and citizenship. Each of these areas of the self is affected by one or several systems of oppression that, at their core, are constituted by societally imposed privileges. An example of this is the system of racism. Racism is maintained and perpetrated by White people who believe that they are superior to others. This system, at its core, is composed of White privilege, a set of unearned opportunities inherited by White people, from White people, through the institutionalization of a racist, hierarchical society (McIntosh 2010).

Systems of oppression are institutionalized in our society through laws and policies. There is an overarching system—the federal government. There is the regional system that differs from state to state. There are also local systems, like counties, cities, towns, and and tiny systems, like the AHC. Each of these systems has commonalities and differences. Historical processes such as colonization and Manifest Destiny make up the foundation that serves as the ethos of commonalities within systemic oppression. This commonality sustains the belief that White is the superior of the races. Northern European is the desired ethnic background. Men dominate over women. Heterosexuality is moral. Rich and affluent is the way to be. Able bodies are the only types of bodies. Christianity, specifically Protestant values, is the righteous way of living. Individuals need legal citizenship status. However, this common belief structure also varies slightly because of variants such as state laws, demographics, and political inclinations. At the individual and institutional levels, a power dynamic exists between oppressor and the oppressed.

According to Roberts (1975), within any of the areas of the self, a distortion or a blind spot to an oppression system can occur. These distortions are caused by having a lot of privilege or not having enough. The more privilege you hold, the more challenging it will be for you to experience or recognize systemic oppression. Access to privilege gives you access to power, which allows you to negate the existence of systematic oppression. The most privileged individuals, those who are most likely blind to all oppression systems, are White, Northern European, male, hetero, rich, able-bodied Christians who hold legal citizenship status.

As stated, oppressive systems exist and affect people, at complex and multifaceted intersections. It is possible for an individual to be oppressed in one area of the self (race), and extremely privileged in another (gender). Psychological stress occurs when an oppressive system, within an area of the self, is at a heightened state. We work in a system that demands that each of us fits this perfect privilege notion, when, in reality, few of us do. When you do not fit any part of the pre-described privileged notion, it causes that area of the self to heighten. This can cause stress, anxiety, depression, and a continuous strain, which could lead to posttraumatic stress disorder (PTSD).[1]

I like to think of the intersecting areas of oppression as an electric grid that exists around us; I often picture it is an electric chain link fence. Each column and row of the grid is a different oppressive system that connects together in parallels and intersections.

As Roberts (1975) attests, each system either heightens or decreases depending on different factors. In Laramie, the system of oppression that heightened for me was race. I believe that this automatically happens to people of color when they enter systems that are overwhelmingly White. This can happen at any place and time throughout one's life. It happened to me at the AHC. I had never been the only Mexican in the room, at all times, in all places. As I write this, I remain the only person of color in almost all situations. According to Roberts's (1975) identity traits, my personal system, my societal identity is Brown (race), Mexican (ethnicity), female (gender), queer (sexual orientation), poor (social class), abled (ability/disability), heathen (religion), and legal (citizenship). My societal identity holds ZERO privileges but needs to work within these macro systems: United States of America. Wyoming. Laramie. University of Wyoming. American Heritage Center.

WYOMING AND THE AMERICAN HERITAGE CENTER

In the attempt to demonstrate conditions of the system of the state of Wyoming, I have applied the eight identity traits that Voorhees (2008) attests hold privileges. While Wyoming is clearly not an individual, I believe that delineating systems using these traits allows individuals to create a visual map of the system they are entering or living in. When I mapped the traits to the state, I found that Wyoming was a very privileged place, therefore, it was very oppressive to the traits that represent my social identity.

Wyoming, the least populated state in the nation, is also known as the equality state. With a population of 585,501, it is overwhelmingly (84 percent) White.[2] Residents of Wyoming are predominantly of European ethnic decent, and men hold a slight majority.[3] In May 2015, a nondiscriminatory city ordinance was passed in Laramie that protects LGBTQ community members from discrimination in housing, workplaces, and public accommodations; at the time of this writing, it was the only ordinance of its kind in the state. Wyoming has never had a gay establishment outside of the University of Wyoming. In the summer of 2017, nineteen years after the death of Matthew Shepard,[4] both Laramie and Cheyenne, Wyoming, will host their first Pride festivals. Because of this, I assume Wyoming is a straight, hetero individual.

Wyoming's median household income is $60,214, which places it on the top tier in the state rankings.[5] It is not cheap to live in Wyoming. In terms of ability, Wyoming is an able-body individual. I make this assumption because although the previous director of the AHC was handicapped, it was only last year, one year after he retired, that our parking lot received the upgrades necessary to become compliant with the Americans with Disabilities Act (ADA). Although this may not be sufficient to serve as substantial proof, it is fair to say that if you walk the streets of Laramie, you can see how hazardous they would be to someone in a wheelchair. Wyoming is Protestant, Catholic, and Mormon, and it is the only state in the nation that does not have any refugee protection laws, making it a very legal, citizen-oriented, political state. Lastly, Wyoming is one of five states that does not have any hate crime laws.[6]

THE TOKEN

I grew up in the border cities of El Paso, Texas, and Ciudad Juarez, Chihuahua, Mexico. El Paso's population is overwhelmingly Latino (81.3 percent).[7] I am the only child of Mexican immigrants. I grew up surrounded by Mexican culture. I am the first generation to attend college, earning my bachelor degrees (anthropology and history) from the University of Texas at El Paso (UTEP), a Hispanic-Serving Institution (U.S. Department of Education 2016). After graduating from UTEP, I moved to Casa Grande, Arizona, where I lived for five years. Thirty-nine percent of Casa Grande's demographic is Latino.[8] Upon graduating with my master's degree in information resources and library science, I left Arizona for a job at the University of

New Mexico (UNM) in Albuquerque, where the Latino population is just over 45 percent.[9] In all these geographic areas, my electric chain link fence was consistent in the areas of race.

Leaving the system of Arizona caused me to realize that my electric fence had continuously been at a heightened state within the intersecting systems of gender, class, and race. At UNM, I was able to seek help for the anxiety attacks I had experienced since leaving Casa Grande. Once I left, I came to realize that I had been in an emotional and manipulative relationship for eight years. My male partner had kept me in isolation, and abused me psychologically, emotionally, and financially, for eight years. As a UNM employee, policy mandated that I be granted time to attend my appointments at Counseling, Assistance and Referral Services (CARS).[10] UNM created a safe place for me with this office and this policy. UW had no such policy. Seeking help for my mental health resulted in a PTSD diagnosis, and I received therapy treatment that significantly decreased my anxiety and allowed me to build confidence, which resulted in my being a little more outspoken.

The move from Albuquerque to Laramie, where the number of Latinos dropped to nearly 10 percent,[11] felt like I had been slammed face first into an electric fence. I was figuratively electrocuted by race because I had never been in a location where I was the overwhelming minority. I realized that I had lived a long life being Mexican, but I had never been *the Mexican.*

TOKEN IN THE SYSTEM: AN ABUSIVE RELATIONSHIP

I began to think that I might be living in another abusive environment when I noticed that my reaction to returning to Laramie from anywhere was eerily similar to the reaction that I had returning home from graduate school. When I lived in Casa Grande with my partner, I would drive five days a week to attend classes in Tucson, nearly 150 miles, roundtrip. My partner thought it was unnecessary for us to live in the city where I attended school. For him, school was a choice; for me, my education represented the American Dream. We had to live in Casa Grande because his job was there; moving to Tucson would have been a burden for him. He continuously reminded me that he paid the bills and that I had promised to pay half of our rent. If I wanted to live in Tucson, I would have to pay the rent that I had promised him, as well as my rent in Tucson. Living on a student's salary, I could not afford to pay both, so I drove, an hour and a half each way.

The Duluth Model, a batterer intervention program housed at the Domestic Abuse Intervention Project, developed the Power and Control Wheel, which outlines common behaviors an abuser uses to maintain control over an individual.[12] My partner used geographic isolation to control who I saw and to limit my involvement with the outside world. He used his male privilege to delineate women's and men's roles. He employed economic abuse and denied me knowledge of his income, although he knew mine. It was only after I left that I learned the difference between our contributions to household expenses was only about seventy-five dollars. For five years, I lived under the impression that he supported me economically in an extravagant way.

On the drive home from Tucson, almost always, I would cry. The tears would flow because I was tired, or I was thinking of a life that I wanted and knew I couldn't have if I stayed with my partner, or because of the overwhelming stress, or maybe it was a little bit of all those things. Toward the end of my program, the drive became a place where I could practice verbalizing what I wanted—to break up with him and leave. Somehow, I still got engaged; I was only able to call it off with the help of a mental health professional.

On average, it takes seven times for someone to leave an abusive partner (Robinson 2013). Leaving takes preparation and resources that sometimes take time to acquire. We should attempt to abstain from judging someone who stays in an abusive relationship; but it can be difficult not to judge.

I cry every time that I return to Laramie. I cry because I'm tired of having to leave to feel normal. I cry because it makes me nervous to think of working somewhere outside of academia, because that is all I know. I cry because in order to stay in academia, I have to stay at the UW until I find another academic home. I cry because if this does not happen soon, I will have to leave this profession to create a better life for myself. On my drives back to Laramie, I practice leaving. I practice accepting a job. I practice leaving Wyoming behind.

Dominant groups promise mobility to marginalized groups by restricting the flow of the number of tokens into the dominant group and the token's ability to change the system. The relationship is mutually beneficial as long as the boundaries put forth by the sponsors are followed by the token. If you contextualize my partner's behavior within the Power and Control Wheel, you begin to see how the relationship dynamic was one of power and control. If we look at the three psychological effects of tokenism and place them within the Power and Control Wheel, we can see how members of the dominant community, our sponsors, perpetrate tokenism as a means of controlling tokens.

TOKENISM AT THE AHC, LARAMIE, AND WYOMING: SORRY, I GOTS TO GO

At a symposium presentation, the first delineation of differences between my coworkers and me occurred. My German coworker, who moved to the United States to study history, spoke about her experience as a "non-American" in the West. When I asked why she did not use the term immigrant, her response was she had not moved to the United States to work.

I once had a patron tell me that he wished to speak to the real university archivist. On another occasion, a donor told me that I should call back in August when his granddaughter was in town, because she would be able to speak to me in Spanish. At a work function, I introduced myself as the university archivist to a White male on our board of advisors. With an astonished look on his face, he turned and asked my coworker who I was. My coworker verified—not once, but twice—that I did work at the AHC and that I was the new university archivist. At another function, he pointedly ignored me while acknowledging the rest of my coworkers.

Role encapsulation or role entrapment is the constant application of racial stereotypes. Delineation or roles can also occur with the assignment of racial work such as diversity initiatives. In the beginning of my first fall semester at the AHC, I was asked if I wanted to teach a Latino studies course, although I do not possess any academic knowledge on Chicana/o culture. I was also nominated and selected, without my knowledge, to be the faculty advisor for MEChA (Movimiento Estuduantil Chicano de Aztlan).[13] I welcomed both role encapsulations because if I didn't, then who would? I believed I would be rejecting my community. But I am conflicted because I am not compensated for this time-consuming labor that is also emotional work. On the other hand, when diversity initiatives are assigned to my White coworkers, I feel betrayed; and that I should have been consulted. I just don't trust that my White colleagues will do what is best for marginalized communities.

When I first arrived in Laramie, I decided that I was going to be my loud, high heel–wearing, music-blasting self. However, after seven months, the burden of being my fullest self in public exceeded what I could handle. I began to isolate myself. I have never lived in a demographic like this—the contrast is drastic and harsh and led me to isolate myself. I sought mental health support again, and for nearly a year, my week consisted of waking, going to work, maybe going to the grocery store, and going home. My happy, bubbly, extroverted self was replaced with a person who is extremely guarded. I have only stayed because the economic burden of leaving without another job offer is too great.

Minimizing, denying, and blaming, and emotional abuse are two domains within the Power and Control Wheel that I feel are extremely important for White professionals to analyze. These domains are a way of maintaining power and control over the token's reality. Minimizing and denying real situations that have occurred, denying my reality, and then proceeding to create an alternative reality is known as gaslighting—a very common manipulation technique. When I express my concerns to my coworkers, their reactions vary. Some have actually admitted that race is at play. However, others minimize or place blame elsewhere. They don't know where the patron comments stem from, or they just don't understand what I am talking about. Some days I go home feeling dejected, anxious, and just plain crazy—feelings that occur when there is prolonged exposure to gaslighting (Abramson 2014; The Hotline 2014).

Emotional abuse is difficult to recognize because it is so prevalent and accepted in our society. The emotional abuse that I have experienced at the AHC stems from my constant feelings of guilt. In the comments section of the review for my first-year faculty packet, a White faculty member wrote, "People can be just mean regardless of race, ethnicity, gender, education, occupation, etc." While I know that they are right, my White colleagues have the luxury to think that negative actions stem from meanness, or jealousy, and that is that. I get to ponder if it might be jealousy, or if it might be race. I do not have the privilege of dismissing race in any situation. The colleague then added that he did not want me to be one of those assistant archivists who start working at the AHC and then leave after a few years "to another state, for better pay, better weather, or a more comfortable diverse place where they feel like they can fit in better." "I believe that Irlanda can make a much bigger and more positive difference here than in one of those places." And therein lies the source of my guilt—"make the difference."

I attempt to not see myself as a symbol, but my brain insists that I need to make a difference for my community. Not wanting to carry the weight, and having this desire to leave induces this guilt that I carry constantly. I carry the guilt of leaving my dog behind in Casa Grande; I will be able to carry the guilt of leaving an environment that in the last twenty-one years, twenty-five White individuals have left. They, too, could have made a difference in Wyoming for marginalized peoples. I wonder if they, too, carried this immense guilt when they made the decision to leave.

I am no longer optimistic toward dominants. I no longer believe that White institutions are equipped to build support networks that facilitate coping. I do not believe that they want to let go of their power and control. My life here contains many aspects of the life that I lived with my abusive partner; he was not my first. The constant alteration of myself in order to feel accepted, the constant guilt, the inability to leave because of economics, the feeling that I am the one who is crazy, the continuous denial of my abuse by my abuser: these are all aspects of my life that are extremely familiar. I have dealt with these before. It is this familiarity that allows me to know what I have to do to walk out the door.

NOTES

1. Posttraumatic stress disorder is defined by the American Psychiatric Association (2017) as "a psychiatric disorder that can occur in people who have experienced or witnessed a

traumatic event such as a natural disaster, a serious accident, a terrorist act, war/combat, rape or other violent personal assault."

2. Eighty-four percent white (alone, not of Hispanic origin). U.S. Census Bureau, "Wyoming."

3. U.S. Census Bureau, "Wyoming."

4. On October 6, 1998, Matthew Shepard was found tied to a fence near Laramie, Wyoming. He died October 12, becoming a symbol of gay-bashing victims and sparking public reflection on homophobia in the United States.

5. U.S. Census Bureau, American FactFinder, "Median Household Income in 2015 Inflation-Adjusted Dollars."

6. Arkansas, Georgia, Indiana, and South Carolina do not have hate crime laws. See the Anti-Defamation League, https://www.adl.org/50statesagainsthate.

7. U.S. Census Bureau, "El Paso County, TX."

8. U.S. Census Bureau, "Casa Grande, AZ."

9. U.S. Census Bureau, "Albuquerque, NM"; U.S. Census Bureau, "Laramie City, Wyoming."

10. CARS. https://cars.unm.edu/about/index.html.

11. U.S. Census Bureau, "Wyoming." U.S. Census Bureau, "Laramie City, Wyoming: July 1, 2016."

12. See Power and Control Wheel. https://www.theduluthmodel.org/wheels/.

13. MEChA. https://uwyo.campuslabs.com/engage/organization/MEChA.

Part Eight

Warrior Women

WARRIOR WOMEN

Chapter Twenty-One

Shi Shei Iiná Naaltsoos Bá Hooghan

"My Library Life"

Monica Etsitty Dorame

Yá'át'ééh, shí éí Monica Etsitty Dorame *yinishyé. Shi dóone'e éí Tábąąhá nishłį́ dóó Tótsohnii báshíshchíin. Honágháahnii dashíchei dóó Tó'aheedłiinii dashináłí.*

Hello, my name is Monica Etsitty Dorame. I am Edge of Water clan and born for the Big Water clan. The One Walks Around clan is my maternal grand-father's clan and the Water Flows Together clan is my paternal grandfather's clan.

ENGLISH

I always knew I was going to college, because of my mother's influence and her strong belief in education, but I never thought that I would be so unprepared for college. Going to the University of Arizona (UA) in 1981 really opened my eyes to how far behind I was academically. I remember when I was first told that I could not write. I was taking the first of the required English classes during a summer prep program when the teacher told me that I couldn't write. I was placed in an English class specifically for Native American students—English 101 (Indian English). We were taught the basics—grammar, punctuation, and sentence structure. I passed. My classmates had trouble, and some went home after the semester. In English 104, the instructor, again, told me I did not know how to write. He told me to get a tutor. When I did, he accused me of plagiarizing. Even with my tutor at my side defending me, he was determined, and he told me to withdraw from his class. My tutor could not believe his actions. I registered again for an English

191

class but withdrew because I didn't trust the instructor. The irony is that after my freshman year, I went home and got a summer job for $3.50 per hour with the Arizona Bordertown Indian Education Program, as an instructor consultant for a summer school English program.

In 1985, my husband and I moved to Albuquerque, New Mexico. I enrolled and attended the University of New Mexico (UNM). I registered for an English class and failed. I registered again and found myself continuing the same pattern from the UA—go to class and withdraw. In one of my English classes, the instructor passed out graded essays to everyone, and when I didn't get my essay back, I was called out to the hall. The teacher told me that I didn't know how to write and that I should look into tutoring, same old spiel . . . yada yada yada. She wasn't very nice and asked me to withdraw from her class. I hated English to my core!

After I was basically knocked down in defeat, I got back up and registered for Round 6 of English 102. For our first assignment, we were asked to write a personal statement. I dreaded writing about myself. I get to class, and papers were returned except mine. I thought to myself, *Here I go again*. I remember feeling so deflated. My teacher told the class that she was going to read a couple of papers as examples. I sat there thinking there's going to be a good paper and a bad paper. When she finished reading both papers, she said our papers were exemplary and the class should follow suit. I could not believe it. I was so overcome with relief that I let go of all those years of anxiety and cried tears of joy. I received an A+. There *was* hope. I not only passed English 102 but received my bachelor's degree in American studies and my master's degree in public administration.

PARISH MEMORIAL LIBRARY (PML)

In June 1985, my husband saw a student position open at Parish Memorial Library (PML) and suggested I apply. I felt a bit intimidated because I thought working in the library was a job for smart White women who read a lot and could be English teachers. Judith Bernstein hired me as her assistant at $4.00 per hour, and that was the start of my library career. I loved it! I never thought of having a career in the library. That was never an option. She was a great mentor and believed in me, and I didn't get that validation often. I learned the basics of working in a library. I shelved books and fielded reference questions from patrons looking for information on investments, stocks and bonds, and economic statistics. At times, I felt very ignorant because I had never heard of such terms. No one I knew on the reservation had stocks or bonds, much less money to invest; we lived paycheck to paycheck, and some of us had no money at all. I learned so much from Judy, the

PML staff and my peers in the two years I was there. That was the first time people told me that I was smart, and it made me feel confident.

THREE YEARS OLD, DALLAS, TEXAS, 1966

In the midst of the civil rights movement, a twenty-five-year-old Navajo woman moved to Dallas, with her three-year-old daughter and two-year-old son. She left the reservation to study at Draughon's Business College, to become a secretary. One night while she was studying, she noticed it was quiet. She called out to her children, and there was no answer. She looked down only to see her baby under the bed. She pulled her out and saw the child had eaten all the baby aspirin. Panicked, she asked her neighbor to drive her to the hospital, and the neighbor's oldest son obliged. Not knowing she had forgotten her insurance card, she arrived at the emergency room with the neighbor carrying the baby. The neighbor's son was White, and she was Navajo. The nurse looked at them with judgmental eyes and coldly, callously refused to admit her baby because she did not have an insurance card. She begged and begged. The nurse was apathetic. She was panicked because it would be an hour or more before they could return. She had no other choice. They drove back, returned with the card, and the baby was admitted. The toddler was rushed to the emergency room; the doctors on duty pumped her stomach and admitted her. After staying four days with me, my mom returned to school the next day.

CENTENNIAL SCIENCE AND ENGINEERING LIBRARY (CSEL)

In February 1988, I was hired as a student assistant of the newly constructed Centennial Science and Engineering Library (CSEL). I carried out some of the same duties that I had at PML under limited supervision. My government documents experience began when I volunteered to work with the collection because no one liked it. There was a constant stream of documents; they were difficult to shelve and difficult to find, and microfiche seemed to reproduce exponentially overnight. The call numbers were confusing and long with dashes, slashes, colons, periods, and brackets. I loved the investigative nature of finding documents. I always felt a sense of pride when I was able to find the obscure documents that the librarians could not. I breathed government documents.

SIX YEARS OLD, FORT DEFIANCE, ARIZONA, 1969

It's night out. A car drives up to the house. Daddy is home. He enters. We already know what's going to happen. We've seen it before. He has that look, that smell of cheap alcohol. Mom is silent. Dad starts yelling at her for no reason. He looks very angry and is scaring us all. He slaps her across the face, hard enough for her to lose her balance, and he shoves her against a wall. We run into the other room and huddle on the bed. She's crying and begging him to stop. He cannot. His anger and alcohol overtake him and make him a monster. She tries to escape, only to be thrown into a closet. He grabs her by the hair, and she tries to fight him off as he hits her in the face with his fists, over and over, until she's bleeding. I take my brother by the hand, and we run barefoot to my grandma's house. There is no moon. I can't really see, but I know the way. I'm not scared. I don't feel the rocks I step on. Grandma grabs her gun. At four foot eight, she's the bravest and toughest woman I know. He escapes into the night. I was six, my brother five, and sister one; it would be the last time we would be with our dad.

ZIMMERMAN LIBRARY

In August 1989, I was hired as a Library Technical Assistant II at $6.56 per hour ($13,645/year). I was hired to type cards, lists, letters, and reports. I typed thousands of government documents and shelflist cards and thousands of pages of the *Government Information Newsletter* and the *Needs and Offers List* (N&O). I worked the reference desk and became responsible for the reference schedule. After a year, other duties were added. I trained and supervised students, and I learned about serials and bindery, e-mail and early productivity software, and searching databases.

In 1993, after a positive review that read, in part, "I would bet that she [Monica] may be the only LTA II in the system that carries this much responsibility," and the completion of my undergraduate degree in American studies, my position was reclassed to Library Information Specialist III (LIS3), making $19,864 a year. Over the next few years, additional responsibilities were added. I began to teach library instruction, coordinated with twelve state depository libraries providing guidance to ensure federal priorities and regulations were met, and served as the government information subject specialist.

EIGHT YEARS OLD, KINLICHEE BOARDING SCHOOL, NAVAJO NATION

It's 1971, and I remember feeling excited buying new school clothes for the year. The day had come to go to school. I was crying as my stepfather drove me to boarding school in Kinlichee, Arizona, forty minutes away from home. Mom wasn't able to come. She was working a hundred miles away in Shiprock, New Mexico, training to be a nurse. There were many families doing the same, leaving their kids. I was left with my suitcase. No sentiments or hugs. I guess it was understandable since he had only just become my step-father and I was not his child. I wanted my mom there so she could settle me in and tell me it would be okay. I was scared but tried to be brave. I just sat on my bed sobbing quietly. I was confused. I wondered what I did wrong.

For the most part, boarding school for me consisted of waking up at 6:00 a.m., running in the morning darkness, making my bed, and doing my daily assigned detail. Detail often included working in the cafeteria and cleaning everything in sight. I witnessed my best friend get her head kicked in by one of the girls and her gang, and I had to fight my way out because I was next. I ran away with a few girls. I tried to get rid of the never-ending head lice. I tried to keep my things from being stolen. I was alone. I had nightmares and was unable to sleep at night, but I survived third grade.

CENTER FOR SOUTHWEST RESEARCH AND SPECIAL COLLECTIONS

In 2002, having my master's degree solidified my application for a program manager position at the Center for Southwest Research and Special Collections. I felt that this was the perfect timing for me to use my master's degree. The position was to be filled internally. I was told, with affirmation, that the position would be posted when the new dean was hired. I was the only applicant. Because of the skills and experience I had gained working throughout the University Libraries, I was able to assume duties without much supervision. At this time, I also was pregnant with my second child, Nena. I worked in the position for ten months. Two months after I returned from maternity leave, I learned from the dean that there was actually no permanent position. I returned to government documents, resuming my re-sponsibilities as though nothing happened. I was so frustrated at the system, frustrated at the people taking advantage of me, frustrated at myself, for my naïveté. It was as though all my hard work in school, obtaining my master's degree, going above and beyond at work, trying to improve myself profes-sionally, was all for naught. What does a Native woman have to do to move up in this place?

WEDNESDAY, DECEMBER 15, 2010, ALBUQUERQUE HIGH SCHOOL

My husband and daughters, Dinée and Nena, anxiously wait for the clock to strike three. We are nervous. Dinée logs in and nervously looks at the screen, but the page does not load. She exits and logs in a second time; again, nothing. She repeats again and again but to no avail. Unbeknownst to us at the time, thousands of students were also logging in at three o'clock, crashing the website. Finally, after twenty minutes, the page loads, and she clicks the button. Up pops the bulldog and confetti, and the fight song plays:

> Bulldog! Bulldog!
> Bow, wow, wow
> Eli Yale
> Bulldog! Bulldog!
> Bow, wow, wow...
> —Cole Porter

She became a Yalie. That day was one of my proudest moments. It was the best feeling ever knowing that we did our job as parents. I thought about my family (see fig. 21.1)—my mother, Rose Cook; my maternal grandmother, Alice David; my paternal grandmother, Rose Etsitty (not pictured); my maternal great-grandmother, Emma George; and my ancestors—and our struggles, our strength, and our survival. All went into molding Dinée into who she is today. She graduated in 2015 after studying women, gender, and sexuality studies. Dinée is currently the assistant director of Native outreach and recruitment coordinator at Yale University undergraduate admissions (see fig. 21.2).

Figure 21.1.   Five generations of Diné women, 1992. Photo courtesy of the author.

Figure 21.2.   The Dorame family at the 2015 Yale graduation. Photo courtesy of the author.

GLASS CEILING, I THINK NOT . . . MORE LIKE CONCRETE!

In 2012, I had been an LS3 for nineteen years. Although I had received salary and cost-of-living increases, there was no position above LS3 to allow any of the staff the opportunity to increase their salary, until the library services coordinator (LSC) position was added as a step up. With the economic downturn and our salaries stagnant for five years, about ten LS3s applied for a chance at one of the five LSC positions. We were optimistic about an upgrade, an increase in salary, and a change in our careers. We were encouraged to apply. According to UNM's Human Resources' guidelines, "a career ladder is a process designed to formally progress a staff employee to a higher level of job responsibility within his/her current position . . . there is no need for a competitive posting process" (UNM Human Resources 2013). Given this guideline, some colleagues wondered why the positions were posted as career ladders. Nonetheless, I applied for a position at CSEL. I was qualified and interviewed, but I was not one of the successful candidates. With all my years of experience, knowledge, and skill set, I felt a bit betrayed and jilted by the system. The hiring manager told me that I was not the best fit, and that my job was not seen going in that direction. As far as I knew, no one informed me that there was another path planned for me. I applied for the opportunity. I saw it going in that direction. I usually don't make waves, but I felt especially concerned when one of the applicants told me she didn't apply for the CSEL position, that she was interested in one of the others, yet she was offered the position. I was advised to report it to the Office of Equal Opportunity. I wanted to report that the process was unfair, faulty, and misleading. It was not my intention to report discrimination. At that moment, I understood my place. As a Native woman, I was used to combating the system, used to doing twice as much to prove myself, and used to being a statistic. I was tired of all of it—tired of all the negative news regarding Native people at the bottom of the barrel in everything, and sometimes completely absent from the findings, like we didn't exist. This was a pivotal moment. It was time to crush that concrete ceiling!

LOOD DOO NA'ZIIHII
(THE SORE OR WOUND THAT DOES NOT HEAL)

On January 5, 2014, I was attending a funeral when I accidentally felt a small, hard bump on the right side of my neck. I'll never forget February 20, 2014. I was working a reference shift when I got the call. The doctor said, "You have cancer, diffuse large b-cell lymphoma to be exact." All in an instant, I remember thinking, *Am I going to die? How long do I have? Chemo! My family!* I knew in that moment I had to be positive (there was no time to be sad) and start my fight for life, ready to kick cancer's butt.

I learned that of all the cancers, this is the one to have. Luckily, I was able to work during my treatments (see fig. 21.3). After my first chemo treatment, my hair started falling out by the handful. It was a bit startling. Even more distressing was the night my daughter Nena and I went to Dick's Sporting Goods store to shop for a hat to cover my soon-to-be bald head. That was when the biggest clumps of hair were dangling down my back and falling onto the super clean white floor in the store. The lights seemed blindingly bright, as if a spotlight was shining directly on me. I was really embarrassed. Nena saw the look on my face. She scooped up the clumps and quickly stuffed them into her pockets. Clumps and strands of my culture, my mind, and who I am as a Navajo woman were falling all over Dick's clean, pristine floor. As a Navajo, hair represents not only who we are but also our mind, our culture, and our history. I was so proud of Nena because she took care of me and consoled me; she didn't even think twice about the situation. She just reacted. She was eleven years old.

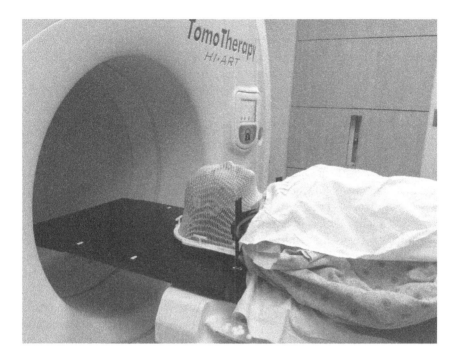

Figure 21.3.   Dorame radiation therapy, 2014. Photo courtesy of the author.

RUNG BY RUNG

On July 1, 2015, after twenty-two years, I finally moved up the ladder. A career ladder was approved, moving me to a library services coordinator position. Also, during this time, the library embarked on a project to review staff salaries and began "addressing equity and compaction issues." With the salary adjustment and career ladder, my salary increased to $49,355 a year. Two months later our head of government information retired. I knew my work as a coordinator required a higher level of knowledge and skills, so I submitted for a reclassification to a library operations manager. Because of our legally mandated responsibilities as a federal depository library, it was now solely my responsibility to operate and manage our regional depository library and reading room collections. After twenty-eight years in the UL, I am a library operations manager with a salary adjustment to $54,291 a year.

BEING NATIVE

Do you live in a teepee? I never met a real Indian! You must be Indian; your skin is red. You don't have to tan. Why are Indians alcoholics, isn't it in their DNA? Don't you get money from the government every month? Why are Natives so poor and their reservations shabby if they get assistance from the government? Indians get everything for free. If you're Native American, people bend over backward to accommodate you because they feel guilty. You got accepted into the program because you're Indian. You must be rich because the Indian casinos give money to their people. These are common statements I hear as a Diné (Navajo) woman. There are three strikes against me as soon as I walk outside, as I enter a classroom, as I apply for a job, or as I apply for a loan—I'm Native American; I'm brown-skinned; I'm a woman.

These harmful, hostile, and negative experiences became the norm, and it wasn't until I was invited to write about myself and my experiences, as a Diné woman, in life, in school, and in the library, that I realized how much I've endured. However, I have made changes and will continue to do so by turning these negatives into positives, educating others about Diné life, teaching my daughters to be impactful, and advising others to never give up.

Recently, I was watching a PBS documentary about Maya Angelou, and she spoke of what it felt like to be looked at with loathing as she walked in the White part of town. Listening to her words, I immediately connected with how she was feeling. How it felt to be Native in a White world. How it felt to be alone at boarding school. How it felt to be relegated to the Native-only English class. How it felt to work really hard and accomplish my academic goals, and then not be considered for promotions or positions. I felt like her. "Surviving it, but my God, what scars does that leave on somebody? I don't even dare examine it myself, and when I reached for the pen, to write [this chapter], I [had] to scrape it across those scars to sharpen that point" (Angelou 2016). Perhaps my writing this chapter may one day influence a Diné woman to finish her degree, stand up against those who doubt her, and know that life is worth living and fighting for.

Chapter Twenty-Two

The Skirt Revolution

Speaking Out as a Mexicana Librarian

Jimena Bretón

A SOCIAL JUSTICE MISSION

I could see naked children laughing at me. I had tripped on a wire and fallen face first to the ground. The wire was set up to trip intruders entering private property. Just a moment ago—while I waited for my *tia*[1] Mary, a doctor on a vaccination campaign injecting pregnant women who did not have access to prenatal care—I was walking down the dirt streets feeling sorry for the barefoot children living in cardboard homes. As I lay there on the dirt ground, I realized how vulnerable I was to the very same people I was pitying. I was ten years old when this happened, and it shaped the rest of my life.

It was the first time I had seen poverty. I traveled from Chicago to Mexico City where I spent my summers with my *abuelita*[2] Crucita. South of the U.S.-Mexican border, I lived in a privileged bubble as a dominant middle-to-upper-class Mexican with fair skin—never giving notice to those who had less. Although I continued to be privileged, my bubble burst, and I could not stop wondering why the children had less than I did.

Little did I know that as a Mexican girl growing up north of the U.S.-Mexican border, I was not all that privileged.

My ten-year-old mind could not stop asking questions: What fault did they have? What is going on with the world? Why doesn't anyone help? Maybe I should write the Mexican president, Ernesto Zedillo, and tell him what I saw. Surely, he would do something. Yes, that's what I'll do.

I grew up, moved to Colorado—with my mother, stepfather, and brother—graduated from high school with a barely-getting-by grade point average, and started college with conditional admission at Colorado State University (CSU) in Fort Collins, Colorado. I decided to pursue a dual degree in international studies with a concentration in Latin American studies and Spanish, and a minor in French. Now, I realize that my degree choices were a long and expensive pursuit to discovering my identity rather than actually choosing a career. Between the courses on Chicano/a history and the International Studies Seminar, I started to see and understand my own experiences of discrimination, microaggressions, institutionalized racism, and machismo.

I struggled to understand how I fit between my white American and Mexican worlds—never quite assimilated enough as an American nor a Mexican, never Chicana[3] enough, pretty enough, smart enough. As a one-and-a-half-generation immigrant,[4] I most identified with Mexican rather than Latina or Chicana. Although I spent hours in the library studying, my grades suffered, and I had a lingering feeling that I was the only one not understanding how to be a successful student; everyone seemed to be one step ahead. It took me nine years to complete my bachelor's degree, and I graduated with a 2.4 GPA.

It was during my second to last course before graduation that I began to find my path to librarianship. I was working as a multicultural services coordinator (library assistant rank[5]) in the public library of Fort Collins, and taking a three-hour course once a week on Tuesday nights with scholar activist Dr. Norberto Valdez. My mostly White classmates and I sat together in a classroom like a secret society listening to what felt like classified information about our world society. One question from a student would send Dr. Valdez on a tangent about yet another inhumane injustice. Every reading brought more questions and more confusion. On Valentine's Day, Dr. Valdez asked if any of us had received a rose—he never missed the chance to inculcate more awareness. Of course, one student raised their hand, and Dr. Valdez followed with the question, "Do you know how that rose made it to your hands?" By now, we knew where this lecture was going, "That rose was picked by an exploited laborer . . ." Dr. Valdez challenged us to investigate where the clothes and shoes we wore and the food we ate came from, and who built the furniture we sat on and the buildings we lived in. I began to believe that just by taking a breath I was contributing to the exploitation of someone else on the planet. I almost became paralyzed with the knowledge.

It was getting close to the end of the semester, and my frustration was only growing. I wanted to be a part of a solution, but the problems were overwhelming. Finally, one night, Dr. Valdez gave me the key that unlocked my future. He said, "When a farmworker is working the land with their heads down and they ask the question, 'Why?,' they seek the answers, begin to lift their heads, look up to the sky, demand justice, and start a revolution."

When people ask questions, they seek information, and that knowledge becomes empowerment. Empowered people mobilize communities for change, and these are forces that challenge and change the status quo. After that lecture, I decided that I would become a librarian with a social justice mission.

LIBRARIAN AS REVOLUTIONARY

After all, my *bisabuela*[6] Maria was a radical educator during the Mexican Revolution who clandestinely taught indigenous children in small towns in Mexico. Education during the Mexican Revolution was used as a political tool to control the masses and legitimize bourgeois rule. Many peasants viewed boycotting schools as an act of resistance (Vaughn 1975). However, there were teachers who thought education for children was necessary, and they secretly taught children. Maria, being one of these teachers, was incarcerated at least once during this time. She remained loyal to her beliefs until she passed away from pneumonia after marching in the rain defending nonreligious education. I did not know this story until after I started my work in libraries, and then I realized that I inherited my mission through three generations of women teachers on my maternal side.

Working in public libraries, never had I felt closer to the frontline of community activism than my day-to-day work serving the public. Residents of Fort Collins, Colorado, approached the reference desk for a variety of reasons. People came with anxiety and needed wisdom to soothe their minds, with curiosity and needed education to learn a new skill, with frustration and needed guidance to relieve their stress, with loneliness and needed a friendly ear to share the novel they just read, with happiness and needed ideas to plan their next milestone, with hopelessness and needed a biography to feel inspired, and with victimization and needed information to advocate for themselves. Being at the reference desk was rewarding, and I felt as if I were in the field equipping people to fight their battle, only the weapons were books and information. While these experiences felt fulfilling, they made the ugly part of my job more tolerable.

In 2009—the year before I started library school—only 3.09 percent of credentialed librarians in the United States self-identified as Latino/a (Godfrey and Tordella 2006). According to the 2010 U.S. Census, 16.3 percent of the U.S. population is Hispanic or Latino. Of those Latinx[7] librarians, I wonder how many identified as Mexican, and, of those Mexican librarians, how many are one-and-a-half-generation Mexican immigrants—a person born outside of the United States but raised in the United States. I was becoming a librarian who thought of herself not only as a conduit for revolutions but also, perhaps, as a revolutionary in my own profession.

WEARING SKIRTS AS AN ACT OF RESISTANCE

Although I was helping others, I faced problems of my own. Being a young Latina woman serving the public meant I encountered men and women gazing me up and down, people seeking me out to teach them Spanish for free, a countless number of comments about the pronunciation of my name and its meaning, uncomfortable looks doubting my competency, remarks about my clothes and the bright colors I wore, and comments about my body shape. The microaggressions did not stop once I was off the floor. They poured into my life during meetings and daily interactions with my colleagues. Well-meaning colleagues felt the liberty to point out differences, question my work ethic, and comment on the way I dressed. I often received demeaning comments about wearing pumps, a norm among the women in my family—I grew up watching my mother wear them all my life as she worked in downtown offices. I was twenty-one years old when I started working at the public library, and, at the time, I did not know that my experiences were not normal and were different from my White counterparts.

My response to these repeated occurrences was to wear skirts more often; to me, skirts accentuate my femininity. In general, I observe the inverse relationship between being perceived as feminine and power; the more feminine society perceives you to be, the less people tend to perceive you as competent. In fact, Heflick et al. (2011) concluded in a quantitative study that "women are evaluated on the basis of their physical appearance more often than men, and further, when women and men are evaluated on the basis of appearance, women face unique detrimental consequences" (2011, 580). I want the world to associate femininity with power, intelligence, leadership, and competence. As my own act of resistance, I wear skirts—my personal expression of femininity—to my most important meetings, interviews, recognitions, and career milestones. Wearing skirts also brings me back to my childhood memory of loving *faldas*[8] and refusing to wear anything else. I am determined to help change society's image of power from a homogeneity of clothing expressions to a heterogeneity of expressions. While I identify as cisgender[9] female and skirts help me express my femininity, I can't wait to see the day that library management and leadership teams show a balanced representation of gender identities and clothing expressions, instead of fearful people with a single expression.

NAMING OUR EXPERIENCES

In 2012, I graduated with an MLIS from the University of Denver with a 3.8 grade point average. It was an ordinary reference desk shift, and I was having a pleasant conversation with a White colleague. Empathizing with each other about our struggles with financing graduate school led me to share how fortunate I felt for having a full-ride scholarship. My colleague's reaction was to say, "I should change my last name to [a Hispanic name]." I quickly scrambled for ways to justify how I earned my scholarship and told her that she could have also applied because anyone was eligible, and that I even had White scholarship colleagues. I was more concerned with trying to convince her that it was not because of my ethnicity that I had earned the scholarship than feeling offended by her hateful comment. A day later, yet another senseless comment from a library user triggered my realization of the awfulness of my peer's words and sent me into a bathroom stall to cry. In this case, my colleague realized what she had done on her own and apologized.

As of this writing, a subject term search for *microaggressions* in the *Library, Information Science & Technology Abstracts* (indexing from the mid-1960s) will result in three articles. One article is a review of a book about assessing information needs (Cooke and Hill 2017), another about students of color experiences on campus (Becker 2017), and the third about microaggressions against LGBT (lesbian, gay, bisexual, and transgendered) individuals, and more specifically, librarians (Wheeler 2016). While research in these areas is critical, none echo my personal experience as a librarian of color. A subject term search for *racial microaggressions* in the *Library Literature & Information Science Index* (indexing from 1980) will give you five results, two of which are actually about librarians' experiences. However, both articles are by the same author published only a few months apart (Alabi 2014, 2015). The term *microaggression* was coined forty years ago in 1977 by Pierce as "subtle, stunning, often automatic, and non-verbal exchanges which are 'put downs' of blacks by offenders" (Pierce et al. 1977, 66). It is telling of the librarian profession when well-founded terms, such as *microaggression*, are not used in the literature. While there are known published books and articles about the experience of discrimination in the profession using different search terms—such as *discrimination*—even yet, the literature review conducted by Alabi (2014, 2015) confirms that the experiences of librarians of color in library and information science (LIS) is sparse. Alabi concludes that academic librarians of color experience racial microaggressions from colleagues in their workplace and are more likely than nonminority librarians to perceive racial microaggressions directed toward colleagues. Outside of LIS literature, regarding the experiences of people of color, the term *microaggressions* is more widely used; it seems as if we are not naming our experiences for what they are. Coming to the point, the absence of research in LIS scholarly literature and the reluctance to use foundational terms that describe different forms of discrimination sustains the environmental microinvalidations of the experiences of librarians of color.

SOLUTIONS FALL SHORT

I have observed that sometimes we as librarians surrender to the idea that nothing can be done for many reasons: there are not enough people of color who apply for positions, there are not enough people of color with a library science degree, there is not enough diversity to justify a diversity program in a mostly White town, the budget is being cut and multicultural services are not what keeps the library doors open, or immigrants in our community do not have voting power and we need to appeal to the voters who support the library.

Even as librarians recognize the problem, they search for answers left and right, not paying attention to viable solutions and, instead, perpetuating the problem. The conclusions about diversity in the workplace drawn by Irvin (2016) is an example of this common recurrence. Irvin (2016) explains how assumptions about culture used to make administrative decisions can be problematic, and clearly recognizes librarianship as an overwhelmingly White profession. However, the article becomes anticlimactic when Irvin provides a solution. Irvin explains that "'multicultural' denotes multiple cultural expressions packaged as one representation. In this view, *everyone* is multicultural." Therefore, "[t]he crux of our goal for public librarianship in the twenty-first century is to heighten our awareness of diversity identities so that we may create an open space for the possibilities that exist within the identities of those we work with and service in the public library" (Irvin 2016, 21). While it is well established that social justice starts with self-awareness, Irvin's solution to recognize diversity within the individual—as a solution to resolve the absence of librarians of color in the profession—is problematic. The "Euro-American" (as the author identifies White American librarians) experience has critical limitations to understanding what it is like to live as a person of color day in and day out. This egocentric solution misses the point that the problem of being a White profession is an issue of equity and the lack of recruitment and retention of people of color. Whether librarians can recognize the diversity within themselves does not address the problem.

LIBRARIAN AS RESEARCHER

Based on my professional experiences and observations—in both academic and public libraries—identifying research scarcities and Band-Aid solutions, I began to consider a career as an academic librarian due to the research component in the position. While at the public library, I noticed how management looked to research to guide their management practices. With few scholarly authors discussing best practices to advance diversity, equity, and inclusion in librarianship, I felt a call and responsibility to leave the front-lines and develop my voice as a researcher. During the last semester of library school, I completed my practicum at the CSU Morgan Library, and the academic librarians there welcomed me. This opportunity led to a full-time non-tenure-track faculty position as a college liaison librarian with the rank of assistant professor. In some ways, I felt that I had arrived; it was 2013, I was twenty-nine, and I had faculty status at a public university.

Now, instead of serving immigrants in the community, I was serving nonnative-English-speaking international students. While the characteristics of this population were more focused—college students—the issues were similar. Instead of immigrants being exploited for labor, international students are being recruited for their tuition money. Just like immigrants are hidden in the city of Fort Collins, international students are tucked away in a corner on campus and expected to adapt. I found campus to be a microcosm of the city of Fort Collins, reflecting and perpetuating similar human relations conditions.

My day-to-day activities changed drastically since I was no longer working with the public and my interactions with most people were through the computer. I was no longer making an instant impression with each contact I made. Instead, my impact transformed from short term to long term through reading, writing, and presenting. It started to get lonely, and I chose to name my office the *capullo*, meaning cocoon. I convinced myself that in this *capullo* I was developing my knowledge to go forth.

SITTING AT THE TABLE

At CSU, I was inspired when I recognized that I was sitting at several tables across campus with people who had influence (whether they recognized it or not) and were well respected in our community and society. It took months to become acquainted with the jargon and to muster the courage to speak at meetings. Even though I had been affiliated with CSU as a student, being at the front of the classroom as a librarian and among faculty, administrative professionals, and staff made the campus feel like unfamiliar territory. I established my goals on campus to serve international students and contribute to retention and persistence efforts for underrepresented and underserved students on campus. I put my efforts toward increasing library visibility and agency for academic success among students of color. One of my favorite campus copresentations was titled "Libraries: The Forgotten Piece in the Diversity Puzzle" (Sagàs and Puig 2014). As I gained confidence, I spoke up more; nonetheless, I knew that my perspectives did not usually resonate with the rest of the group and felt that, unless I was in harmony with the group, my contributions were challenged under my status of junior faculty. It felt as if my voice was being trained to sound like everyone else, and only if I assimilated would I succeed. Sometimes, I wondered why I was welcomed, and I realized that diversity brings discordance. While my colleagues knew that diversity was the right thing to do, they still did not seem to realize how that would change their conversations; they did not appear to be ready for diversity.

WEARING A *CHAL* FOR RESILIENCE

This time my resilience came in the form of a c*hal*. A *chal* is a cloth usually of wool or silk, much longer than it is wide, and women usually wear it over the shoulders to keep warm or as a fashionable piece. The patterns are usually of historical or modern designs by Indigenous peoples. Although I do not wear them daily, I keep a collection of them, and when I most need courage, I imagine I am wrapped by one. Something about being wrapped in a *chal* gives me a sense of power by reminding me of the richness of my *Mexicanidad*.

A NATION OF LIBRARIANS

As librarians continue to improve libraries and cultivate their role in local communities during an age of technology and the Internet, I join the many voices of librarians calling for global partnerships. I had the opportunity to attend the International Federation of Library Associations and Institutions (IFLA) World Library and Information Congress. It was an inspiring experience, and yet, at the same time, it continued to raise my awareness that even on an international stage diversity is lacking; developing countries are sorely underrepresented among IFLA leadership.

To illustrate, the language table is where conference participants can take a sticker to let others know the languages they speak. Instead of a blank sticker where people can write any of the thousands of languages spoken today, we were given seven languages to choose from (Arabic, Chinese, English, French, German, Russian, and Spanish) all identified by a country flag. As a Mexican, having to place a British, French, and Spanish flag next to my name felt as if I had surrendered to my oppressors, or as if I was only allowed to honor a part of my history.

While international librarianship is reflective of local practices (for better or for worse), moving forward as a global driver for social justice and forming the identity of our profession as a nation of libraries and librarians is the next frontier.

LIBRARIAN AS TEACHER

The lack of representation of librarians of color in the United States and librarians from developing countries on the international stage caused me to take a step back and realize that the effectiveness of libraries on improving social equity is compromised. During the 2nd National Joint Conference of Librarians of Color in Kansas City, Missouri, in 2012, I received the familiar encouragement from mentors to continue to seek the next level in my career. As I searched for a doctoral program that would give me the right preparation, I discovered that the PhD in education and human resource studies with a specialization in organizational learning, performance, and change would be the new layer necessary to support my life mission. Now, I believe that by developing and unleashing human expertise in libraries, we undoubtedly improve library systems, which consequently improves the whole of humanity (McLean and McLean 2001). In 2016, I was accepted into this PhD program at Colorado State University.

With three semesters of the program completed as of this writing, I have gained a wealth of knowledge about the implications of organizations in society; countless assessment, diagnostic, and intervention tools; and even more theories. I am eager to become an LIS professor and work with libraries to improve the expertise and performance of individuals, groups, and organizations through teaching and learning, and recruitment and retention of librarians of color. Furthermore, I hope to assist in designing processes and structures that integrate diversity, equity, and inclusion every step of the way.

While the road is long, and the unknown is greater than my understanding, I plan to wear my *chal* and *falda* wherever the next chapters of my librarian life may take me.

NOTES

1. *Aunt* in Spanish.
2. *Grandmother* in Spanish.
3. The use of the name Chicana/o—a person of Mexican birth or decent resident in the United States—is most identified with the rise of the Chicano movement during the 1960s and 1970s. Chávez (2013, 369) describes the period this way: "Never a unified entity, the Chicano insurgency was instead a series of events and actions waged by organizations that use cultural nationalism and Marxist-Leninist ideas to press their demands."
4. An immigrant who was born outside of the United States but raised in the United States.
5. At the public library in Fort Collins, a master's of library and information science degree is required to be at the librarian rank.
6. *Great-grandmother* in Spanish.
7. The gender-neutral alternative to Latino.
8. *Skirts* in Spanish.
9. A person whose sense of personal identity and gender corresponds with the sex assigned at birth.

Chapter Twenty-Three

Reflections of a Long Journey

Mee-Len Hom

Our profession has evolved rapidly since the beginning of my career as a librarian. When I entered library school, the computer was still mainly a tool of circulation and cataloging. Electronic searching was by modem and limited due to excessive cost. By the time I graduated, in 1991, CD-ROMs were considered the future.

Twenty years ago, I wrote about how important my parents, family, and culture were for me. Also, I discussed some problems and challenges I faced at the beginning of my career in librarianship (Hom 1996). The idea of working in an academic institution was exciting; being able to work collaboratively with colleagues who had the similar interests in librarianship was a fantastic opportunity.

During the promotion and tenure process, there was a period of time when I was moved between the main campus and two branch libraries of Hunter College. I was the only librarian who was relocated. The branch libraries are located in our professional schools. The Health Professions Library supports nursing and allied health programs, and the Social Work and Urban Public Health Library supports the School of Social Work and community health education and nutrition. It wasn't because of my major, which was geology, with a minor in elementary school education. The positions at the branches didn't work well, especially at the social work library. The library had problems with the staff and the work environment, and there were changes that the chief librarian needed to implement to make the branch work. I was to report the problems at that branch directly to him, which alienated me from my colleagues. Since I was a new member in this community, I was treated horribly. I was told to sit at the reference desk for most of my working days and help faculty with technology issues, such as using the databases to help graduate students and faculty retrieve their research articles. The faculty and students appreciated learning new ways of acquiring information, and it was professionally fulfilling for me as well. Interaction with the chief librarian and support staff was nonexistent. It made working there very uncomfortable. Escaping to the main campus was my goal. Being in a dysfunctional branch library was not ideal for someone trying to succeed in learning more about the profession. I needed a change.

I really can say I was the only person that I know who was treated this badly, and I don't think, for the most part, administration cared. There was a total lack of nurturing for a new faculty member.

TENURE AND PROMOTION

Striving for tenure was important for me because it was a way to finally prove myself in the profession. Scholarship in the form of publishing has challenges that I faced and wanted to explore. The tenure process was a nerve-racking five years of jumping hurdles in trying to get it done. It was difficult here in Hunter College because there was no mentor to go to or a program to help new librarians. Mentorship was at first discouraged, then later encouraged. A former chief librarian, through meetings with the college's administration, reported to the library faculty that mentorship was not provided because of a lawsuit in which a faculty member was denied tenure due to advice a mentor gave to the faculty member. The faculty advice in question indicated that if the candidate followed what this advisor was asking them to do, then they should receive tenure. Because of this, the chief librarian said mentoring was to be treated cautiously.

What also made the situation more difficult was that many of the tenured faculty who were available to mentor were given tenure at a time when publishing and other tasks were not required. Besides publishing, there was also service to the college community—presentation of papers, joining particular organizations, committee work, and teaching. I survived the tenure process by following the rules of the institution and listening to other colleagues in other city university schools in New York City. It wasn't easy, but I got through it; as of September 1, 2000, I was granted tenure, but I was not promoted to associate professor. I believe this was the case because the chief librarian and other associate professors had little knowledge about the process and my accomplishments in this area, and they held me back.

Teaching was becoming an important part of the profession when I started my career in the early 1990s. The generation of librarians prior to the early 1990s did not function as educators in the classroom. Their role was to supply information to the end user, not necessarily teach the end user research skills and strategies. In my library school, you weren't taught how to teach; however, my minor in education helped a bit. Teaching in the beginning was by trial and error. I remember that the first class I taught was a freshman composition course. I didn't have a computer to use—just an overhead projector with your diagrams, showing the actual reference books the students needed to use to write their research papers. I was a wreck, and for a fifty-minute class I finished my lesson in twenty minutes; I knew something had to change. The expansion of bibliographic instruction helped move instruction from the physical aspects of the library into the new digital world.

Service at Hunter College was to participate on committees. One committee that I participated on was the disciplinary committee. At the end of the semester, a faculty member may bring a student up on charges of plagiarism or cheating, and a student may bring up charges against a faculty member for failing a course. I was on the committee to hear both sides and decide with the panel how to resolve the problem.

Another service opportunity was the Presidential Award for Teaching Excellence Committee that annually awards deserving faculty members who exhibit excellence in teaching or who are helpful to students in some outstanding way. I worked with a panel of faculty members from across the curriculum to decide who should win the award. The panel used the letters of support written by students and colleagues on behalf of nominees to make their decisions. My service to Hunter College also included the Hunter College Senate, and as one of the two elected senators representing the libraries, I participated in this college-wide body.

I've served on other committees outside of Hunter College, including the Library Association of the City University of New York (LACUNY). I served as secretary of LACUNY for four years and was responsible for recording and sharing the minutes of our meetings. Additionally, I was the managing editor of *Urban Library Journal*, the organization's journal. I was also responsible for responding to questions about missing issues, and I managed subscription contracts.

Scholarship, besides publishing articles, also included writing and receiving grants. Grants are helpful in financing attendance at conferences. My institution tries its best to support us, but this is an avenue to obtain additional funding. A colleague of mine (who is no longer at Hunter College) and I were interested in applying for the Shuster award, an internal award given to junior faculty. The award offers recipients up to $500 to further research goals. At the time, the library administration was very negative. We were told that we weren't going to get the award because that's not what the award was used for. We both applied, and we both received the money and used it to attend a conference. Of course, other librarians applied and received funding. This incident was a sign to me about the covert racism in the workplace. This was a case of two librarians of color trying and getting funding while library administrators went out of their way to discourage us. Everything one accomplished or tried was dismissed by those in power.

I have to say publishing was not my strongest suit, but I published an article in *Collection Building* and contributed a book chapter for *IOOV* 1996 (Hom 1996). I also wrote and received a few grants, including the Professional Staff Congress–City University of New York (PSC-CUNY) Research Grant and the Hunter College Presidential Travel Grant. I also gave a presentation that discussed being a librarian of color shortly after the publication of *IOOV* 1996 at the ALA Conference in San Francisco (Hom 1997). Overall, I feel that I did well in surviving the tenure process and prepared for the next part of my journey.

The lack of guidance and advice during my tenure experience left me making decisions that haunt me to this day. I should have gone for promotion when going for tenure. At the time, the library administration claimed that you could not do both at the same time. Shortly afterward, the same individuals who claimed it could not be done began advancing others. I take responsibility for not pursuing advancement—I was tired of fighting for ways to get promoted. I finally realized that I was being rejected in the workplace.

Trying to work in a place where you're always watched to see if you're doing the wrong thing and where you don't feel that you are treated like a colleague takes a lot out of you, but I just focused on the students and faculty I served. In the twenty plus years that I've been working at Hunter College, little has changed. I always make a joke in saying the only two things here that change are death and furniture. The top-level administration is composed of the same people who were my colleagues working in the reference office. All that has happened is that they get promoted with a new title and perhaps a new job, but their mentality on everything remains the same. The poisoned culture continues. The policies of my library are stuck in the 1970s and 1980s and have not kept up with changes in the needs of a twenty-first-century library.

A major problem with my institution is the lack of representation of people of color. When I started, there were at least two Latino, two African American, and two Asian American librarians on staff. Currently, there are only three Asian Americans. The library just can't seem to hire or keep people of color. In a school that prides itself on diversity, the statistics are mind numbing. An informal survey of the library faculty at City College of New York, a sister school, reveals there are fewer total faculty (twenty-three at Hunter College vs. twenty at City College), but the latter institution is much more diverse (see table 23.1).

I was elected by my peers earlier in my career to serve on a library committee called Personnel and Budget (P&B). It's a two-year commitment and an important committee because this group deals with approving research leave, hiring, renewal of untenured faculty, tenure, and library faculty promotion. I was elected twice, and I have seen what goes on in these meetings and how candidates are selected; it can be an eye-opener.

Table 23.1. Library Faculty at Two CUNY Schools

Ethnicity	Hunter College Library Faculty	City College of New York
White	20 (86.95%)	9 (45%)
Black	0	4 (20%)
Hispanic	0	4 (20%)
Asian	3 (13.04%)	3 (15%)
Totals	23	20

During my time on the committee, I observed that the process takes too long, selects too few finalists, and has preconceived ideas on the candidates. One of the most disturbing things I've witnessed is the way some candidates' résumés are critiqued by my colleagues. If someone on the committee found even one or two errors in grammar or punctuation on a résumé, or did not like the way the résumé was typed, the applicant would be dismissed as a candidate.

In all the years that I've been working at Hunter College, only one Latino has served on this committee, and I am the only Asian American to have served. Also, the committee is the same group that selects which candidates to interview. It was always interesting to hear my colleagues comment on organizations that the candidates belonged to, or schools they attended, or even neighborhoods they lived in. If a candidate was Latino or Asian, comments would be made about not understanding their accents even if they were American born. Sadly, prejudice is embedded in the library's DNA. This could be a good reason why we can't get or keep librarians of color in any position. I'm not surprised. To survive here, you must have a thick skin and turn away when racist remarks are said or implied. Those who leave feel they just don't need to tolerate this atmosphere.

RACISM: "STATISTICALLY, YOU DON'T EXIST"

At a library's faculty meeting early in my time at Hunter College, some faculty members of color raised the issue of the lack of diversity in the library. One of the administrators blurted out a comment that has set the culture of the Hunter College Libraries. As the administrator looked directly at me and an African American librarian, he told us that the library could not be any more diverse because "statistically, you don't exist." I remember that the few librarians of color present looked at each other to acknowledge what we had all heard. The writing was on the wall. The person who was making the claim was stating that there were not enough people of color who were applying for the chief librarian position that was available at that time. I often wonder about that comment made long ago, and I ask myself, *Was that truly the case?* It may have been twenty years ago, but the comment still stings today.

Right now in the library we have only three Asian American librarians. We recently lost an African American librarian who was our web designer. From the time she was hired, she was not made to feel comfortable. I wasn't surprised that she left. When she accepted the position, the library administration needed to find her an office space in the reference department. Hunter College's reference department is a large room where sections are divided by low partitions. The workspace is a typical 120 square feet with room for a desk, computer, and a file cabinet. Privacy is nonexistent.

The library administration made it clear that she was not to have a working area near me because I was trouble. I would influence her in a negative environment. Thus, she was situated in a more isolated area of the floor with higher, makeshift walls. This could be one of the reasons why she didn't feel welcomed. She was literally not allowed to blend in with the other librarians. The administration's main problem is that they don't know why they can't keep new minority faculty.

STATISTICALLY, WE DO EXIST

In a 2013 article titled "Ethnic and Racial Diversity in Academic and Research Libraries: Past, Present, and Future," Chang writes,

> The number of professional staff in ARL university libraries by race and ethnicity for the fiscal years 1981, 1991, 2001–10 and 2011–2012 shows the same ethnic and racial distribution by percentage. In 1981, the ethnic and racial representation of professional staff was comprised of 90% Caucasian, 3.1% Black, 1.39% Hispanic, 5.40% Asian/Pacific Islander, and 0.09% American Indian/Alaskan Native. When viewed across time, the percentage of racial and ethnic representation has shown slight increases. Between 1981 and 2011 overall minority representation has only increased from 10% to 14.2%. The percentage of library professionals who are black has increased from 1.39% to 2.6%, Hispanic has increased from 1.39% to 2.6%, Asian/Pacific Islander has increased from 5.4% to 6.8%, and American Indian/Alaskan Native increased from 0.09% to 0.30%. During the same period the percentage of white library professionals has fallen only from 90% to 85.8%. (Chang 2013, 273)

I can say that the Hunter College Library has consistently had problems retaining librarians of color. I truly believe the problem is the treatment they receive from the administration. The perception is that there are two sets of rules for the library faculty—one for the majority and another for those individuals of color. An example of this lack of equity occurred when I was preparing this chapter. As a tenured library faculty member, you have time off for research. There is a biannual window of time where you can apply for a reassignment leave to pursue your research. You can have up to five weeks off to do the research. This is a contractual right. I'd mentioned to the chief librarian that I'd received a contract from Rowman & Littlefield to write a chapter in a book and I would like to apply for a reassignment. His answer was that since in our new contract we received two more additional weeks toward our vacation, maybe I can use that time to write it. I couldn't believe he suggested this, and he repeated it again later when he informed me that P&B did not approve my reassignment. He told me the problems were with the application, and I really had no choice but to accept the outcome. However, as I was being denied reassignment, other faculty members in my department received the reassignments without having to use annual leave. The university's PSC-CUNY contract clearly states:

> The parties agree to establish a paid leave not to exceed five weeks during any year commencing September 1st and ending August 31st for the purpose of permitting members of the instructional staff who serve in the libraries to be reassigned for research, scholarly writing and other recognized professional activities that enhance their contribution to City University. [1]

Following this definition, how can I not feel that the roadblocks I faced in requesting time for research were biased based? Without a systematic overhaul of the culture, the Hunter College Libraries will continue to lag in equality.

CHANGE MAY BE COMING . . .

Chang (2013) writes,

> In 2021 by race and ethnicity, college and university campuses are projected to be comprised of 17.24% of students who are Hispanic, 16.83% of students who are Black, 6.78% of students who are Asian/Pacific Islander, 0.87% of students who are American Indians. . . . What are the implications for academic and research libraries? Although projection data for ARL libraries is not available, based on slow progression of racial and ethnic representation in the library profession during the past 30 years, it remains certain that academic libraries will have a lot to catch up [on] in recruiting more diverse library professionals, perhaps in particular Hispanic and Black minorities, to reflect the academic communities we are serving in the future. (Chang 2013, 189–90)

Hunter College is in the process of finding a new chief librarian, and I hope changes are possible. I'll be here for a few more years, and then I will retire. I don't think I would ever return to Hunter College even though it has been a major part of my life for close to forty years. From a student in the 1970s, to a faculty member for the last twenty-five years, I have experienced the good, the bad, and the ugly, and frankly, I am tired of fighting for a place at the table. As mentioned by Jaena Alabi regarding racism in the library workplace, racial microaggressions can be found here (Alabi 2015). Microaggressions are defined by Sue et al. (2007) as "brief, everyday exchanges that send denigrating messages to people of color because they belong to a racial minority group" (Sue et al. 2007, 273). It would be wonderful to hear that things have changed; sadly, I will not be here to see it.

NOTE

1. City College of New York, Professional Staff Congress (2017).

Chapter Twenty-Four

What Do I Have to Be?

Tanya Elder

Very recently, I faced a split-second, ongoing dilemma. I was at a justice rally for a man named Timothy Caughman, a fellow New Yorker who was mercilessly stabbed to death with a sword while picking up cans and bottles from street recycling. As he was bending over foraging for cans, a White man from Maryland approached him and, without cause, plunged a sword—*a sword*—into him. Mr. Caughman, who was Black, walked two blocks to a police station, where he died. His assailant had traveled to the "media capital of the world" to kill a Black man, any Black man. Mr. Caughman was his unfortunate victim of hate (Kleinfeld 2017).

My dilemma is nothing compared to what happened to Mr. Caughman. His death shook me deeply, as reports of the stabbing, which did not make a dent in the news until two days afterward, focused on Mr. Caughman's troubled past, even as a Twitter selfie emerged of him proudly standing on a New York City (NYC) street, in line to vote in 2016, proclaiming that he "loved America." Video cameras around town pinpointed the White man—his intentions unknown at the time—who turned himself in before "he could kill again." He told police he traveled to NYC to kill Black men, whom he had hated since childhood—particularly those who dated White women.

My "dilemma" occurred during a demonstration sponsored by a coalition of activists under the banner of NYC Resists Hate Crimes, which marched thirty-six blocks from Union Square to Herald near where Caughman died. Organizers asked White members of the march to stay silent while Black members recited eleven times, "I am somebody, and I deserve full equality, right here, right now."

What was my dilemma, if only for a moment? I'm like former president Barack Obama, born of a White mother and a Black father. From there I differ from President Obama in a few ways: I was born in Detroit, not

Hawaii; I am adopted, not raised by either biological parent; white-skinned, not obviously Black (or "foreign," if you will); and most importantly, I am an archivist, not former president of the United States of America. It crossed my mind that people might wonder why I chanted along with the Black folks, being so light and passable. It may sound odd, but after years of living in America and being me, it's something I think about constantly.

This chapter is a personal one about my life and work experiences from my first position as children's librarian at the West Oak Lane Library of the Free Library of Philadelphia and my current position as senior archivist of the American Jewish Historical Society at the Center for Jewish History. My positions from then and now are completely different. A children's librarian works with kids. An archivist works with a vast array of documents, organizing them, protecting them, and disseminating them to the public. My chapter for the original *IOOV* 1996 focused on my enthusiasm for my new job and attempted to define phases of my work from that of enthusiasm to frustration (Elder 1996). Ultimately, I failed as a children's librarian.

I look back on that chapter, which I wrote after leaving New York and heading to Detroit to become a children's librarian, and I shudder about my gung-ho attitude (Elder 1996). I became a children's librarian mostly because I was a good storyteller, but I hoped to become a performing arts librarian or archivist after my career trajectory swerved from studying theater in high school to studying theater in college. The only thing I ever wanted to do was act. Sadly, I hated auditioning, so that was a problem. I worked too much and was going through major depression and a crippling lack of confidence. Lots of Jesus thinking and worry about the Second Coming didn't help either.

I was born into an African American home in 1964. My dad owned a bar while my mom ran an open-pit barbecue restaurant. Mom wasn't super religious for many years, but sometime during the late 1970s she began attending a Pentecostal church that believed in a literal hell. Due to circumstances that I did not find out about until later, my mom, born in the 1920s, did not talk about her family or growing up on a sharecropping farm in Georgia. Snippets of her life as a child emerged here and there; her father was a hellfire pastor, her mom a housewife and sharecropper. There were seventeen kids; my mother was the youngest.

Dad's family hailed from Tennessee and North Carolina. He was born in 1930, the oldest of five children. His dad, Matthew, was very light skinned, as was his mother, Vertie. No one ever really talked about Vertie except that she was a schoolteacher and played the piano. Matthew remarried after Vertie's death to a darker-skinned woman, Grandma Charlie, and they had three daughters together.

I never got to ask Matthew, but I am going to assume that being light skinned in the early twentieth century was both a blessing and a curse. Born about 1912 in Arkansas, he raised his first family in North Carolina. There is only one photo of Vertie that I know of. She died in 1937 after having five children, and while she was light of color, no one would mistake her for White like they did Matthew. Dad was young when she died and never really talked about her. The more I asked questions, the more dad clammed up.

Dad served in the Korean War, and at some point, he and Mom met after making the Great Migration trail of Black folks who left the south and headed northward to Detroit for jobs and a little respite from the racism of the south. They married in 1955.

Dad told one story as a child standing on a street in Tennessee, eating an ice cream cone on a scorching hot summer day. A school bus of White children passed them; some spit at him, and spittle landed on his cone. Instead of throwing the cone away, he wiped the spit off and continued eating. He said that it was really good ice cream and he wasn't going to waste good ice cream. Later in life, Mom said that it was suspected one of her brothers was killed by Whites in Georgia, but since Mom sometimes made things up, I never knew what to believe.

I do not remember when I felt different in my family. Maybe it was when I fell in love with the Bay City Rollers, the Scottish plaid band of the 1970s, when my cousins were into the Jacksons. Dad owned a bar from 1954 until 2004, and as a kid, I remember that the jukebox was filled with the soul and blues tunes of the day that eventually turned into the disco and R&B sounds of the 1970s and 1980s. For me, though, I gravitated toward *American Bandstand* more so than *Soul Train*, though I religiously watched both. When KC and the Sunshine Band and David Bowie finally hit Dad's jukebox, I found myself playing them much more than Bobby Blue Bland or the Ohio Players.

Maybe it was my first time as a kid seeing *Imitation of Life*, versions of which came out in 1934 and 1959. It was the story of a Black maid who had a light-skinned daughter who turned away from her mother and her Blackness and, while "passing," dated a White man. When the man found out she was Black, he beat and left her, and then her mother died, and she was doubly devastated. I remember vividly when mixed-race couples would come into my dad's bar. No one ever said anything to their face, but when they left the bar, all sorts of comments about Black men (it was always Black men dating white women in my dad's bar, not the other way around) dating out of their race flew around, with comments ranging from "tsk tsk" to outright derogatory remarks about Black men straying outside their race and White women taking Black men away from Black women.

In 1977, when I was in the eighth grade, we moved from a mixed-race, middle-class neighborhood to the apartment over dad's bar on Grand River. I left a mixed-race school where no one openly seemed to give a hoot regarding race, to an all-Black middle school not far from the bar. My previous middle school was academically stringent, and my new one academically struggled. Middle school is always traumatic, but coming from my previous school, it was like being hit in the face with a giant pie of racial encounters. Being new in the school, no one knew my parents were Black. It may not have mattered even if they did. That year, I was called a honky by a white-skinned albino student. That wasn't the worst thing that happened during that hellish year.

In February 1978, the miniseries *King* was televised. I remember watching it with my parents. I was four years old when Martin Luther King Jr. was assassinated in 1968, so I had questions that my parents were unable to answer. It hadn't occurred to me that I would be considered an enemy due to my skin color. I was Black, with Black parents, living in a Black neighborhood, thinking Black thoughts, even if I liked the Bay City Rollers and *American Bandstand.*

After an episode that showed King leading the March on Selma across the Edmund Pettus Bridge, I was standing outside of our classroom, eating, of all things, an ice cream sandwich . . . you know, white on the inside, black on the outside. . . . As we sat down, while my teacher contained the after-lunch mayhem, a kid by the name of Jerry jumped on one of the desks and shouted, "Hey, we're gonna march on Alabama and kill all the White folks, but first we're gonna kill the White girl in our class. Who's the White girl in our class!?" He turned and pointed at me (I'm still eating the ice cream sandwich), and almost every child in that room yelled, "Tanya . . . kill the White girl in our class . . . kill the White girl . . ." I don't remember what happened after that. It is all a blank of humiliation and a "what, who, me?" moment that I blocked out. The next year I got into another mixed-race high school, where moments like that never happened again.

I know Black people have suffered much worse indignities, up to and including death. From that time forward, I made sure everyone I knew was aware of my racial makeup, but I also knew I would never be Black enough for some and White enough for others. It is a quandary that affects every part of your being. If you're in a room full of White people, it's at the forefront of your mind; if you're in a room of Black people, it's the same. You are wary of what you say and how you say it, what you agree with and what you don't. One day I was working at a clothing store in New York, chatting with some coworkers, and I brought up the fact that during World War II, my granddad Matthew was traveling on a troop train in Europe, seated with Black non-coms. A White officer came along and told him to move to the White car. He did. One of the girls I was talking to was Black, and she said, "Of course he did, because that's what they do" and walked away. The other girl was White, and she turned away in embarrassment. For my grandfather's part, he said that he could never tell his commanding officer anything to the contrary, plus the food and accommodations were better, though in war nothing is great. He also said that when he got back to Newark, New Jersey, where my grandparents had moved by then, his White fellow military men were shocked when Grandma Charlie walked up and hugged him. Granddad said that with a gleam in his eye, like he had gotten away with making White people feel stupid for their assumptions. It was the 1940s after all; what could you do but try and make people feel their own racial bias and have better accommodations at the same time?

My parents weren't wealthy, even if they owned a bar for years. The economy of Detroit during Mayor Coleman Young's administration, combined with never-ending racial tensions between Detroit and the suburbs, took a toll on everything. Frankly, I wanted to get away from everything Black and White, and just be.

In 1984, I moved to NYC to attend a theater program and stayed with my grandparents for three months in Newark. It was good to be with them, but the commute from NYC to Newark, plus long days of theater training and working nights in a restaurant, took a toll on me, so I moved to Manhattan. It was the best three years of college ever. As a friend of mine at New York University (NYU) told me, "You are in a place where you can be anything you want to be. I suggest you take full advantage of it."

New York, at the height of its delight for me, was magical. No one really gave a shit, for the most part, who you were. They were mostly interested if you were talented or had money. I worked so hard between school and plays that I had a slight breakdown in which I became very religious. I became scared to death of going to hell, and I told all my friends that they were going to hell. I had never really dealt with my mom's religiosity, nor the years of being subjected to a church that made everything a sin and emphasized hell as the only recourse for sinners. My mom told me that I wasn't doing well in the city because I had left Jesus, and my dad kept telling me that I may have talent but did not have what it takes. Ultimately, I realized Dad said things like that because he knew that being in show business was rough for women. My mom wanted to save my soul. Working to pay rent and do theater exhausted me. Needless to say, my favorite years of my life soon became my least favorite. I was zealous, depressed, disgruntled, and dismayed. In 1991, I moved back to Detroit.

By the time I moved back, I was at a loss as what to do with my life. My parents wanted me to become a teacher, but I could not tell them that I was not smart enough or committed enough for it. Shortly before I left New York, I saw a pamphlet on the street for NYU's Archives and Historical Editing program and thought that I would love to be a performing arts archivist. So I went to Wayne State University and talked to one of the library science professors who convinced me to apply for a scholarship to specialize in urban children's librarianship, a five-semester program just starting up. I could be out of graduate school and Detroit in a little over two years, if all went well. I applied, got in, graduated, moved to Philadelphia, and became a children's librarian.

"Urban" children's librarianship is what one would think it is: working with youth in cities, particularly in minority areas. I never told anyone how frightening this was to me, not because I was afraid of cities, but because I had never shaken off the feeling of Jerry jumping up on a table and screaming at me. People look at you and make a judgment: skin—White, hair that's straight and stringy—White, etc. The only thing that really gave people a moment to think about my nationality was that I have a slight southern accent mixed with northern, a trait that my voice teacher told me sounded "too Black."

I had become a little afraid of working in places where everyone was Black (or all White for that matter), frankly. I am not naive about the type of treatment I may encounter, and I know that I can pass. Then, as now, I ensure that my coworkers and friends know that I am, if not skin-wise, then culturally Black, even if I gravitate to rock and roll or punk music. But people like me, or people like Barack Obama, physically Black but genetically mixed, walk a thin line of being too Black or not Black enough. And there are many people who will hold both against you, no matter what you say or do. It's a no-win situation. After a while, you just stop trying.

At the library branch in Philadelphia (Philly), one of my coworkers was a person who held it against you. When I told this person my background, they said that they were wary of people like me because we couldn't be trusted and would always eventually show our "true color." They did try their best to be open minded, but ultimately, they, and probably I, failed.

I did theater while in Philly, and prior to leaving NYC, I created some one-woman shows. I decided to pursue a new one based on my storytelling skills, one of the few strengths I had as a children's librarian. The one I was most proud of was called *Storytime with Tanya*, where I told children's stories to adults, using slides for picture books, and the end featured a rousing children's rhyme where I got the entire audience to quack like ducks. It was the first time that I had been back on stage with an audience mostly filled with friends that I hadn't seen in years. My coworkers surprised me by making the trip to NYC to see the show. I saw them in the audience and mentally acknowledged that they were there, but if you ask anyone who has done a show, they'll tell you that once you come off the stage, you're not thinking completely straight; you're swamped with emotions and hellos. When I finally got it in my head that my coworkers actually came to the show, I tried to find them to say thanks for coming, but they were gone.

Back in Philadelphia, the first person I saw was the head librarian. She mentioned that I was in big trouble with my coworkers. When I asked why, my boss said it was because they thought I ignored them in front of my White friends and audience and that I was ashamed of them being there. I had, in their eyes, betrayed them like every other light-skinned person. There was no telling them that was not the case, though I have asked myself many times if that's what I did. I was hyped up on adrenaline and had not expected my coworkers to be there. Maybe they wanted me to fail at being the Black person they knew I was going to be. Maybe it was a little of all the above.

The question that I usually ask myself about the event is this: If they knew me as White, would they have had the same reaction? Or would they have been mad at me for ignoring them without the Black part thrown in? If I did ignore them, why was race the first thing to come to mind regarding their anger? From my viewpoint, a million things were happening at once, and yes, maybe I was ashamed of them, but maybe I had not caught my breath in time to acknowledge them.

I left Philadelphia not long after that. I found that while I loved the kids, I didn't love the pressure of stopping fights between children or feeling that I had fallen into the trope of the (White) savior going into an urban setting and helping kids. I found the city racially paralyzed, and the City of Brotherly Love a misnomer. I went back to NYC where people already knew me—black and white—and really didn't give a crap that I was either. As long as I didn't tell them they were going to hell again, it was all good.

Returning to New York, I lived in New Jersey and needed a new driver's permit for my car. I had lost my copy of my birth certificate, and I needed to get a new one. I was always a little fascinated about my birth certificate. The original certificate was filed more than a year after my birth. When I asked my mother why, she told me it was because the original spelled my name wrong, and it had to be refiled. This was the first major lie my mother told me about my birth. The other was that whenever I asked why I was so light skinned, she told me to look at a picture of Matthew to see how much I looked like him. The only thing about us that was alike was the color of our skin. I stopped asking about it, but my grandmother Charlie let the cat out of the bag when I was about fifteen: I was adopted, but I would have to ask my parents about the details. When I asked Dad, he told me to ask Mom. When I asked Mom, she told me it wasn't true. What are you going to do as a kid when no one tells you the truth? You stop asking.

I was now thirty-three years old, grown, and I needed my birth certificate, and my mother in Detroit needed to get it. She tried to get a copy from the Detroit Board of Health, but she had to go to Lansing instead. I asked her why she had to go to Lansing for it. She said that she should tell me in person, knowing that I wouldn't be coming home for months. I put my foot down and asked her to tell me then and there. After much hesitation, she told me I was adopted. Finally, confirmation of what I had always suspected.

Here's where a bombshell came: she said that the reason no one would tell me was that my father was my biological father. Back in 1963, Dad had always talked about an Italian woman who worked at the bank, with whom he had had an affair; she had gotten pregnant, and somehow, Dad was able to arrange an adoption. Everyone in the family knew this but me. Ultimately, even that was not the truth.

In Michigan, closed adoptions are closed to the adopted child. In order to find information regarding your birth, you must petition the court for a fee, who then hires an intermediary who contacts the birth parents on your behalf. If the birth parents want contact, they agree to meet you or to accept a written letter. In most cases, the birth mother, not the father, wants contact. In my case, it was my birth father who said yes, while my birth mother said no.

I found out my original first name and that my birth parents met in the Peace Corps in Pakistan. He was Black, and she was White. He was a divinity student from Kentucky; she was from Bay City, Michigan, and a librarian.

When I met my birth father (a time when I broke my adoptive dad's heart), he was the nicest fellow ever. He was a minister in Washington, DC, married, and had two children. He told me my birth mother's name. I sometimes search for it on the Internet, but I have never attempted to reach out to her. The intermediary told me that my birth mother was active in civil rights issues prior to the Peace Corps. She said that her family was very racist and would never accept that she got pregnant by a Black man. He said that they were the only two English-speaking people in that area of Pakistan and that the summer was hot and that they had a short affair. He went to Afghanistan for two weeks, and when he came back, she was gone. The intermediary said that my birth mother was told by mutual friends that he never felt anything for her, and only wanted to take revenge on a White woman by getting her pregnant. When I told him that, he was shocked and said it wasn't the case. I have always had a difficult time reconciling the two differences of opinion, particularly as he was a minister and he wanted to meet me, while she didn't. He and I met only once, but I did get to meet one of my biological sisters.

Needless to say, this rocked my world. What do you do when everything you've known turns out to be a lie? How do you turn around after telling all your friends all your life that you were one thing and you turned out to be another? Does that even matter? How do you encounter the world once the world turns out to be much different than you thought? I'm still trying to answer these questions.

Eventually, I became an archivist, but so far, I haven't fulfilled my dream of becoming a performing arts archivist. Somehow I ended up at the American Jewish Historical Society (AJHS), where I confronted an entirely different set of racial and ethnic norms. I had to learn a lot about American Jewish history that I didn't know. I had to confront biases about Jews that I encountered in my youth, particularly since there is some animosity between Jews and African Americans. Much of this was tied up in White privilege, issues of landlords versus tenants, and religious bias. My mother, as a Pentecostal Evangelical, was overjoyed that I worked for a Jewish organization.

She looked at it as a gift from God, that God had chosen me to work with his own Chosen, and I would be in good stead with God himself. If I could evangelize a little, that was a bonus. I never told my mother that I had stopped believing in God, or at least religion, around 1999. Mom died in June 2017.

Working at the AJHS at the Center for Jewish History (CJH) is unlike working at the Free Library of Philadelphia. Many people assume that everyone who works at the CJH is Jewish or devoutly Jewish. Neither is necessarily true. No one has ever said derogatory things to me because I am not Jewish or because I am Black or light skinned. I don't have to be anything except the archivist, who happens to not be Jewish.

I was three years old in 1967 and don't remember the Detroit riots, but Dad told me that we had to stay in the bar for at least three days. He painted "black owned" on the facade to warn fellow Blacks from burning or looting the bar. He said he sat inside with his shotgun, and us, waiting and ready for anything, as the bar was not far from the riot epicenter. While I don't remember any of this, I do have in myself a fear of being caught up in a race or religious war and having to choose sides—especially in these times of racial tension in the United States where White supremacists are rising at the beck and call of American Nazis and railing against Muslims in America. Where White men who recently stood up to said supremacists had their throats slashed on a train in Portland, Oregon (Wang 2017). Where a recent spate of Black men like Timothy Caughman are chopped down for no other reason than the color of their skin and being in the path of White men with hate in their hearts, egged on by social media and a president who does not seem to care. It is scary to say the least.

For my birthday recently, a friend got me a home DNA kit from 23and-Me. My overall results came back as 72 percent European and 28 percent African. Culturally, I am the opposite, but no one will see my culture in the middle of a riot; they will only see my skin. I only hope when, not if, that time comes, I have the courage not to pass, the courage to bend my knee with the other Black folks and say, "I am somebody, and I deserve full equality, right here, right now."

Part Nine

Bringing Us Home

Bringing us HOME

Chapter Twenty-Five

My America

Ngoc-Mỹ Guidarelli

Mes amis, je dois m'en aller
Je n'ai plus qu'à jeter mes clés
Car elle m'attend depuis que je suis né
L'Amérique

L'Amérique, l'Amérique, si c'est un rêve, je le saurai
Tous les sifflets des trains, toutes les sirènes des bateaux
M'ont chanté cent fois la chanson de l'Eldorado
De l'Amérique

My friends I have to leave
I only have to throw away my keys
Because she's been waiting for me since I was born
America

America, America, if it is a dream, I will know it
All the train whistles, all the boat sirens
Sang to me a hundred times the song of El Dorado

—The song of America (Dassin 1970)

HISTORICAL CONTEXT

Like the famous American-born French singer, Joe Dassin, who passed away unexpectedly at the height of his career, in August 1980, I had my American dream at a very early age. It may have something to do with my name, "Mỹ," which means "beautiful" or "American" in Vietnamese. Thus, I am destined to go and live in the United States and my dream will be fulfilled. That moment of epiphany came later, during a French class I have been teaching for over ten years at my current institution, Virginia Commonwealth University (VCU), in Richmond, Virginia. I confided in my students that I had always dreamed of studying in an American university, and here I am, thirty-four years after graduating from high school in Vietnam, working and studying in an American institution of higher learning. I have achieved my American dream. The trajectory of that dream started in Vietnam, went across France, Switzerland, and England; made a ricochet in Harrisburg, Pennsylvania; and ended in Richmond, Virginia. Like Joe Dassin, I finally found my voice in this "land of the free" and "home of the brave."

My fascination with American academe in particular and American culture in general also has its roots in the American involvement in the Vietnamese conflict. I was born in the year of the Geneva Convention that put an end to French colonization in Vietnam. The signing of this treaty also marked the beginning of the American intervention in Southeast Asia to prevent the spread of communism based on the domino theory. For example, if Vietnam were to become communist under Ho Chi Minh, the other countries of former French Indochina, Cambodia, and then Laos would eventually fall into communist hands. As our house was located not far from the Armed Forces Radio and Televison Services station—the film *Good Morning Vietnam* may offer you a glimpse of the programming that my family and I enjoyed as did several hundred thousand GIs posted throughout Vietnam—I was nourished with a solid diet of radio and TV series and shows, just like the ones Americans would watch back in the United States. After the 1975 debacle, when North Vietnamese troops finally took control of the whole country, from the border with China in the north to the cape of Ca Mau in the south, over a million Vietnamese fled their country. The great majority of Vietnamese refugees were resettled on the West Coast from Sacramento and San Jose to Orange County. In a manner of speaking, they, too, had their share of "California dreamin'." A generation of Vietnamese refugees is growing old while a new one has been fully integrated into the fabric of American life.

ON BECOMING VIETNAMESE AMERICAN

While we witnessed the 2016 appointment of Dr. Carla Hayden, the first female, African American, and African American female librarian as librarian of Congress, the most prestigious position any professional librarian would have aspired to, in my own Vietnamese community, Professor Viet Thanh Nguyen achieved the rare distinction of being the first Vietnamese writer to have been awarded the Pulitzer Prize for his thriller *The Sympathizer* in 2016. Since the end of the Vietnam War in 1975, marked by a massive influx of Vietnamese refugees into the United States, two generations have come of age and thrived in this country. New writers and artists appeared on the cultural scene. Some were writing about their refugee experience and how they have adapted to their new country. The first Vietnamese-born writer and journalist I heard of when arriving in the United States in the early 1980s was Andrew Lam, son of a general, a University of California–Berkeley graduate who traded medical studies for a career in journalism. I enjoyed listening to his reports on National Public Radio (NPR) about West Coast Vietnamese Americans. Later on, I had the opportunity to teach a class about the Vietnamese diaspora using as textbooks his two collections of essays, *Perfume Dreams: Reflections on the Vietnamese Diaspora* (2005) and *East Eats West* (2010). Mr. Lam has garnered many awards for his writing and reporting, among which are two PEN prizes, an Outstanding Young Journalist Award, and a Best Commentator Award. Alongside early pioneers like Lam, a Vietnamese American literary and artistic community has grown. There was also Andrew X. Pham, author of *Catfish and Mandala* (2000), who forsook his training as an engineer in orbital mechanics to become a writer and now a food critic. Aimee Phan's novel *We Should Never Meet: Stories* (2005) describes the lives of Vietnamese orphans who resettled in Orange County, near Los Angeles, where one can find one of the largest concentrations of Vietnamese in the United States. According to a study of the Migration Policy Institute, the Los Angeles-Long Beach-Anaheim metropolitan area counted the largest concentration of foreign born from Vietnam with 237,000 immigrants between 2010 and 2014. San Jose-Sunnyvale-Santa Clara came in second with 101,000 immigrants (Zong and Batalova 2016). Vietnamese authors are still writing about the refugee experience, the Vietnam War, and its aftermath, but they adopt new forms like GB Tran's graphic novel *Vietnamerica: A Family's Journey* (2011). I discovered the poetry of Ocean Vuong, recipient of the 2016 Whiting Award, in the pages of the *New Yorker*. As a guest lecturer for another course titled "Modern Migrations" at my institution, I had the opportunity to do research in our collections and discover the aforementioned authors whose works I was proud to present and discuss in class.

In my daily cataloging work, I also came across a growing number of Vietnamese artists whose art was reproduced in exhibition catalogs, a genre that we collect heavily. Photographer Dinh Quang Le is well known for his "woven photographs," where photographic strips are woven to form an image. The originality of his creations can be enjoyed at the PPOW Gallery, in particular one titled "Untitled: From Vietnam to Hollywood."

ON DIVERSITY IN CATALOGING

In addition to the competencies detailed below, metadata professionals are responsible for advancing diversity issues within the broader information community. Human beings unavoidably assign value judgments when making assertions about a resource and in defining (via metadata standards and vocabularies) the assertions that can be made about a resource. Metadata creators must possess awareness of their own historical, cultural, racial, gendered, and religious worldviews, and work at the identifying where those views exclude other human experiences. (American Library Association 2017)

The above excerpt came from a recommendation submitted by the Cataloging Competencies Task Force to the Board of Directors of the Association for Library Collections and Technical Services (ALCTS) at the 2017 American Library Association (ALA) Midwinter Conference. As a metadata professional, I have made every effort to keep my own bias from interfering in my assignments of subject headings. Over the past twenty years, I have been able to observe transformations in our culture through the use of subject headings. It is essential in a multicultural society to name its constituent groups accurately instead of lumping them in one indistinguishable mass. About a decade ago, the term *Afro-American* was changed to *African American*. In the summer of 2015, the Library of Congress launched a pilot test of 380 demographic group terms to enhance access to library materials while leveraging faceted search capability (Policy and Standards Division 2017). The terms *Vietnamese Americans* and *Vietnamese speakers* are now part of the controlled vocabulary. As a Vietnamese American, I felt vindicated. Henceforth, Asians will no longer be coalesced in one homogeneous group. Another development related to subject headings was the Library of Congress proposal to replace the term *illegal aliens* with two terms: *noncitizen* and *unauthorized immigration*. The change was made at the request of a Dartmouth College student, Estefani Marin, and a librarian, Jill Baron, who found the term offensive and inaccurate (Sananes 2016). That move was stalled, however, by a group of conservative House Republicans who wanted the former term reinstated in a report accompanying a legislative appropriations bill (H.R. 5325) for funding such agencies as the Library of Congress for Fiscal Year 2017. The report includes this stipulation: "To the extent practicable, the Committee instructs the Library to maintain certain subject headings that reflect terminology used in title 8, United States Code."

The period of comments about this heading change was extended by the Library of Congress by three months, until August 2016. However, as things stand, *illegal aliens* remains currently an authorized heading in the Library of Congress authority file. This controversy illustrates how subject headings use has the power to mobilize public opinion. As immigration remains the subject of heated debates, it is unlikely that the motion to change will pass in the current conservative climate. Unlike the heading *handicapped people*, which was quickly replaced by *people with disabilities*, it is improbable that loaded terms like *illegal alien* will be replaced in a deeply polarized political environment. In my daily work as a metadata librarian, especially with regard to authority control, it is important to identify people and subjects correctly to avoid ambiguities. Each work has to be connected to its proper creator and subject headings. While establishing names or other entities in the authority file, it is essential to give enough attributes, among which nationality or other demographic information, and occupation to help distinguish one creator from another. A quick check of WorldCat will reveal numerous iterations of similar Chinese and Vietnamese names that, in fact, belong to different authors writing on different topics.

In the realm of diversity in the workplace, I have observed a shift of focus during the last five years at my institution, from diversity and multiculturalism to diversity and inclusion. In the early days of my career at Pennsylvania State University as a member of the Diversity Forum, we were concerned mostly with racial/ethnic differences. Nowadays, diversity is related also to social status, gender, sexual orientation, ability level, and religious and political affiliations. "Tolerance" for differences has been substituted with an "appreciation" of diversity and inclusion. In my area of technical services in an academic library, I already worked with staff and faculty from very diverse backgrounds. However, the staff/faculty divide causes some friction among some of my coworkers. For that reason, following Virginia Commonwealth University Libraries leadership's example, I strive to include staff in everything that I do and often seek their expertise in activities they are familiar with. In an era of outsourcing, we spend most of our work day in the library downloading vendor records that accompany shelf-ready books and checking the quality of the loaded records. Records need to be checked to see if the file went through properly, links to e-books need to be verified, updates to our headings need to be monitored daily through OCLC WorldShare. Gone are the days when catalogers cataloged each volume individually. Librarians and staff alike share the responsibility in the maintenance of the catalog, work that has become increasingly automated and complex, if one considers the sheer volume of records being ingested every day. We all have to learn to manipulate files and run programs and reports. Technical services tasks are labor intensive, and we hire a substantial number of students as a consequence. Again, I try to recruit students with diverse backgrounds to create synergy. They also bring their knowledge gained through their major to bear on the work they do in the library. In the wider professional field, it is heartwarming to meet more and more Vietnamese Americans embracing librarianship as a career, participating actively in professional organizations, and holding responsible positions in their institutions. Although I could not obtain statistics concerning librarians of Vietnamese descent in the profession, according to ALA, Asian and Pacific Islanders, Native Hawaiian, and Other Pacific Islanders make up 2.74 percent of credentialed librarians (American Library Association 2012, table A-1). I felt heartened by the growing number of Vietnamese librarians whose names appeared on listservs and whom I encountered at library conferences.

FOCUS ON DIVERSITY IN THE LIBRARIES AND UNIVERSITY

As chair of the Library Diversity Committee at Virginia Commonwealth University Libraries for the academic year 2016–2017, I had the opportunity to offer training in diversity and collaborate with departments on campus to promote diversity and inclusion at VCU. Our Diversity Mosaic Workshop enabled faculty and staff to know each other better and helped them develop empathy. Using the "Diversity Wheel," based on the "dimensions of diversity" (Gardenswartz and Rowe 2003), participants learned about their identity and the values they cared about. Empathy is crucial in maintaining good relationships with those with whom you disagree. All through this workshop, we were engaged in the difficult process of opening ourselves up and discussing race, sexual orientation, and political affiliation. During Black History Month 2017, which is celebrated at our university all through February, Virginia Commonwealth University Libraries were invited to cosponsor an African American Read-In with the Office of Multicultural Student Affairs (OMSA). Virginia Commonwealth University Libraries provide books in different genres written by African American authors, from Frederick Douglass to Henry Louis Gates, with a special focus on women authors such as Nikki Giovanni and Maya Angelou. For five hours, faculty, staff, and students would take turns reading excerpts from their favorite novels, essays, or poems. It was interesting to note that most participants preferred reading from their smartphones rather than the books we provided. This was only the second year of the Read-In at VCU, and the event is gaining popularity. I was encouraged to see so many readers from all backgrounds and ethnicities streaming in to participate in this communal event.

Reflecting on my years as an international student who came to the United States as a Rotary fellow representing France in 1980 to complete a master's degree in American studies, I found myself very fortunate not to have to carry the burden of a graduate tuition. In classes that I taught as an adjunct faculty, I often noticed some students falling asleep after staying up all night to finish a paper or work a graveyard shift to pay their tuition. For that reason, I joined a VCU scholarship committee to select candidates for the Diversity Scholarship. Most of our students are first generation and have to support themselves through college. Applications for the Diversity Scholarship are accompanied by essays, many relating tales of hard struggles and also remarkable achievements considering the many obstacles they had to overcome: poverty, ill health, juggling work and studies, sometimes family responsibilities, or lack of familial support. I also collaborated with the VCU Honors College to help students from underprivileged backgrounds to apply for the year-long Fulbright Fellowship; the Boren Scholarship, which focuses on national security; or the three-month international residential Critical Language Scholarship. Thanks to those scholarships, needy students have an opportunity to experience study abroad without the onus of additional school debt.

One way to reduce the cost of college education is to make textbooks less expensive. Riding the wave of Open Education Resources (OER), I joined a group of foreign-language-speaking faculty who are native speakers to create learning modules based on authentic foreign language materials culled from the Internet. In the summer of 2017, thanks to a library grant, we will be able to recruit students to assist us in finding relevant resources to make up those modules. Our presentation on the creation of those OERs—"Student Curated Authentic Online Language Learning Resources I & II"—was well received at the Modern Language Association (MLA) and the Association of College Teachers of Foreign Languages (ACTFL) conferences.

PROMOTING DIVERSITY IN THE COMMUNITY

I have cultivated the spirit of inclusion not only in the library and in the classroom but also in my daily life off campus. Since my arrival in the United States in the early 1980s, I have always stayed in touch with the Vietnamese community. While working for Pennsylvania State University, I served as an advisor to the Vietnamese Student Association. As a group, we would reach out to other associations such as the X-GIs Club or the Graduate Students Association. After moving to Richmond, I joined the board of the Asian American Society of Central Virginia, an umbrella group that unites representatives from thirteen Asian countries, including Japan, India, China, and Kazakhstan. Every year in May, we would celebrate Asian-Pacific Heritage month by setting up a one-day extravaganza of food, cultural hands-on activities, and nonstop folk dances from the various member countries at the Richmond Convention Center. The event, dubbed "Asian American Celebration," has always been well attended, not so much by the Asian community itself, but by many non-Asians. It was an opportunity to showcase the rich diversity of our different cultures and to dispel the misconception that all Asians are Chinese. I also stayed in touch with my community by teaching Vietnamese as a second language to American Vietnamese children, aged five to fifteen, so that they would be able to communicate with the elderly people in their lives, like their grandparents, in Vietnamese or travel to Vietnam and talk to their countrymen. Classes were held at the Vietnamese Language Center, familiarly called the "Vietnamese School" in contrast to the "American School" students attended during the week, a building located on the grounds of Hue Quang Buddhist Temple in a Richmond suburb. Although classes were held for only two hours a week every Sunday during the academic year, students learned to speak, read, and write fluently after five years at this Vietnamese school. To celebrate Têt or the Vietnamese

New Year, the school's students would perform traditional Vietnamese dances and songs. Members of the community were invited to join in this very joyful and colorful event where everything is in red to symbolize good luck.

Sometimes, inclusion is harder to practice due to ideological differences, even if we all belong to the Vietnamese community. In the aftermath of the collapse of the Republic of South Vietnam in May 1975, over a million Vietnamese fled communism and found their way to the United States as refugees. Ironically, in 2004, when I returned to Vietnam after spending three decades abroad, I landed for the first time in Ha Noi, capital of a reunited Vietnam, and formerly considered as the enemy's headquarters. Two charter members of the Library Education Foundation of Vietnam (or LEAF-VN for short) and I came to offer training in cataloging based on AACR2 (Anglo-American Cataloging Rules) to the staff of the National Library of Vietnam in Ha Noi. It was an eye-opening experience because I discovered that not all Vietnamese living in a communist country like Vietnam would toe the party line. Returning to the microcosm of the Richmond (VA) Vietnamese Association, of which I am a member, I realized that some former refugees' distrust of communism was so deep seated that they look upon later Vietnamese immigrants to the United States as spies or sympathizers of the current communist government. The latter are therefore not welcomed in their midst. If we care about diversity and inclusion, we should demonstrate this spirit within our own community. Unfortunately, diverse views are not so easily appreciated, let alone accepted, among my expatriate countrymen. If some Americans are still waging the American Civil War in Richmond, the former capital of the Confederacy, the wounds inflicted on the vanquished South Vietnamese may need more time to heal, since this North-South conflict only ended a little over four decades ago.

FROM REFUGEE TO CITIZEN

Like author/professor Viet Thanh Nguyen, I often consider myself as a refugee first and foremost. This reminds me of the debt I owe to France, my first country of asylum, and to the United States, where I made my home. A Vietnamese proverb admonishes one that "if you eat the fruit of a tree, you should give thanks to the one who planted that tree." I am thankful for the opportunities to learn and thrive in a profession that allows me to develop my full potential as a cataloger, a linguist, and a bridge builder. In my librarian work, I connect library patrons to the resources they need via descriptive records and links placed in the catalog. As a linguist, I connect students to French culture through my teaching. Off campus, I reach out to various Richmond communities to introduce them to Vietnamese culture. I appreciate working in an environment that encourages the free expression and exchange of ideas, and that promotes diversity and inclusion in all its forms.

An image remains etched in my mind the day following the 2016 United States presidential election. It was nine o'clock in the morning, the sky was overcast, a light rain was falling, and there was no one in the Compass—an open tiled area in front of our library that contains a mosaic representing a compass—but two forlorn-looking female students carrying a sign that read, "Need a Hug?" I wanted to hold them tight in my embrace just as I never wanted to let go of our institution's values of diversity and inclusion. After all, I spent one week in the summer of 2015 at Virginia Commonwealth University Institute of Inclusive Teaching where participants were invited to explore all facets of diversity and learn various teaching techniques to serve a diverse student body. Community members off campus also remind me to continue upholding these values that seem to be threatened every day with new government edicts. Charles M. McGuigan, publisher of a local newspaper in my hometown, wrote very movingly in the conclusion of his article "A Nation of Immigrants," in reaction to Executive Order: Protecting the Nation from Foreign Terrorist Entry into the United States (The White House 2017):

> For in the end we are not a nation of thugs and bullies, of fear-mongers and haters, of conspiracy theorists and liars. We're quite the opposite. We are a nation of others. And the stranger among us is always a manifestation of God. (McGuigan 2017)

In the same vein, I noted another comment from a foreign visitor to my hometown. Pierre-William Glenn, a French cinematographer, came to Richmond to celebrate the twenty-fifth edition of our very popular French Film Festival, which is the biggest manifestation of its kind on the east coast. In the festival's program, he confessed his love for American movies because "they exalted virtues such as individual courage in a democratic society, aspirations for social emancipation, justice and equality." He also wrote: "To say that political reality has brutally awakened me, that the dream has turned into a nightmare, that the awakening from that *American dream* was infinitely painful sounds obvious."

Richmond, where I live and work, is only one hour away from Monticello, where one of the country's founding fathers wrote the Declaration of Independence. It is ironic that a slave holder would declare that it is a "self-evident truth that all men are created equal." By the same token, although I am surrounded by historical monuments that constantly remind me of the values of freedom, democracy, honesty, and truth, they also represent a history of colonization, oppression, slavery, deportation, and walls. Truth in particular is becoming a rare commodity in this era of fake news. The voices of those who speak the truth, which is not always pleasant to hear, have been drowned out in the cacophony of fake news spewed by a plethora of sources on social networks. As an information professional, it behooves me to seek the truth and share this value with the constituencies I serve. I have the opportunity to guide students, staff, and faculty and steer them toward reliable and unbiased sources of information. Now, more than ever, I am conscious of my role and responsibility as a librarian. As professional information brokers, we are trained to find, obtain, and evaluate information before we provide it to our patrons. They in turn expect the information to be accurate and reliable. Having witnessed the psychological warfare that took place simultaneously on the frontlines in Vietnam and on the people of Vietnam for the first twenty years of my life, I cannot help but see the similarity between the propaganda battle that is being carried out at this moment, more than sixty years later, on radio and television with alternative facts, and the fake news war being waged on the Internet. Can aspirations to greatness be achieved using tactics familiar to Third World dictatorships?

Chapter Twenty-Six

I'm Still Here

An Addendum to a Personal Perspective
of Academic Librarianship

Lisa Pillow

Writing this chapter was a very difficult process for me—there were more than a few times when I considered throwing in the towel and not contributing to this new collection. I struggled with which approach to take and with what I felt comfortable sharing. A straightforward recounting of my career since 1996 peppered with lessons learned would be snooze worthy and not very authentic. On the other hand, I worried about writing something that could possibly sour future job opportunities for me or come across as angry, thus negating any prospect that my perspective would be taken with serious consideration in this important collection of essays. I did toy with writing "retention" thirty-five hundred times while in the throes of frustration due to writer's block; that approach would have definitely resulted in the editors throwing the towel *at* me. So, I went back and read my contribution (Pillow 1996) to *IOOV* 1996 as well as essays of my fellow contributors (see appendix A). I was struck not only by my youthful optimism, but by the detailed shared experiences and heartfelt various visions for future careers in librarianship. Back then, when I was a fairly new librarian, I can remember embracing the profession's egalitarian, service-oriented, and neutral values when providing information and service equally to all. These are the deeply held values of the profession. Yet, even as time has passed, I recognize that these cornerstone beliefs about librarianship do not always extend to increased inclusion and retention of librarians from historically underrepresented groups. Now that there exists a common vocabulary to name experiences and coping mechanisms in the workplace, is it easier for me to discuss the state of diversity in the profession beyond private conversations with like-minded colleagues or trusted allies? More often than not I have accepted that these issues are par for the course, and I try to focus on the work and my role in the profession at large. My personal perspective on librarianship and particularly academic librarianship has matured since I wrote the first chapter. Creating a diverse workforce and managing organizational change evokes a construction metaphor. Much like constructing a new home, managers need to pay attention to not only opening the door but also building an honest and safe work environment to affect organizational climate. Workplace inclusion has a history in U.S. academic libraries that those new to the field should understand.

RETENTION VERSUS RECRUITMENT

Twenty years ago, I would have expected the profession to have, by now, progressed in its understanding that recruitment is merely the first step in increasing diversity within the profession, and to have realized retention is key. Retention requires a nuanced understanding of the role of race and exclusion in the workplace, and an honest effort by individuals and institutions not to treat librarians of color as exotic or remedial. Recruitment is a start in diversifying the profession, but there is an elephant in the room. The approach of centering recruitment as the crux of the issue provides great optics that the profession takes diversity in the ranks seriously but ignores that inclusion requires more than getting underrepresented groups in the door. So what happens once we get them in the door? Do they only get as far as the lobby? Do they decide to leave an institution rather than persevere? Are individuals treated as a monolith of a specific ethnic or racial group instead of as individuals? Are we creating institutional cultures that allow for these questions to be asked? And if so, are we ready to listen to answers that might be uncomfortable for some to hear?

In my 1996 chapter, I wrote, "Many institutions are guilty of hiring minorities to serve merely as silent poster children for affirmative action. The profession needs to look at retaining minorities instead of temporarily increasing statistics only to see them plummet in two to three years" (Pillow 1996, 201). Not much has changed when looking at the general approach to diversity in the profession. It continues to be a numbers game with occasional updates about the latest demographic profiles of the profession, which demonstrate that not much has improved since the last statistical analysis. Panel discussions at various library conferences about the issue, and what to do about it, occur with some frequency. Well-intentioned programs aimed at increasing the number of librarians of color in the profession via scholarship and leadership programs for early career librarians are laudable. A number of academic libraries have established postgraduate residencies, internships, institutes, and conferences targeted toward underrepresented librarians for varying reasons, including a sincere desire to support creating a representative workforce, fulfillment of institutional requirements to demonstrate diversity initiatives, or in some instances, simply to gain praise, prestige, and pats on the back.

Looking back on the various positions I've held at different institutions, I have some personal observations of what works for keeping at least this librarian of color engaged and feeling a sense of belonging in the workplace—and it is not as difficult as some might imagine. It by no means involves special treatment; rather, it entails extending the same opportunities, information, and courtesy that are extended to anyone on staff. When I began as interim head of the Black Studies Library at the Ohio State University Libraries (OSUL), my new supervisor told me his job was to make sure I did everything I needed to do in order to get tenure and promotion. And he meant it. He honestly critiqued my drafts for articles I submitted; he gave honest annual reviews regarding my progress toward building a solid publishing record. Nothing in the reviews were things we hadn't been discussing regularly, so there were no surprises. He sent opportunities to publish my way, and when I would tell him an article had been accepted for publication, he would always say, "Good. So what are you working on now?" He extended this kind of support for everyone he supervised, tenured or untenured, as he didn't believe in resting on laurels. I had colleagues at OSUL who were also supportive, in particular, the head of the Women's Studies Library, who had successfully undergone the tenure and promotion process before me. One sage piece of advice she gave me was to find research projects I was really interested in because I would reach a point in the writing process where I would grow tired of working on the manuscript and having a true interest would help get past those moments of frustration. She shared her experience going through the process, and her dossier, so I could have a good example of what the committee was looking for in terms of the personal narrative and other documentation. Identifying allies early on to understand the unwritten rules of the process was instrumental in my receiving promotion and tenure at OSUL.

Being treated as an adult who has the required degree and experience for a position goes a long way as well. I have found that some libraries that have not had a Black librarian/manager or have only hired black librarians for postgraduate internships or residencies can end up treating one as a novice even when said novice has years of experience and progression through the ranks. While I have always entered new positions with a degree of humbleness, knowing that every library has its own culture, policies, and procedures that may be new to me, I have also brought experiences and skills that are transferrable regardless of when and where I acquired them. One would assume this upon being offered a position that you were, without reservations, the best candidate for the job. As a collection development librarian, I have patiently read e-mails from coworkers regarding major book award announcements along with explanations of what the award is and why it is important to add these award-winning books to the collection. The habit of some to ask questions they already know the answers to in order to test if I know what I am doing can be trying, but remaining professional has always been the option for me.

Years ago when I was transitioning out of a position, the human resources (HR) person for the library invited me for a lunch that turned into an informal exit interview. I remember as we were walking back to the library, she asked, "So why couldn't we keep a young, talented librarian like yourself?" "Because I don't think the library really wants one," I replied. We talked about my experiences with my then supervisor, which were challenging, and the culture of the library in general. At one point, I mentioned that the library director met with me to discuss a related issue, and as I was leaving the meeting, the director said it would not hurt for me to smile more. The HR person said she did not think the director meant any harm and that, in the American south, men often think smiling is an indication of a woman's happiness. I responded that the library director was from Chicago, born and raised, to which she laughed and said *touché*. I share this story because (1) this was the first and last time a library administrator seemed to really want to have an honest discussion about why I was moving on and to hear about my impressions about working at an institution; and (2) the director's comment about smiling demonstrates how initial support can be diminished by a tone-deaf piece of advice.

The theory of six degrees of separation is the idea that everyone is separated from everyone else on the planet by six links. I think that theory holds true among academic libraries and librarians. Odds are that I can call a couple of people and ask if they know a particular person, or know of a particular library and about the organizational climate and political landscape. When it comes to librarians of color, the situation is more like two degrees of separation, and some institutions are viewed as not conducive for librarians of color to thrive.

KEEPING IT REAL

A recurring documentary-style sketch featured on Dave Chappelle's comedy series *Chappelle's Show* was called "When Keeping It Real Goes Wrong," which were cautionary tales of characters who perceive some form of disrespect or slight and are faced with the option of letting the offense go or reacting honestly in the moment. The character would always opt to keep it real, which always backfired and resulted in the character ruining his/her life. One particular installment in this series of sketches featured the character Vernon Franklin, the youngest person to become a vice president at his company, who also happened to be Black. During an executive board meeting, Vernon's White mentor commends Vernon on a job well done with an awkward comment, "You the man. Give me some skin!" (*Chappelle's Show* 2004). At that moment, the frame freezes, and the expression on Vernon's face can best be described as an internal sigh, which seems to indicate this is not the first time he has had to weigh the decision of whether to express dudgeon over a microaggression, or to let it go. Vernon decides to keep it real and relays how he really feels in not-suitable-for-work language and actions. At the end of the sketch, we see Vernon in a new job—gas station attendant. It is a funny yet poignant sketch because it encapsulates in less than three minutes what it sometimes feels like when a person makes an unfiltered comment that intentionally, or unintentionally, has an undertone that gives one pause to rhetorically ask, "Really?" What is also all too familiar is immediately after Vernon expresses his dislike about what was said, those present are taken aback, and his mentor exclaims in so many words that *this* is not the Vernon they know. For me, this sketch captures the absurdity that can come with navigating race and racism with a well-honed ability to calibrate actions and tone to situations that may or may not be worth addressing honestly. It is easy to extol the virtues of diversity and inclusion abstractly, but matters of race, marginalization, inclusion, and diversity in the workplace are rarely easy to openly discuss with a general audience, let alone with administrators or coworkers who sincerely attest to believing we are in a post-racial world. Privilege is when you think something is not a problem because it is not a problem to you personally.

While Vernon's reaction is played to the hilt for comedic effect, the situation he finds himself in is not unfamiliar to many people of color. I believe that *everyone*, to an extent, has to compartmentalize thoughts and feelings while at work; however, for those who are not from the dominant culture, it becomes a second-nature coping mechanism. Modulating tone, carefully choosing one's words, and being aware of one's body language to essentially not be viewed and/or dismissed as the angry Black person is exhausting. While a White counterpart's work behavior may be seen as assertive, inquisitive, and passionate with a serving of irreverence, those same attributes for the underrepresented person may be seen as aggressive, combative, uncooperative, and insubordinate. Since going full Vernon is not a realistic option, I take more of a relax, relate, and release approach to situations or interactions that I find may require some degree of parsing. For me, this means either compartmentalizing or simply having a so-this-happened telephone call or discussion with a trusted colleague or friend. Such a call or discussion serves a dual purpose of safely unpacking the situation (relax and relate) and simply expressing whatever feelings the situation has elicited (release) without repercussions. This is when being authentic is not acceptable for everyone and one seeks support in one's community to de-stress.

I'M STILL HERE

When I began thinking about writing this chapter in terms of what I felt comfortable sharing, or what would even be worthwhile to share about my academic library career since 1996, I considered how I would answer this question, "After nearly twenty-five years in the profession in different positions at various institutions, what has been your greatest accomplishment?" My immediate thought was, *I'm still here.* I've had moments where I considered leaving academic libraries and/or librarianship altogether to try something else; these moments occurred during bad patches where I felt my career-dissipation light was flickering. However, I concluded long ago that there are no utopian libraries where change is easy and greeted with total jubilation. There are no perfect libraries free of idiosyncrasies, dysfunction, or library intrigue. Likewise there are no perfect library administrators. The new car smell eventually fades, and any ideas of finding the perfect job in a perfect library at a perfect institution can only lead to disappointment. If one is looking for a *supercalifragilistic* experience, one may as well consider engaging in some *Disney* cosplay in the backyard with hopes that the squirrels don't pelt you with nuts because they have better things to do than watch you prance around and yodel. What I have learned over the years is to recognize what I can and cannot tolerate in a work situation. Toxic environments that perpetuate bullying, marginalization, and false competition are not for me. Meetings that consistently necessitate a ritual of preparation that includes two or more of the following—listening to a playlist, visualization of my happy place, aromatherapy, and/or meditation—beforehand because the culture is one of fear and retribution might signal a need to seek out new opportunities and challenges.

I'm still here because I enjoy what I do. After a few false starts, I have settled into collection development, which builds on a foundation of years in different roles including reference and management. Libraries and librarians play an important role in contributing to an informed and information-fluent citizenry. During a time when facts are seen as an inconvenience, this role is even more critical. Historically, people of color have not been strangers to the quest for social change. Having a library workforce that is representative of the population is vital and important to the profession's commitment to hold itself to a higher standard and conduct.

Chapter Twenty-Seven

How Never to Be a Librarian

A View from Retirement

Zora J. Sampson

CHOCTAW PATH

Growing up in a small town in Oklahoma, I was aware of the way Indians were mistreated and the prevailing assumptions about their laziness and alcoholism. All of that I knew long before I discovered my Choctaw ancestry, and none of it ever touched my pride in our family. My aunt, Virginia, was fairer than my dark-complected mother, her sister, Imogene, whose coal black hair always shone. Aunt Virginia told people that obviously Imogene got all the Indian blood, thus, she had none. When her first-grade teacher asked Virginia to confirm her Indian blood—schools received additional payment for teaching Native students, presumed to be difficult to educate—she denied it, explaining, "One day I poked my finger with a needle and squeezed it all out." To our family, her stories of denial are amusing. Life with my mother, aunt, and grandmother was rich in kindness, humor, and generosity. With so much to take pride in, I grieve that they lost their joy of sharing our Choctaw culture.

Over time, I came to understand that denial. Some injuries are almost too painful to share. My mother waited decades to tell me about how she lost her grandmother. My great-aunt woke Bertha, my grandmother, frantically urging her to dress and hurry if she wanted to see her mother one last time. Their mother had been stuck by a stray bullet that penetrated a wall in the Indian community of Whitebead, Oklahoma. My great-aunt had driven a horse and wagon the five miles to Pauls Valley to fetch the doctor, only to be turned away, with "I ain't going nowhere to work on a filthy Indian." Horrified, she

247

and Bertha rushed to the bedside where, with no doctor, my great-grand-mother died before morning.

That was my grandmother Bertha's world; she lived with that understand-ing. To work and worship with people who feel that way about you is hard. To send your children to school to be taught by teachers who harbor such sentiments is hard. Writing these words is uncomfortable for me. I under-stand how painful it was for my mother and grandmother to share this. The few times my mother talked about our Choctaw family, forced to walk to Indian Territory[1] on the "Trail of Tears,"[2] she spoke only of the children who died along the way. Mother told me that her great-grandmother "bathed and dressed her babies for burial all alone; she would not let anyone help her." Their names and graves are added to the weighty burden of loss we carry. The loss of homeland, culture, possessions, and trust, all gone when the U.S. government forced our "removal."

Still, the knowledge of who we are strengthens us, even when remember-ing and retelling are painful. What we have endured makes us who we are. Denial does not protect anyone. I understand the desire to protect children as long as possible from the hurts that minority status brings. But those children still grow up amid the negative stereotypes. Cultural misunderstandings re-sult when others do not know our history. How can the larger society know what we don't even tell each other?

Yet my family held to Choctaw and Christian truths that they saw as self-evident. "Goodness is its own reward." During the Depression, my mother, still a child, had a job. Her home (the same house I sit in writing this) was just a couple of blocks from the railroad depot. Jobless men traveling the rails would come asking for food. Poor though they were, my grandparents never turned away the hungry. But after each such visit, Mother's job was to walk the sidewalks for blocks around and erase the chalk or charcoal "hobo marks" that might send even more such visitors their way. Growing up, I learned that missing items of clothing, books, or toys were likely to have been given away by Mother to someone who had "needed it much more." Most all we had was hand-me-downs from family or church-folk, but we always knew good people who had much less. In Mother's eyes it was just part of the flow of life.

LIBRARY PATH

My first impression of libraries was a positive one. Before I even knew what reading was, I saw my parents drawn to something found in books and newspapers that held their attention and led to lively discourse. It was mys-terious and something I wanted to discover. By age four, I was reading. My father would drop me at the library on his way back to work from lunch, and

I would stay till he picked me up after work. I would sit and read book after book in the children's section, rereading my favorites. I tried not to bother the librarian, to whom I rarely spoke. I knew the daddy-long-legs spiders who trembled in the corners of the bathroom better than I knew that woman who occasionally replaced falling hair barrettes, retied ribbons, or reached books from shelves too high for me. The public library was my great treasure.

When I wrote "How Not to Be a Librarian" (Sampson 1996) early in my library career, I had finished my master's degree in library and information science (MLIS), completed a library media specialist certification, and was about to begin a doctoral program in educational technology. I could not secure a position as an academic librarian. I felt that being a Native American librarian at the University of Oklahoma (OU), serving a relatively large Native student population, should be a positive. At that time, none of the campus librarians claimed any tribal affiliation.

Responding to my frustration, a kind librarian, Patricia Weaver-Myers, told me what my library classes had not: how to write a successful cover letter for the current job selection processes. She explained that simply stating that I met "all qualifications" for the advertised position "as detailed in my résumé" was insufficient. She directed me to specify in the cover letter how I met each and every qualification just to make it past the first sorting of applications by selection committees. After that correction, and after visiting the Equal Employment Opportunity Office (EEOC), I did get interviewed at OU, but not hired.

Sitting in the waiting area at the EEOC office, I could not help but overhear one side of a phone conversation. The EEOC officer was explaining how he was hired by the university after retiring from the federal oversight agency to ensure that nothing the university did, or put in writing, could be construed as a violation of federal law. He was a compliance officer, not a champion for minority hiring. Instead of ensuring equal opportunity, he saw his job as institutional protection or keeping the university out of court. He listened to my complaint, and I lost my innocent expectation of finding an advocate of any true equity. Perhaps that experience committed my career to promoting and growing diversity in the profession.

One day Wilbur Stolt paid me a visit. He was the director of public services at OU, a good man and brave advocate for minority professionals. He informed me that I was yet again not the candidate selected. In the course of our conversation, he kindly explained to me that, in my library technician position as Physics/Astronomy branch supervisor, I was already working at librarian level for less than half the pay. I was keeping an academic department happy assisting their highly technical research needs. If the OU libraries were to hire me into a librarian position, they could not replace me for the budgeted salary without a loss of service. I immediately began to apply elsewhere. Soon after, I was hired at a two-year campus of the University of Wisconsin system, moving from library technician to director in one leap. Thus I have never been a librarian, as far as job title is concerned, though I remain a librarian at heart, always.

Many others have learned that to move up you must relocate. As library director, supervision of all campus technology was added to my duties in the first year, including implementing a distance education program. My friend Alice Alderman had taught me that the future of libraries required mastery of advancing technologies by vigilant professionals who never allow the human mind to serve technology, but who instead bend technology to the service of knowledge and learning. By the time I left my first directorship, thanks to the talents of my staff and my money-seeking/saving skills, every classroom on campus was a "smart classroom." The distance education program grew to receive classes from two- and four-year campuses and sent classes out to high schools throughout Wisconsin. Over time, I was able to secure funding for my own professional development, encourage and support two staff members to get master's degrees, and recommend one who moved on to her own directorship.

MIXED DISCRIMINATION

Was I ever discriminated against as a Native American? Probably, but as a small-town kid who grew up poor, I knew I would have to work hard to attain anything in life. I focused on learning society's rules and meeting my own goals. I was not skilled in recognizing the nuances of discrimination. I knew I had to overcome the assumptions and low expectations associated with my income status and gender. My mother taught me, "It's a man's world. Men make the rules. You have to work very hard to get anywhere as a woman."

As a freshman at OU in 1969, meeting with my undergraduate advisor in engineering, his first words to me were, "I must tell you that I know why you are here, and I have say there are much easier ways to find a husband." Every time I sought help on assignments during office hours, one of my professors repeated, "There are no women in my class." I was so young and naive that I actually decided that the problem was my short haircut, so I wore more lace and dresses to class, then fuller skirts, only to hear the same response, word for word and no help, end of discussion. Second semester, when I finally figured out the clear message, that I was not wanted in the engineering department, I changed my major. I graduated with a bachelor of fine arts in drama with an emphasis in theater history, which prepared me well for public presentations. I had so many interests that choosing a major had been diffi-cult. I was much happier working and studying where I was wanted. As a graduating senior, I applied for a study abroad program scholarship. After I explained those first semester engineering grades, one of the interviewers replied, "Why young lady, we are all amazed that you have made it this far. You should be proud." I knew by his condescending tone that I would not get the scholarship, but whether it was because of my poverty, sex, or Choctaw heritage I could not say.

When I was working as a full-time staff member, a fellow minority employee at OU warned me, "If you want to stay out of trouble you cannot speak up to the bosses. Just say 'yes, yes, thank you for telling me.'" She feared that I would be fired for not being afraid to politely explain my work processes. In other words, I suffered from a deficit of deference. One day the woman who supervised my work told me to "wear your best Bib and Tucker tomorrow." Apparently we were having important visitors. I explained that my aim was to dress professionally every day but would certainly keep her advice in mind. She stared at me and said, "Well, that's damn White of you." I never thought I would hear language such as that at any institution of higher learning. As a very dark-skinned child, I was, on occasion, called "nigger." Later in life, there were times, like this one, when the word was not spoken aloud but was clearly implied.

Over the years as I advocated for diversity, I came to appreciate my minority professors at OU—including Melvin B. Tolson Jr. (PhD in French) and George Henderson (PhD in sociology)—as well as several others I met along the way. I have since met so many people—scholars, administrators, and educators—who never had one professor of color during their postsecondary educational pursuits. Luckily, I also came to know Lotsee Patterson, PhD, a Comanche faculty member in the OU School of Library and Information Studies and my mentor. She believed in my abilities, encouraged and supported me, and, for her trouble, ended up serving as my job reference for over thirty years. I encountered another Native American faculty member in the OU School of Education. As a graduate student, I heard rumors that questioned the rigor of his scholarship. I have heard too many such rumors about Native American faculty and scholars to ignore the pattern echoing the lazy Indian stereotype. I saw many of these scholars work twice as hard for half the recognition. This treatment was what we had come to expect. Native scholars tend to be quieter than some faculty, which seems to earn suspicion. Even though I was never required as director to publish, I did so, in part, to earn the respect of faculty, who were required to do so.

As new chancellor of the University of Wisconsin–Platteville, Dennis J. Shields started a program to hire minority PhD candidates who had completed all coursework. These scholars were hired as temporary faculty for up to two years, teaching a half-time load for full pay while finishing their dissertations. The program increased diversity on campus and benefited the participants as well as their students. Such temporary positions, while a first step, are a revolving door and the campus culture does not have to adapt, nor do any faculty or staff have to engage with them, both necessary next steps in order to benefit from their perspectives. Despite the Platteville program's success, over time many people noticed the number of permanent minority faculty seemed to be shrinking. Were minority faculty now associated with temporary status? If campuses and institutions have a mental culture, it may be that we need to care for such mental health.

GENDER BIAS

As an administrator, being a woman was my greatest challenge. Conditioned by society and by our system of advancement and reward, we all expect more of women for less. We are all part of the problem, you and me, too. The OU campus libraries established a new award to be given by staff to a fellow staff member. When the winner was announced, a coworker confided to me, "I knew the first award would go to a guy in spite of the fact that women are the majority of our staff." Her remark caused me to cringe. I had nominated and voted for a man. Analyzing my own motives I did not like my conclusions. Thinking over the females I admired on staff, several clearly exceeded my nominee's qualifications and contributions. Why had I passed over them? Because I truly expected their level of generosity and persistence, while I gave a man extra credit just for coming close. I had somehow decided that it was harder for a man to be as giving and painstaking as a woman. Of course that sentiment is sexist to the core. I was ashamed.

I continue my struggle to understand and overcome sexism, in myself and in society. I hold up the shame I felt that day like a backboard to bounce my assumptions against. Recognizing the nuances of discrimination is hard for me. I admire people who, like my coworker, are better at it. To fight for the majority (which is what women are in librarianship and in the world) seems counter to my inner "champion of the underdog." But glass ceilings are real, and even when breached, they tend to re-form. I was hired for both my directorships by women heads of universities. Before a year was gone, so were they, both replaced by men. I have seen general advances by women into executive positions over the course of my career, but I have also seen advances lost with every downturn in the economy. When times are uncertain, we retreat back to the more conservative past.

One fall I secured funds to remodel the reference desk in order to better serve both students who were physically disabled and those of small stature. The university carpenters, all males, came to a planning meeting with me, as well as the heads of reference and technology. Later that day both of those librarians showed up in my office to explain why they had abruptly left the meeting. My librarians felt they had no choice but to walk away, embarrassed, because the carpenters, all males, were ignoring my every word while turning to them, as men, to affirm the carpenters' preferred plan. At the time, I was aware that there was a communication problem, but I was focused on explaining why we needed to meet the published guidelines for accommodation and presenting my proposed alterations. In the end, the work had to be done twice because the carpenters originally ignored the guidelines I gave them and had made smaller, easier changes.

In the late 1980s, Professor W. Michael Havener, PhD, taught a class I took at OU on the use of technology. I was impressed by his skills handling the network troubles so frequent in those early days of the Internet. He always explained what had happened, unperturbed, then would move smoothly on to the backup plan he always had prepared. In reply to my praise, he surprised me, confessing that he was nervous every time. Thanks to him, I have great compassion for the pressures faculty feel trying to use technology to teach any class, especially one where the subject is not technology. So, as director of library and campus technology, when a faculty member reported trouble trying to show a movie, with all my staff busy fixing other problems, I rushed to set up a portable unit that bypassed her teaching console. As I was quickly leaving so the lights could be dimmed and class could proceed, she loudly ordered me to "get back down there and fix what is broken." I was stunned and confused. Was she asking me to squat in the dark and work on equipment while she showed a movie over my head? It made no sense. I turned back and assured her, "I will send a technician." Trying to leave again I heard her approaching, yelling loudly at me, "Are you telling me you are incompetent to do your job?" I felt sure that she was frustrated and embarrassed about her own perceived incompetence. I simply repeated, "I will send a technician," and marched out the door. The incident brought students to my door, all week long, to apologize for their professor. My staff all felt that she would have never treated any male technician like that even though she taught women's studies. My final exit to retirement was hastened by a woman, a new administrator, my new supervisor, who characterized my firm defense of library principles and philosophy as "being a bully."

HOPES AND HELPS FOR YOUR PATH

Minority administrators are not a guarantee of progress. Some fail to hire other minorities or do not engage with and/or support those they do hire. I have wondered if some minorities desire to be the sole "voice of diversity." Business schools used to recommend moving up, or on, every five years as sound career strategy. My advice is to update your resume the day you accept a new position and never stop looking for better jobs. Keep sample job descriptions that you like (you may want to refer to them when you have to write job descriptions), and interview occasionally, if only to keep in practice. Professional associations (local, state, and national) are great places to get advice on how and where to apply, to begin friendships among inspiring peers, and to develop a network to call on for help. If you secure a job where professional development funds support participation in and travel to conferences and meetings, you might want to stay longer. A position that pays more can look like advancement, but if it offers little commitment for professional development it can be a career trap, particularly if even that support lessens over time. Professional growth and support for development is a bellwether for the potential to do good.

I never regretted supporting professional development for any staff. Even when they left my institution, they remained my colleagues. You may find that administration changes can, at any time, give you no choice but to move on. Keep and nurture as many advocates as you can. I advise librarians to plan for advancement into directorships, boards, or other leadership positions. When you get there, promote diversity, hire minority staff and mentor minorities, buy books and materials authored by diverse scholars, and encourage young people. As a director of an academic library, I tried to meet and stay in contact with area public and school librarians and understand their plan for the students they sent us and to better continue their work. As a director of a library on an academic campus, with or without faculty status for librarians, you are an odd bit of the administration and you may find that no one considers you their peer.

At the two-year campus, I found the perfect spot to fund and allow time for my participation in library associations. This became increasingly difficult when I moved on to a four-year campus. Budgets on the whole were not favorable for the library there. During the selection process, all candidates were informed that the advertised salary range had been lowered. When I was offered the job and began to negotiate, I was told that some candidates had left the pool when the stated salary had been lowered and they could not legally negotiate salary. (I did wonder how often that is used as a ploy.) Rather than turn down the job, I took it contingent on full support for my obligations in multiple professional associations, and I immediately filed a letter of protest detailing the comparable positions in the state system that used a higher salary range. A year later the chancellor raised the salary back to the initial higher range just before she retired. The vice-chancellor to whom I had reported eventually retired during a time of administrative reorganization. My new supervisor decided to deal with a budget downturn by eliminating my position and appointing a librarian to perform my duties as an acting director. Be ready and don't take budget reorganizations personally.

Over the course of my career, the most personally rewarding work included my work with the American Library Association (ALA), supporting

ALA's Spectrum Institute, and planning and attending ALA programs, especially the Martin Luther King Sunrise Breakfasts where you can meet powerful advocates for diversity. I was most honored to work with the American Indian Library Association, which supports tribal libraries and tribal librarians. Much of the expansion of community engagement seen these days in public libraries mirrors what I have seen in tribal libraries for a long time. Public librarians may find, like tribal librarians have, that such engagement may bring archives and artifacts their way, which add complexity to our jobs but add value to community service.

As I read each book as a child, I had the habit of creating a mental image of the author. The words left an imprint of the mind behind the story. In college, I visited the National Portrait Gallery in Washington, DC. There I delighted in matching, or contrasting, the face on the wall with my mental creations. Supervising the Physics/Astronomy branch library, I watched the sharing of information advance from line editing on monochrome terminal screens, to personal computers, to searching the Internet with Mosaic, to browsing with Google; from articles shared as preprints requested by mail, to open-source sharing of articles online prior to publication.[3] It was clear to me that the power of these advances was the connection of human minds. Librarians will always be part of the best, most effective progress in information seeking, knowledge creation, storage, and access. Our respect for the source, the human mind, rewards us with enduring awe.

Thank you, student/scholar/reader for the work you do to honor all who quest for knowledge.

NOTES

1. What is now the State of Oklahoma was part of the Indian Country called Indiana Territory but was never a true territory of the United States.

2. A description of the Trail of Tears of the Choctaw can be found at http://www.choctawschool.com/.

3. LANL.gov at the Los Alamos National Laboratory Research Library and Q-Spires (now replaced by INSPIRE) from the Stanford Linear Accelerator Laboratory, still known as SLAC, which was once called a center. Q-Spires research sharing was a crucial tool used by Tim Berners-Lee in the promotion of the nascent World Wide Web. Yes, there was a time when people had to be convinced that the World Wide Web would be useful and worth doing.

Chapter Twenty-Eight

Letter to New People of Color in LIS

Sofia Leung

Dear New Librarian, Library Worker, or Library Student of Color,

I'm writing this, not just for me, but for you, every one of you who has no idea or maybe some misconceptions about what you're about to encounter in this profession. This letter is the letter I wished I had received when I was in library school. When I started my first academic library job, I was hopeful and excited to be in what was then my dream job. I would get to create programs and events for undergraduates that would ease their entry into college and help them find and build community. Although it wasn't a part of the job description, I purposefully sought to create programs and spaces for students on the margins of campus: first-generation; low-income; students who identified as lesbian, gay, bisexual, trans, queer, intersex, or asexual; and/or students of color. I wanted to be who I, and many others with marginalized voices, needed when I was younger. I still want to do that.

But first let me tell you who I am and why I needed this letter when I was in your shoes. I am the child of immigrants. In 1965, when he was fourteen or sixteen (no record of his birth), my father immigrated to New York City from Hong Kong by way of a small village in China. My mother, also Chinese, came to America from Indonesia for college. They each had to teach themselves a new language, a new culture, and acclimate to a new country. To give us a leg up, my two brothers and I were raised with English as our first language with minimal Cantonese. Neither my brothers nor I have a Cantonese accent when we speak English, although sometimes a Brooklyn accent might creep in. My parents did whatever they could to make sure we would benefit from them having figured out America and its White people to a certain extent. They had observed how White Americans confidently asserted their place in the world and taught me to speak up for myself, especially in instances of injustice. However, as newcomers to America, they did not yet recognize how structural oppression operated in this country or could not fully express that to me. Thanks to microaggressions from classmates, teachers, and strangers, I learned how to fit in and tamp down or hide any tendencies that made me different. Even New York City, with its wealth of diversity, has its way of reminding you that you're still Other.

After graduating from Barnard College, I lived in San Francisco, California, and then Seattle, Washington, where I attended the University of Washington and earned two master's degrees, one in library and information science, and the other in public administration. I also spent a summer in Raleigh, North Carolina, as part of the Association of Research Libraries (ARL) Career Enhancement Program (CEP), a fellowship that no longer exists. Joining the ARL family of diversity programs introduced me to one of my mentors, Mark Puente, without whom I wouldn't be where I am today. I cannot emphasize enough the importance of finding your champions who will lift you up and recognize your value and labor. Find those people and support them when you can.

I was working as a temporary instruction librarian at a small, private college in Seattle when I was offered my first permanent position at a large public institution in the Midwest. I knew it was going to be tough to live in a small college town in the middle of the country, but really, I was not prepared for how tough. I don't want to scare anyone away from working in a place they never thought they'd ever be; I want you to *be prepared*. I honestly can't say I have any regrets from moving there; I met some of the best people I have ever known and learned so much more about myself and others. I grew as a woman of color and a leader, especially important in a predominantly White profession and institution.

To be fair, I don't think I was prepared for what I was to encounter, and some of the library administrators weren't prepared for me. In my interview, I didn't directly mention that social justice was the core value around which I practice librarianship. I mistakenly thought people who join this profession would feel the same way or, at least, respect the notion. Maybe I'm too naive or optimistic, but it still amazes me when I meet librarians or archivists who don't believe that social justice is the foundation of our work.

I don't need to tell you what tokenism feels like, but I have never experienced it as strongly as I have being the only person of color in my department. Growing up in New York City did not prepare me for the juxtaposition of color-blindness and invisibility at work with the blatant stares I received in public spaces. One of the disadvantages to moving to a new place (depending on how far away you end up) for a new job is the cultural shock of being in a different part of the country, away from anything or anyone familiar. However, if you're someone who is willing and able to move elsewhere for your career goals, this is something you'll be forced to do, especially if you want to stay in academia. Intellectually, I understood this; emotionally, I was not anywhere near prepared for this. As an East Coaster, moving to the West Coast was already a bit of culture shock for me. Moving to the Midwest was almost like moving to another country or even another planet in some ways. I couldn't spend too much time outdoors without being eaten alive by the various bugs. People stared blatantly at me whenever I left the relatively "safe" environs of campus. The food culture was severely lacking. The town was way too small; I would run into people from work more often than not. And where were the people of color (POC)?!

In addition to these environmental distractions, I quickly discovered that my new position required me to be much more of a self-starter and self-learner than I originally anticipated. No one was going to tell me what was expected of me, set up introductions to external (to the library) partners, or give me guidance on the cultural norms and organizational culture. I was partially more adrift than other new librarians because I had an interim supervisor while a search was conducted for that position, and I was the only librarian located at my branch location. After much emotional labor, stress, and sometimes after getting into trouble, I figured things out for myself.

One thing to be aware of, and it still surprises me that I have to warn you of this, is colleagues who will want to take advantage of your newness and your initial eagerness to be liked and useful as a new employee. On the very rare occasion that you encounter a person like this, you may be *volun-told* that they've been "waiting for you" in order to hand off certain projects. If this strikes you as weird because your supervisor told you nothing of the sort, listen to that instinct! You will need to set boundaries and protect your time, especially if you're in a new position within the library that you get to create. Don't get caught up in their false sense of urgency. Your colleagues should be making time and space for you as a new employee to get acclimated before giving you projects, especially in your first week! Of course, if that does happen, go to your supervisor immediately. If your supervisor doesn't step in to protect you, you'll know there's a side relationship between the supervisor and that colleague—one that you shouldn't trust—and you'll also know that you should stay far away from that colleague. That's office politics in a nutshell.

I probably don't need to tell you that you will encounter microaggressions and just straight-up racist bullshit from colleagues, supervisors, and superiors at work. But just in case you didn't think that was possible in a so-called values-based profession, librarians of color continue to experience microaggressions from the best of the well-meaning White folks (Alabi 2015, 2015a). So refreshing.

As a new librarian, it's super important to have a supervisor who advocates for you and protects you from administrative bullshit, especially as a person of color. Mediocre White people with insecurities will always be looking for ways to diminish us and our work. They will feel intimidated by our sheer work ethic, instilled in us by the fact that we had to work twice as hard to get to the same place. In some cases, it ends up being your supervisor or administrator who feels threatened by you. Instead of supporting you or lifting you up, they may bully you in subtle and not-so-subtle ways. Pay attention to changes in their behavior and reach out to a mentor to help you navigate those pitfalls.

A FEW LESSONS

One of my favorite faculty members, Shannon Portillo,[1] a badass woman of color who earned tenure before she turned thirty, shared a valuable piece of advice from her mentor: save the best of yourself for yourself. The only person looking out for you is *you*. I still have a hard time taking that advice myself, but I recognize the value in it. DeEtta Jones[2] gave my Minnesota Institute[3] cohort some wisdom that really complements what I learned from Shannon: the only person your anger hurts is you. I have to tell myself that over and over almost daily. It's a really difficult realization to come to terms with because that kind of anger can feel so good. DeEtta told us to redirect that energy into something more productive; otherwise, it will just feel like repeatedly hitting a brick wall, which is just more frustrating. This is a lesson I have had to learn over and over again. Kathryn Deiss,[4] DeEtta's cofacilitator at the Minnesota Institute, did warn me that it would take practice, one step at a time.

Many librarians of color find themselves being asked to join, lead, or create their library's diversity committee or they find themselves bringing up "the diversity question/issue" more often than their White colleagues. Many folks of color already know that it's important to make changes in order to improve things for those who come after us. We say to ourselves, "Be the person you needed when you were younger and the person you need now." For a lot of us, to *not* make social justice a part of our daily work would be worse than doing it and suffering for it.

I am not saying do not take on the "diversity work" of educating your colleagues and your institution. What I am saying is to understand the risks of that work and to be strategic when you do it. While it may not seem like it sometimes, recognize that this is a choice that comes with many risks to our career and our mental health. First, you're putting yourself in a vulnerable position by "standing out" and gaining recognition, whether it be positive or negative, from colleagues, managers, and administrators. It's possible that it'll paint a target on your back. On the other hand, you could still garner unwanted attention by being told you're "doing too much," if your contributions to the profession threaten the insecurities of your supervisor or administrators. At the same time, you will not be getting recognition for the difficult work of educating your peers and the emotional labor you're putting in. You will be expected to shoulder that burden, as if it *is* your work and no one else's. Your managers and administrators won't actually listen to anything you have to say. However, your administrators will happily take credit for your unpaid labor, especially when it makes the library look good.

HOW TO SURVIVE

> Hope is not at the expense of struggle but animates a struggle; hope gives us a sense that there is a point to working things out, working things through. Hope does not only or always point toward the future, but carries us through when the terrain is difficult, when the path we follow makes it harder to proceed. Hope is behind us when we have to work for something to be possible.
> —Sara Ahmed, *Living a Feminist Life*

Living and working in this environment, as you may imagine, was detrimental to both my mental and physical health. To help prevent a similar cycle of negativity and despair from happening to you, I am offering up some tips and advice on how to survive if you find yourself in such a situation. Obviously, these may not all work for you, but I hope you are able to find solace in one of these or through one of your own forms of self-care.

1. First and most important, find your community—outside of the library, if necessary. *You are not alone.* It's a sad, depressing, but hopeful truth—POC in this profession and higher education share many of the same experiences of tokenism, microaggressions, and the backlash attributed to White fragility.[5] You will need to create what Nicole Cooke (2014) calls "counterspaces," a term she borrows from Daniel Solórzano, Miguel Ceja, and Tara Yosso, where you can be your whole self and not have to submerge your racial identity. Reach out to library school students of color and other librarians of color to support and co-mentor one another. Connecting with faculty, students, and other staff of color on your campus can also be a source of refuge and comfort. The relationships that I've built just from shared experiences with other POC have sustained me and given me the strength to continue in this field.

2. Look beyond your institution for professional development opportunities in the form of service committees and publishing and presenting opportunities. If you have the time or it's part of your job description, get your name out there by volunteering for various professional organizations, submitting proposals to conferences or for articles and chapters, joining the editorial board of a journal, or becoming a peer reviewer. There are so many opportunities to do all of that. There are also quite a few leadership programs and scholarships out there for early-career librarians, less so for mid-career folks, so get them in while you can. Another mentor of mine emphasized the importance of name recognition for POC in this profession and, honestly, it's so true.

3. Motivate yourself by envisioning an outrageous goal. If work life is a struggle, get inspiration from this almost unattainable goal to help you find the desire to get out of bed every day. This piece of wisdom came from the wonderful, inspirational DeEtta Jones. For example, my career goal used to be going into library administration as a dean or director of a research library. But after learning from DeEtta, I decided that wasn't enough. It didn't mean anything for me to be a dean without my fellow POC beside me. Once I made that decision, I made lifting up other POC in the profession a part of my goals. Not once have I regretted that decision, and every win for another POC is a win for all of us. Every time I'm able to lift another one of us up, I feel more fulfilled and motivated to stay in this profession.

4. Recognize your self-worth and value, not just to the institution but also to students, faculty, and staff. It's important to remember that as POC, we have already had a harder time, in varying degrees, than White people in these same spaces, but this isn't the Oppression Olympics. We have had to work twice as hard, if not more, to get to the same place as many of these White people. We deserve to be here. In a presentation at ACRL 2017, Dr. Nicole Cooke noted that "although the profession is eighty-seven percent White, most of the communities we serve are not" (Cooke 2017). By being ourselves and having our lived experiences, we are already valuable to the library profession, more so than our White colleagues would like to admit. When a student of color sees you and sees themselves in you, you've already made a difference, just by being there.

5. Many of the suggestions above are forms of self-care, but the following are activities rather than strategies.

- Get a therapist, if you're able to afford it, or get it from your health insurance. Work is giving you mental health issues; work should pay for it. Obviously, this is not an affordable choice if your insurance doesn't cover it. But talking with others about what's happening to you, whether it's with family or friends or colleagues in other departments or institutions, can be a form of therapy as well. I found it less helpful to talk to White colleagues who didn't get it, because then I had to explain why I found my experiences difficult.
- Listen to podcasts[6] or watch TV shows[7] that speak directly to the experiences you're having. I found it incredibly helpful to listen to podcasts where race was discussed regularly. It helped me to feel as though I wasn't imagining my experiences; that women of color in all professions have similar struggles.
- Take a vacation or mental health day. I was reminded by a good friend of mine, another POC survivor in higher education, that we become so trau-

matized by White spaces that our bodies react viscerally to returning to those spaces. So give yourself a break from those White spaces!

• Exercise and/or meditate regularly. Both activities helped to clear my mind and make me feel physically and mentally stronger.

• Read to liberate. I did so much reading in and around critical theory, particularly critical race theory, to teach myself the language to explain what I was experiencing. Over and over, I heard and read how important it is to be able to name the thing that's happening to you and others, so that you can call attention to it and do something about it. Some readings that resonated with me include Ahmed's *On Being Included: Racism and Diversity in Institutional Life* (2012), Cooke's "Pushing Back from the Table: Fighting to Maintain My Voice as a Pre-Tenure Minority Female in the White Academy" (2014), Crenshaw's "Mapping the Margins: Intersectionality, Identity Politics, and Violence against Women of Color" (1991), and hooks's *Teaching to Transgress: Education as the Practice of Freedom* (1994).

Good luck and stay strong. We need all of us in this fight. But if you find yourself really unhappy with no end in sight or no motivation to stay, then maybe it's time to think about leaving this profession. We'll miss you, but you'll always be a part of this family.

NOTES

1. Shannon Portillo, PhD, is an associate professor in the School of Public Affairs and Administration at the University of Kansas.

2. DeEtta Jones is the founder and principal at DeEtta Jones and Associates (DJA) Consulting: Next Generation Leadership. See www.deettajones.com.

3. See Minnesota Institute for Early Career Librarians, https://www.lib.umn.edu/sed/institute..

4. Kathryn Deiss is senior facilitator and consultant at DeEtta Jones and Associates (DJA) Consulting: Next Generation Leadership. See www.deettajones.com.

5. *White fragility*, a term coined by Dr. Robin DiAngelo, a consultant and trainer on issues of race and social justice, is defined as "a state in which even a minimum amount of racial stress becomes intolerable, triggering a range of defensive moves." See http://robindiangelo.com/about-me/.

6. Some podcasts I recommend (in no particular order) are *Another Round, Still Processing, The Mash-Up Americans, Code Switch, Politically Re-Active with W. Kamau Bell & Hari Kondabolu, 2 Dope Queens, Sooo Many White Guys,* and *Otherhood.*

7. Some TV shows I would recommend (also in no particular order) include *Being Mary Jane, Jane the Virgin, Insecure, The Mindy Project* (specifically the episode "Mindy Lahiri Is a White Man"), *The Crown* (I acknowledge that this show is problematic because it's about a white woman who continues to enable white supremacy and colonialism, but many of the struggles she faces are very relatable and it's still interesting to see what strategies she employs to deal with them).

Epilogue

Jorge R. López-McKnight

I held these stories up to a mirror, and they reflected light. When the *I* became *us*, the Collective, communicating to you, it was alive and we had all come home.

These days, I don't believe in much, but I believe in our stories, in those chapters you just read. All the truth and power of these voices, together as one; it was terrifying because it was so beautiful, so bright. Burning. An impossible force, transcending time, space, and boundaries. And these voices, they're for us, they're for each other, and they're for folks who will come after us and for some, who our even among us, now. I hope they find you.

I was taught much from these voices. Recognizing the value of community and mentoring is so important; we must continue to do that. It's vital we support and love each other. We must keep looking toward theory, frameworks, and knowledge systems to interrogate the structures in our society, in our profession, that maintain White supremacy. We are going to have to keep passing knowledge from one generation to the next, we are going to have to decolonize our thinking, and we must continue to understand the importance of language if we are going to grow and get stronger. We learned to not be afraid of the dangerous times we are living in, because these voices reminded us that we have been living our entire lives in dangerous times.

Part 1, Back in the Day, reminded us that these times we find ourselves in are, sadly, nothing new. We have seen this situation before, but if we follow the questions and words of these voices, we will know how to move in a different direction.

Part 2, They Have Magic, showed us to not be afraid of our light, to imagine and expand the possibilities of our identities and roles in this profession. That we are exactly the ones we have been waiting for. These voices have demanded that their selves and bodies are enough and of critical importance, and because they have been liberated, they can walk into the sun.

Strength (part 3) is needed, and it takes time to grow; it requires sacrifices and choices, of the self and of family. When it is gained, we must share it with our communities so they can get stronger and healthier. These voices told us; they showed us.

The voices in part 4, Leading by Reflection, are at the top and we trust their vision, because they can *see*. They have been experiencing and learning, and that will shape their directing and our directions.

Family (part 5) requires love and understanding. These voices showed us how to create spaces that allow ourselves to be ourselves, so we could hold each other intimately, fully. To be seen, to be vulnerable, to be human.

In part 6, Disrupting the System, freedom fighters are doing the work and will continue to, in this lifetime and in the next. These voices boldly stand in opposition to the structures of domination in this society that come after marginalized communities. We should be in awe of their efforts.

The voices in part 7, They Persisted, showed us there was no other course of action but through. Even with challenges and difficulties, they did not back down; they did not give up.

The Warrior Women in part 8 are brave and strong. If we follow their lead and speak out about our life, our journey, we will know what we need to be.

In part 9, our anchors, our guides, are always *Bringing Us Home*. Grounded in clarity, tenderness, wisdom, and a fierce love of our communities, they carried us to a place that was beautifully familiar.

What just happened in these pages? What were those voices trying to tell you? How are you now supposed to move, knowing what you now know? Our stories have told you what happened and what is happening. You have to ask yourself, now armed with this knowledge, what *will happen*? It doesn't depend entirely on us.

We hope you're asking yourself these questions, because if you are committed to any type of social justice effort in our profession, you need to ask yourself an even more difficult question: Am I contributing to the continued oppression of folks in the profession and the communities we serve? Your efforts in committees, workplace culture, hiring, educating, and creating spaces and services will need to consider that.

Many of you will have to wake up to read this. You're going to have to believe certain truths about the world and recalibrate your senses in a particular way that will challenge you. You're going to need to listen. You're going to need to take up less space. You'll need to identify your own spaces of oppression. You have to want to give up power.

To the folks already doing the work—in your communities, in your home, in the profession—we see you; we thank you and hope you continue. We don't know what's going to happen in this profession. It was never made for us or by us, and only very recently did it start to include us. There's much work to do.

So, you have been witness to our stories. We share those with you. Our voices are not forgotten; they do not need to be chased. They are right here.

Appendix

In Our Own Voices: The Changing Face of
Librarianship *(Scarecrow Press, 1996)*

Preface, by E. J. Josey
Introduction, by Teresa Y. Neely
Part I: Academic Librarians
Chapter 1: Reflections from the Past, Present, and Future, by José A. Aguiñaga
Chapter 2: An Accent on Reference, by Gloria De Alfaro
Chapter 3: Mexican American Mountaineer, by Monica Garcia Brooks
Chapter 4: Internships/Residencies: Exploring the Possibilities for the Future, by Jon E. Cawthorne and Teri B. Weil
Chapter 5: The Content of My Character, by Vicki Coleman
Chapter 6: To Be Young, Maybe Gifted, and Truly Black—Notes from a New Librarian, by Edna Dixon
Chapter 7: Running through the Doors of Opportunity, by Dexter R. Evans
Chapter 8: Learning to Be: An African American Experience in Academic Librarianship, by Madeline Ford
Chapter 9: My Name Is America, by Ngoc-Mỹ Guidarelli
Chapter 10: On the Ambiguous Side: Experiences in a Predominantly White and Female Profession, by Deborah Hollis
Chapter 11: Invisible Presence: An Asian American Librarian's Experience, by Mee-Len Hom
Chapter 12: The Jackie Robinson of Library Science, by Teresa Y. Neely
Chapter 13: Academic Librarianship: A Personal Perspective, by Lisa Pillow

269

Bibliography

Abramson, Kate. "Turning up the Lights on Gaslighting." *Philosophical Perspectives* 28, no. 1 (2014): 1–30.

Adams, Maurianne, Warren J. Blumenfeld, Carmelita Rosie Castañeda, Heather W. Hackman, Madeline L. Peters, and Ximena Zúñiga. *Readings for Diversity and Social Justice.* New York: Routledge, 2013.

Administration for Native Americans. "American Indians and Alaska Natives—the Trust Responsibility." March 19, 2014. https://www.acf.hhs.gov/ana/resource/american-indians-and-alaska-natives-the-trust-responsibility.

Aguiñaga, José A. "Reflections from the Past, Present, and Future." In *In Our Own Voices: The Changing Face of Librarianship*, edited by Teresa Y. Neely and Khafre K. Abif, 3–19. Lanham, MD: Scarecrow Press, 1996.

Ahmed, Sara. *Living a Feminist Life.* Durham, NC: Duke University Press, 2017.

Alabi, Jaena. "This Actually Happened: An Analysis of Librarians' Responses to a Survey about Racial Microaggressions." *Journal of Library Administration* 55, no. 3 (2015a): 179–91.

———. "Racial Microaggressions in Academic Libraries: Results of a Survey of Minority and Non-Minority Librarians." *Journal of Academic Librarianship* 41, no. 1 (2015b): 47–53. doi:10.1016/j.acalib.2014.10.008.

ALS Association. "The Ice Bucket Challenge." 2017. http://www.alsa.org/fight-als/ice-bucket-challenge.html.

American Association of Museums. "The Museum Workforce in the United States (2009): A Data Snapshot from the American Association of Museums." November 3 2011. http://aam-us.org/docs/center-for-the-future-of-museums/museum-workforce.pdf?sfvrsn=0.

American Libraries. "Civil Rights Pioneer, Librarian E. J. Josey Dies at 85." 2009. https://americanlibrariesmagazine.org/blogs/the-scoop/civil-rights-pioneer-librarian-e-j-josey-dies-at-85/.

American Library Association. "Table Series A: 2009–2010 American Community Survey Estimates Applied to Institute for Museum and Library Services and National Center for Education Statistics Data." 2012. http://www.ala.org/aboutala/sites/ala.org.aboutala/files/content/diversity/diversitycounts/diversitycountstables2012.pdf.

———. "Diversity Counts 2009–2010 Update." December 5, 2012. Accessed March 13, 2017. http://www.ala.org/offices/diversity/diversitycounts/2009-2010update.

———. "ALCTS Endorses Cataloging and Metadata Core Competencies." *ALA Member News*, March 15, 2017. http://www.ala.org/news/member-news/2017/03/alcts-endorses-cataloging-and-metadata-core-competencies.

American Psychological Association (APA) Zero Tolerance Task Force. "Are Zero Tolerance Policies Effective in the Schools? An Evidentiary Review and Recommendations." *American Psychologist* 63, no. 9 (December 2008): 852–62.

American Psychiatric Association. *DSM-5. Diagnostic and Statistical Manual of Mental Disorders.* 5th ed. Washington, DC: American Psychiatric Association, 2013.

———. "What Is Posttraumatic Stress Disorder?" 2017. https://www.psychiatry.org/patients-families/ptsd/what-is-ptsd.

Angelou, Maya. *Maya Angelou: And Still I Rise.* Documentary film. Directed by Bob Hercules and Rita Coburn Whack. People Poet Media Group, LLC, American Masters Pictures, and ITVS, 2016.

Association for Library Service to Children. "Together with DiA!" Accessed April 27, 2017. http://dia.ala.org/content/about-d%C3%ADa.

Association of College and Research Libraries. "Framework for Information Literacy for Higher Education." February 9, 2015. http://www.ala.org/acrl/standards/ilframework.

Association of Research Libraries. "ARL Statistics Questionnaire, 2014–15 Instructions for Completing the Questionnaire." 2015. http://www.libqual.org/documents/admin/15instruct.pdf.

Association on American Indian Affairs (AAIA). "Frequently Asked Questions: What Is Blood Quantum?" 2006. https://www.indian-affairs.org/general-faq.html.

Becker, Jenifer. "Active Allyship." *Public Services Quarterly* 13, no. 1 (2017): 27–31. doi:10.1080/15228959.2016.1261638.

Bennett, Jacob. "White Privilege: A History of the Concept." Thesis, Georgia State University, 2012. http://scholarworks.gsu.edu/history_theses/54.

Biesta, Gert J. *Beyond Learning. Democratic Education for a Human Future.* Boulder, CO: Paradigm, 2006.

Black-Parker, Kimberly. "The Importance, Review and Holdings of Contemporary African-American Women's Poetry and Fiction in ARL Libraries, 1980–1990." PhD diss., Florida State University, 2003, https://diginole.lib.fsu.edu/islandora/object/fsu:181963/datastream/PDF/view.

Bomey, Nathan. "Coal's Demise Threatens Appalachian Miners, Firms as Production Moves to West." *USA Today,* May 4, 2016. Accessed March 14, 2017. https://www.usatoday.com/story/money/2016/04/19/coal-industry-energy-fallout/82972958/.

Bosman, Julie, and Monica Davey. "'Everything's in Danger': Illinois Approaches 3rd Year without Budget." *New York Times,* June 29, 2017. https://www.nytimes.com/2017/06/29/us/illinois-state-budget-impasse.html.

Boylorn, Robin M. "Working While Black: 10 Racial Microaggressions Experienced in the Workplace." *Crunk Feminist Collective* (blog), November 11, 2014. http://www.crunkfeministcollective.com/2014/11/11/working-while-black-10-racial-microaggressions-experienced-in-the-workplace/.

Bretherton, Inge. "The Origins of Attachment Theory: John Bowlby and Mary Ainsworth." *Developmental Psychology* 29, no. 5 (1992): 759–75.

Brooks, Monica Garcia. "Mexican American Mountaineer." In *In Our Own Voices: The Changing Face of Librarianship,* edited by Teresa Y. Neely and Khafre K. Abif, 30–44. Lanham, MD: Scarecrow Press, 1996.

Brown, M. Christopher, and T. Elon Dancy. "Predominantly White Institutions." In *Encyclopedia of African American Education,* edited by Kofi Lomotey. Thousand Oaks, CA: Sage, 2010. http://sk.sagepub.com/reference/africanamericaneducation/n193.xml.

Brown, Malore I. "I Fell into Librarianship and Fell in Love." In *In Our Own Voices: The Changing Face of Librarianship,* edited by Teresa Y. Neely and Khafre K. Abif, 360–71. Lanham, MD: Scarecrow Press, 1996.

Brown, Sarah. "As Illinois Budget Impasse Ends, So Does a 'Nightmare of Total Uncertainty' for Its Public Colleges." *Chronicle of Higher Education,* July 6, 2017. http://www.chronicle.com/article/As-Illinois-Budget-Impasse/240553.

Buckingham, Marcus, and Curt Coffman. *First Break All the Rules: What the World's Greatest Managers Do Differently.* New York: Simon & Schuster, 1999.

Bureau of Indian Affairs. "Indian Affairs | Zuni Agency." 2017. Accessed July 26, 2017. https:/ /www.bia.gov/WhoWeAre/RegionalOffices/Southwest/WeAre/Zuni/index.htm.

Burwell, Lisa A. "A Dream Fulfilled: The Power of Mentoring." In *In Our Own Voices: The Changing Face of Librarianship*, edited by Teresa Y. Neely and Khafre K. Abif, 267–81. Lanham, MD: Scarecrow Press, 1996.

———. "Too Old to Surf?? No Way! An Internet Course for Seniors." *American Libraries* 32, no. 10 (2001): 40–42.

Castillo-Padilla, Edward, Nancy K. Dennis, Linda K. Lewis, and Frances C. Wilkinson. "The Zimmerman Library 2006 Fire that Led to the 2007 Library Flood: An Overview." In *Comprehensive Guide to Emergency Preparedness and Disaster Recovery*, edited by Frances C. Wilkinson, Linda K. Lewis, and Nancy K. Dennis, 145–59. Chicago: Association of College and Research Libraries, 2010.

Cawthorne, Jon E., and Teresa Y. Neely. "ARL's Leadership Career Development Program for Underrepresented Mid-Career Librarians." In *Creating Leaders: An Examination of Academic and Research Library Leadership Institutes*, edited by Irene M. H. Herold, 107–22. Chicago: Association of College and Research Libraries, 2015.

Center for Tax and Budget Accountability. "Illinois' Significant Disinvestment in Higher Education." January 27, 2017. http://www.ctbaonline.org/file/449/download?token= QhlCYpvG.

Centers for Disease Control and Prevention. "Helping Patients Cope with a Traumatic Event." 2017. https://www.cdc.gov/masstrauma/factsheets/public/coping.pdf.

Chang, Hui-Fen. "Ethnic and Racial Diversity in Academic and Research Libraries: Past, Present, and Future." In *Imagine, Innovate, Inspire—the Proceedings of the ACRL 2013 Conference, Indianapolis, Indiana, April 10–13, 2013*, edited by Dawn Mueller, 182–93. Chicago: Association of College and Research Libraries, 2013. http://www.ala.org/acrl/ sites/ala.org.acrl/files/content/conferences/confsandpreconfs/2013/papers/Chang_Ethnic. pdf.

Chapa, Arcely. *Zimmerman@75: The Heart of Campus*. Film. Directed by Arcely Chapa. Albuquerque, NM: UNM, Center for Regional Studies, 2015.

Chappelle's Show. "When Keeping It Real Goes Wrong—Vernon Franklin—Uncensored." Comedy Central, March 3, 2004. http://www.cc.com/video-clips/t0brk3/chappelle-s-show- when-keeping-it-real-goes-wrong---vernon-franklin---uncensored.

Chávez, E. "Chicano Movement." In *Encyclopedia of Race and Racism*, vol. 1, 2nd ed., edited by P. L. Mason, 369–71. Detroit: Macmillan Reference USA, 2013.

City College of New York (CUNY). "City College of New York Fast Facts Fall 2016." February 23, 2017. https://www.ccny.cuny.edu/sites/default/files/2016_Fast_Facts_02.23. 2017.pdf.

City College of New York, Professional Staff Congress. "Research, Fellowship, and Scholar Incentive Awards." Accessed March 15, 2017. http://www.psc-cuny.org/contract/article-25- research-fellowship-and-scholar-incentive-awards.

Collins, James C. *Good to Great: Why Some Companies Make the Leap . . . and Others Don't*. New York: William Collins, 2001.

Constantine, Madonna G., Laura Smith, Rebecca M. Redington, and Delila Owens. "Racial Microaggressions against Black Counseling and Counseling Psychology Faculty: A Central Challenge in the Multicultural Counseling Movement." *Journal of Counseling & Development* 86 (Summer 2008): 348–55.

Cooke, Nicole A. "Pushing Back from the Table: Fighting to Maintain My Voice as a Pre-Tenure Minority Female in the White Academy." *Polymath: An Interdisciplinary Arts and Sciences Journal* 4, no. 2 (2014): 39–49.

———. "How Do You Want to Be Remembered?" Keynote presented at the Association of College and Research Libraries National Conference, Baltimore, MD. March 2017.

Cooke, Nicole A., and Renee F. Hill. "Considering Cultural Competence." *Knowledge Quest* 45, no. 3 (2017): 54–61.

Crenshaw, Kimberle. "Demarginalizing the Intersection of Race and Sex: A Black Feminist Critique of Antidiscrimination Doctrine, Feminist Theory and Antiracist Politics." *University of Chicago Legal Forum* 1989, no. 1 (1989): 139–67.

———. "Mapping the Margins: Intersectionality, Identity Politics, and Violence against Women of Color." *Stanford Law Review* 43, no. 6 (1991): 1241–99.

Creswell, John W. *Educational Research: Planning, Conducting and Evaluating Quantitative and Qualitative Research*. Boston: Pearson, 1998.

Crisp, Gloria, Amanda Taggart, and Amaury Nora. "Undergraduate Latina/o Students: A Systematic Review of Research Identifying Factors Contributing to Academic Success Outcomes." *Review of Educational Research* 85, no. 2 (2015): 249–74.

Croom, Natasha N. "Promotion beyond Tenure: Unpacking Racism and Sexism in the Experiences of Black Womyn Professors." *Review of Higher Education* 40, no. 4 (2017): 557–83.

Curtin, Michael. "Chicago State University, Special Board of Trustees, Full Board Meeting Minutes." February 4, 2016. https://www.csu.edu/boardoftrustees/meetingminutes/year2016/SBM-Feb04-2016.pdf.

Damasco, Ione T., and Dracine Hodges. "Tenure and Promotion Experiences of Academic Librarians of Color." *College & Research Libraries* 73, no. 3 (2012): 279–301.

Dassin, Joe. "L'Amérique." English Translation. *La fleur aux dents*. 1970. http://lyricstranslate.com/en/l039amerique-america.html.

David, E. J. R. *Brown Skin, White Minds: Filipino/American Postcolonial Psychology*. Charlotte, NC: Information Age Publishing, 2013.

Davis, Denise M., and Tracie D. Hall. "Diversity Counts." American Library Association, Office for Research and Statistics, Office for Diversity, January 2007. http://www.ala.org/aboutala/sites/ala.org.aboutala/files/content/diversity/diversitycounts/diversitycounts_rev0.pdf.

Davis, James F. *Who Is Black? One Nation's Definition*. University Park: Pennsylvania University Press, 1991. Excerpt posted on *Frontline*. http://www.pbs.org/wgbh/pages/frontline/shows/jefferson/mixed/onedrop.html.

Dhillon, Kiran. "The 10 Worst-Paying Jobs that Require a Master's Degree." *Time: Money*, September 10, 2014. http://time.com/money/3318635/worst-paying-jobs-requiring-a-masters/.

Dickson, Katherine Murphy. "A Work Journal." *Library Trends* 50, no. 4 (2002): 687–701.

Dill, Kathryn. "The Best and Worst Master's Degrees for Jobs in 2016." *Forbes*, August 12, 2016. https://www.forbes.com/sites/kathryndill/2016/08/12/the-best-and-worst-masters-degrees-for-jobs-in-2016/#3d9bb30a7435.

Dishman, Lydia. "Best and Worst Graduate Degrees for Jobs in 2016." *Fortune*, March 21, 2016. http://fortune.com/2016/03/21/best-worst-graduate-degrees-jobs-2016/.

Donovan, Roxanne A., David J. Galban, Ryan K. Grace, Jacqueline K. Bennett, and Shaina Z. Felicié. "Impact of Racial Macro- and Microaggressions in Black Women's Lives: A Preliminary Analysis." *Journal of Black Psychology* 39, no. 2 (2012): 185–96. doi: 10.1177/0095798412443259.

Drash, Wayne, and Max Blau. "Heroin: The Scarring of the Next Generation." CNN.com, September 16, 2016. http://www.cnn.com/2016/09/16/health/huntington-heroin/.

Earle, Harry. "I'd Rather Be a Nigger than a Poor White Man." Lester S. Levy Sheet Music Collection. New York: M. Witmark and Sons, 1894. http://levysheetmusic.mse.jhu.edu/catalog/levy:141.079.

Elder, Tanya. "Hip v. Nice v. Traditional v. Nasty v. AAAARRGGGHHH." In *In Our Own Voices: The Changing Face of Librarianship*, edited by Teresa Y. Neely and Khafre K. Abif, 282–305. Lanham, MD: Scarecrow Press, 1996.

Eltagouri, Marwa. "Chicago State University Sends Layoff Notices to All 900 Employees." *Chicago Tribune*, February 26, 2016. http://www.chicagotribune.com/news/local/breaking/ct-chicago-state-university-layoff-notices-20160226-story.html.

Ervin, Hazel A. *Handbook of African American Literature*. Gainesville: University Press of Florida, 2004.

Espinal, Isabel. "A New Vocabulary for Inclusive Librarianship: Applying Whiteness Theory to our Profession." In *The Power of Language/El Poder de la Palabra: Selected Papers from the Second REFORMA National Conference*, edited by Lillian Castillo-Speed, 131–49. Englewood, CO: Libraries Unlimited, 2001.

Ettarh, Fobazi. "Vocational Awe?" *WTF Is a Radical Librarian, Anyway?* (blog), May 30, 2017. https://fobaziettarh.wordpress.com/2017/05/30/vocational-awe/.

Evans, Dexter R. "Running Through the Doors of Opportunity." In *In Our Own Voices: The Changing Face of Librarianship*, edited by Teresa Y. Neely and Khafre K. Abif, 94–103, Lanham, MD: Scarecrow Press, 1996.

Ewing, Charles Patrick. "Sensible Zero Tolerance Protects Students." *Harvard Education Letter* 16, no. 1 (January/February 2000).

Figueroa, Julie López, and Gloria M. Rodriguez. "Critical Mentoring Practices to Support Diverse Students in Higher Education: Chicana/Latina Faculty Perspectives." *New Directions for Higher Education* 2015, no. 171 (2015): 23–32. doi:10.1002/he.20139.

Foucault, Michel. "Truth and Juridical Forms." In *Essential Works of Foucault, 1954–1984*. Vol. 3, *Power*, edited by J. D. Faubion, 1–84. New York: New Press, 1994.

Gardenswartz, Lee, and Anita Rowe. *Diverse Teams at Work: Capitalizing on the Power of Diversity*. Alpharetta, GA: Society for Human Resource Management, 2003.

Gershenson, Seth, Cassandra M. D. Hart, Constance A. Lindsay, and Nicholas W. Papageorge. "The Long-Run Impacts of Same-Race Teachers." EconPapers, March 21, 2017. Accessed April 11, 2017. http://econpapers.repec.org/RePEc:iza:izadps:dp10630.

Godfrey, Thomas, and Stephen J. Tordella. "Librarians, Library Technicians and Assistants: Diversity Profile 2000 and 1990, Library Employees Living in Same Sex Partner Households, First Look from the American Community Survey." Arlington, VA: Decision Demographics, 2006. http://www.ala.org/aboutala/offices/diversity/diversitycounts/2009-2010update.

Graf, Jeffrey. "The Word *Hoosier*." Indiana University Libraries, November 1, 2000. Last modified July 28, 2016. http://www.indiana.edu/~librcsd/internet/extra/hoosier.html.

Gray, Jody. "Community Building for Success." In *Choosing to Lead: The Motivational Factors of Underrepresented Minority Librarians in Higher Education*, edited by Antonia P. Olivas. Chicago: Association of College and Research Libraries, a division of the American Library Association, 2017.

Griffin, Karen. "Pursuing Tenure and Promotion in the Academy: A Librarian's Cautionary Tale." *Negro Educational Review* 64, no. 1–4 (2013): 77–96.

Grimm, Jacob, and Wilhelm Grimm. *German Popular Stories*. Translated by Edgar Taylor. London: James Robins, 1826.

The Guardian. "The Counted: People Killed by the Police in the U.S." 2015. https://www.theguardian.com/us-news/ng-interactive/2015/jun/01/the-counted-police-killings-us-database.

Hancock, Dawson R., and Robert Algozzine. *Doing Case Study Research: A Practical Guide for Beginning Researchers*. 2nd ed. New York: Teachers College Press, 2011.

Harris, Clifford Joseph, Michael Cox, Lamar Dauente Edwards, and John Wesley Groover. "We Will Not." By T. I., in *Us or Else: Letter to the System*. MP3. Atlanta, GA: Grand Hustle Records and Roc Nation, 2016.

Hart, Alfred A. *Piute Squaws and Children, at Reno*. 1875. Albumen silver print. J. Paul Getty Museum. http://www.getty.edu/art/collection/objects/82920/alfred-a-hart-piute-squaws-and-children-at-reno-american-about-1875/.

Haskins, Natoya H., and Anneliese Singh. "Critical Race Theory and Counselor Education Pedagogy: Creating Equitable Training." *Counselor Education and Supervision* 54, no. 4 (2015): 288–301. doi:10.1002/ceas.12027.

Heflick, Nathan A., Jamie L. Goldenberg, Douglas P. Cooper, and Elisa Puvia. "From Women to Objects: Appearance Focus, Target Gender, and Perceptions of Warmth, Morality, and Competence." *Journal of Experimental Social Psychology* 47, no. 3 (2011): 572–81.

Higher Learning Commission. "Public Disclosure Notice on Chicago State University." July 12, 2016. http://www.hlcommission.org/download/_PublicDisclosureNotices/Chicago%20State%20PDN%207-2016%20FINAL.pdf.

Hill Collins, Patricia. *Black Feminist Thought: Knowledge, Consciousness, and the Politics of Empowerment*. 2nd ed. New York: Routledge, 2009.

Hollis, Deborah R. "On the Ambiguous Side: Experiences in a Predominantly White and Female Profession." In *In Our Own Voices: The Changing Face of Librarianship*, edited by Teresa Y. Neely and Khafre K. Abif, 139–54. Lanham, MD: Scarecrow Press, 1996.

———. "Affirmative Action or Increased Competition: A Look at Women and Minority Library Deans." *Journal of Library Administration* 27, no. 1–2 (1999): 49–75. doi: 10.1300/J111v27n01_05.

Hom, Mee-Len. "Invisible Presence: An Asian American Librarian's Experience." In *In Our Own Voices: The Changing Face of Librarianship*, edited by Teresa Y. Neely and Khafre K. Abif, 155–63. Lanham, MD: Scarecrow Press, 1996.

———. "In Our Own Voices: Ethnically Diverse Librarians and Librarianship in the 90s." LAMA Cultural Diversity Committee, Panel Presentation at the ALA Annual Conference, San Francisco, June 18, 1997.

The Hotline. "What Is Gaslighting?" National Domestic Violence Hotline, May 29, 2014. http://www.thehotline.org/2014/05/what-is-gaslighting/.

Hughes, Langston. *The Dream Keeper and Other Poems*. New York: Knopf, 1932.

Hurston, Zora Neale. *I Love Myself When I Am Laughing . . . and Then Again When I Am Looking Mean and Impressive: A Zora Neale Hurston Reader*. Edited by Alice Walker. Old Westbury, NY: Feminist Press, 1979.

Indiana State Assembly. "Senate Bill 101—Religious Freedom Restoration." 2015. https://iga.in.gov/legislative/2015/bills/senate/101.

Indiana University, University Institutional Research and Reporting (UIRR). "Student Diversity-Minority Proportions/Two or More Races Breakdown." Indiana University, 2016. https://uirr.iu.edu/doc/facts-figures/enrollment/diversity/ipeds-base-sets/bloomington-base.pdf.

Ingraham, Christopher. "Three Quarters of Whites Do Not Have any Non-White Friends." *Washington Post*, August 25, 2014. https://www.washingtonpost.com/news/wonk/wp/2014/08/25/three-quarters-of-whites-dont-have-any-non-white-friends/?utm_term=.50a88cfdedb6.

Irvin, Vanessa. "We Librarians: Our Many, Necessary Selves." *Public Libraries* 55, no. 1 (2016): 21–22.

Jacinto, Irlanda. "Being a Super Token at the American Heritage Center." Panel Presentation, Joint Conference of the Art Libraries Society of North America and Visual Resources Association, Seattle, Washington, March 10, 2016.

Jackson, Andrew P., Julius Jefferson, and Akilah Nosakhere. *The 21st-Century Black Librarian in America: Issues and Challenges*. Lanham, MD: Scarecrow Press, 2012.

Jackson, Pamela Braboy, Peggy A. Thoits, and Howard F. Taylor. "Composition of the Workplace and Psychological Well-Being: The Effects of Tokenism on America's Black Elite." *Social Forces* 74, no. 2 (1995): 543–57. doi:10.2307/2580491.

Johnson, Kelli. "Minority Librarians in Higher Education: A Critical Race Theory Analysis." PhD diss., Marshall University, 2016.

Johnson, Peggy. "Retaining and Advancing Librarians of Color." *College & Research Libraries* 68, no. 5 (2007): 405–17. doi:10.5860/crl.68.5.405.

Josey, E. J. *The Black Librarian in America*. Lanham, MD: Scarecrow Press, 1970.

———. "Foreword." In *In Our Own Voices: The Changing Face of Librarianship*, edited by Teresa Y. Neely and Khafre K. Abif, xi–xiv. Lanham, MD: Scarecrow Press, 1996.

Josey, E. J., and Marva L. DeLoach. *Handbook of Black Librarianship*. 2nd ed. Santa Barbara, CA: Libraries Unlimited, 2000.

Josey, E. J., and Ann Allen Shockley. *Handbook of Black Librarianship*. Santa Barbara, CA: Libraries Unlimited, 1977.

Kanter, Rosabeth Moss. *Men and Women of the Corporation*. New York: Basic Books, 1993.

Killough, Ashley. "Jonathan Gruber: 'I Am Embarrassed, and I Am Sorry.'" CNN.com, December 9, 2014. http://www.cnn.com/2014/12/09/politics/gruber-hearing/.

Kleinfeld, N. R. "A Man who Hated Black Men Found a Victim Who Cared for Others." New York Times, March 23, 2017. https://www.nytimes.com/2017/03/23/nyregion/james-harris-jackson-timothy-caughman.html?_r=0.

Kübler-Ross, Elisabeth and David Kessler. *On Grief and Grieving: Finding the Meaning of Grief through the Five Stages of Loss.* New York: Scribner, 2005.

Lakshmi, B. Samrajya. "Reflective Practice through Journal Writing and Peer Observation: A Case Study." *Turkish Online Journal of Distance Education* 15, no. 4 (2014): 189–204.

Lanas, Maija, and Tomi Kiilakoski. "Growing Pains: Teacher Becoming a Transformative Agent." *Pedagogy, Culture and Society* 21, no. 3 (2013): 343–60.

Lartey, Jamiles. "Ben Carson Incorrectly Suggests African Slaves Were 'Immigrants' to US." *Guardian*, March 6, 2017. https://www.theguardian.com/us-news/2017/mar/06/ben-carson-african-slaves-immigrants-housing-speech.

Lasko, Diana. "Educators Restructure Curriculum for Revamped GED." *Herald-Standard*, January 23, 2014. https://www.heraldstandard.com/news/local_news/educators-restructure-curriculum-for-revamped-ged/article_fefd4f08-f6a9-5b6c-ae81-84117ab1869c.html.

Laws, Judith Long. "The Psychology of Tokenism: An Analysis." *Sex Roles* 1, no. 1 (1975): 51–67.

Library Journal. "Awards, Past Winners." http://lj.libraryjournal.com/awards/past-winners#librarian.

Liptak, Kevin. "Michelle Obama Says 'Angry Black Woman' Label Rooted in Fear." CNN.com, CNN Politics, December 19, 2016. http://www.cnn.com/2016/12/19/politics/michelle-obama-oprah-angry-black-woman/.

Livingston, Jennie. *Paris Is Burning.* Directed by Jennie Livingston. Documentary Film. Santa Monica, CA: Miramax Films, 1990.

López-McKnight, Jorge R. "My Librarianship Is Not for You." In *Topographies of Whiteness: Mapping Whiteness in Library and Information Science*, edited by Gina Schlesselman-Tarango, 257–66. Sacramento, CA: Library Juice Press, 2017.

Louie, Sam. "Working While Black." *Psychology Today*, April 6, 2017. https://www.psychologytoday.com/blog/minority-report/201704/working-while-black.

Mack, Justin L. "Hoosier Hospitality Takes Center Stage at Final Bicentennial Celebration." Indystar.com, December 12, 2016. http://www.indystar.com/story/news/2016/12/12/hoosier-hospitality-takes-center-stage-final-bicentennial-celebration/95300752/.

Marshall University, Office of Institutional Research and Planning. "Blue Book 2016–2017." 2017. https://sharepoint.marshall.edu/sites/irpweb/_layouts/15/WopiFrame.aspx?sourcedoc=/sites/irpweb/Shared%20Documents/2016-17/Bluebook%20(2016-17).pdf&action=default.

———. "Institutional Research Data." 2004–2018. http://www.marshall.edu/irp/institutional-data/.

Masterson, Matt. "Illinois Weighing Down National Higher Ed Spending Numbers." *Chicago Tonight*, May 4, 2017. http://chicagotonight.wttw.com/2017/05/04/illinois-weighing-down-national-higher-ed-spending-numbers.

McCartney, Robert. "Changes in GED Test Make It Harder for Adults to Get High School Credential Needed for Jobs." *Washington Post*, March 29, 2014. https://www.washingtonpost.com/local/changes-in-ged-test-make-it-harder-for-adults-to-get-high-school-credential-needed-for-jobs/2014/03/29/2145da8a-b6d9-11e3-a7c6-70cf2db17781_story.html?utm_term=.ee2ff29d208d.

McFarland, Joel, Bill Hussar, Cristobal de Brey, Tom Snyder, Xiaolei Wang, Sidney Wilkinson-Flicker, Semhar Gebrekristos, et al. (2017). "The Condition of Education 2017." (NCES 2017-144). U.S. Department of Education. Washington, DC: National Center for Education Statistics. https://nces.ed.gov/pubsearch/pubsinfo.asp?pubid=2017144.

McGuigan, Charles. "A Nation of Immigrants: Embracing the Other." *North of the James* 23, no. 3 (March 2, 2017). http://northofthejames.com/nation-immigrants-embracing/.

McIntosh, Peggy. "White Privilege and Male Privilege: A Personal Account of Coming to See Correspondences through Work in Women's Studies." Wellesley Centers for Women. 1988. https://www.wcwonline.org/images/pdf/White_Privilege_and_Male_Privilege_Personal_Account-Peggy_McIntosh.pdf.

———. "Examining Unearned Privilege." *Liberal Education* 70, no. 1 (Winter 1993): 61–63.

————. "White Privilege and Male Privilege: A Personal Account of Coming to See Correspondences through Work in Women's Studies." In *The Teacher in American Society: A Critical Anthology*, edited by Eugene F. Provenzo, 121–34. Newbury Park, CA: Sage, 2010.

McLean, Gary N., and Laird McLean. "If We Can't Define HRD in One Country, How Can We Define It in an International Context?" *Human Resources Development International* 4, no. 3 (2001): 313.

McLeod, Heather, and Cecile Badenhorst. "New Academics and Identities: Research as a Process of 'Becoming.'" *Brock Education: A Journal of Educational Research and Practice* 24, no. 1 (September 1, 2014): 65–72.

Meissner, Dennis. "Bare Necessities: A Presidential Address." *American Archivist* 80, no. 1 (2017): 6–18. http://americanarchivist.org/doi/pdf/10.17723/0360-9081.80.1.6.

Mezirow, Jack. *Fostering Critical Reflection in Adulthood: A Guide to Transformative and Emancipatory Learning.* San Francisco, CA: Jossey-Bass, 1990.

Moore, Dinty W. *The Truth of the Matter: Art and Craft in Creative Nonfiction.* London: Pearson/Longman, 2006.

Moran, Barbara. "The Impact of Affirmative Action on Academic Libraries." *Library Trends* 34, no. 2 (Fall 1985): 199–217.

Morris, Shaneka. "ARL Annual Salary Survey, 2015–2016." Washington, DC: Association of Research Libraries, 2017. http://publications.arl.org/ARL-Annual-Salary-Survey-2015-2016/.

Myers, Vernā. "About Vernā." The Vernā Myers Company, 2017a. https://vernamyers.com.

————. "What if I Say the Wrong Thing? Interrupting Bias in Ourselves and Others." Keynote presented at the Chair's Choice Session, Association of College and Research Libraries National Conference, Baltimore, MD, March 24, 2017b.

Najmabadi, Shannon. "What the 21st-Century Library Looks Like." *Chronicle of Higher Education*, July 2, 2017. http://www.chronicle.com/article/What-the-21st-Century-Library/240494.

National Coalition against Domestic Violence. "What Is Domestic Violence?" http://ncadv.org/blog/posts/quick-guide-what-is-domestic-violence.

Natvig, Jonathan. "UNM Records Highest Number of Hispanic and American Indian Faculty Members in the Country." *Daily Lobo*, September 15, 2016. http://www.dailylobo.com/article/2016/09/15-unm-faculty-diversity.

Neely, Teresa Y. "The Jackie Robinson of Library Science." In *In Our Own Voices: The Changing Face of Librarianship*, edited by Teresa Y. Neely and Khafre K. Abif, 164–89. Lanham, MD: Scarecrow Press, 1996.

————. "Diversity in Conflict." *Law Library Journal* 90, no. 4 (Fall 1998): 587–601.

————. "Diversity Initiatives and Programs: The National Approach." *Journal of Library Administration* 27, no. 1/2 (1999): 123–44.

Neely, Teresa Y., and Khafre K. Abif, eds. *In Our Own Voices: The Changing Face of Librarianship.* Lanham, MD: Scarecrow Press, 1996.

Neely, Teresa Y., and Lorna Peterson. "Achieving Racial and Ethnic Diversity among Academic and Research Librarians: The Recruitment, Retention, and Advancement of Librarians of Color: A White Paper." *College & Research Libraries News* 68, no. 9 (October 2007): 562–65.

Novack, Sophie. "Arkansas Just Funded Its Medicaid Expansion—but the Fight Isn't Over." *National Journal*, March 4, 2014. http://www.nationaljournal.com/health-care/arkansas-just-funded-its-medicaid-expansion-but-the-fight-isn-t-over-20140304.

Oates, Evangela Q., and Teresa Y. Neely. "Job Offers, Negotiations, and All the Wonderful Things You Can Ask For!" In *How to Stay Afloat in the Academic Library Job Pool*, edited by Teresa Y. Neely, 111–26. Chicago: American Library Association, 2011.

Obama, Barack. *The Audacity of Hope: Thoughts on Reclaiming the American Dream.* New York: Three Rivers Press, 2007.

Office of Institutional Analytics (OIA). "UNM Fact Book." 2016. University of New Mexico. https://oia.unm.edu/facts-and-figures/.

————. "The University of New Mexico Spring 2017 Official Enrollment Report." 2017. Accessed May 31, 2017. https://oia.unm.edu/facts-and-figures/oer-spr-2017.pdf.

Ondatropica. *3 Reyes de la Terapia*. Streaming Audio. Produced by Mariano Galeano and Quantic. London: Soundway Records, 2012.

Padilla, Amado M. "Ethnic Minority Scholars, Research, and Mentoring: Current and Future Issues." *Educational Researcher* 23, no. 4 (1994): 24–27. doi:10.2307/1176259.

Patrick, Megan E., Patrick Wightman, Robert F. Schoeni, and John E. Schulenberg. "Socioeconomic Status and Substance Use among Young Adults: A Comparison across Constructs and Drugs." *Journal of Studies on Alcohol and Drugs* 73, no. 5 (2012): 772–82. doi:10.15288/jsad.2012.73.772.

Pen or Pencil. "PEN or PENCIL." http://www.penorpencilmovement.org/about.php.

Pew Research Center. "Multiracial in America." 2015. http://www.pewsocialtrends.org/2015/06/11/chapter-1-race-and-multiracial-americans-in-the-u-s-census/.

———. "Pew Research Center's Hispanic Trends Project." Pew Research Centers Hispanic Trends Project RSS, February 23, 2017. http://www.pewhispanic.org/.

Pfeuffer, Charyn. "Best-Paying and Worst-Paying Master's Degrees." Monster.com, n.d. https://www.monster.com/career-advice/article/best-and-worst-paying-masters-degrees.

Phan, Aimée. "New Voices in Vietnamese American Literature: A Conversation with Viet Thanh Nguyen, Andrew Lam, and Aimee Phan." *World Literature Today*, September 2016. https://www.worldliteraturetoday.org/2016/september/new-voices-vietnamese-american-literature-conversation-viet-thanh-nguyen-andrew-lam.

Pierce, C. M., J. V. Carew, D. Pierce-Gonzalez, and D. Wills. "An Experiment in Racism: TV Commercials." *Education and Urban Society* 10, no. 1 (1977): 61–87.

Pillow, Lisa. "Academic Librarianship: A Personal Perspective." In *In Our Own Voices: The Changing Face of Librarianship*, edited by Teresa Y. Neely and Khafre K. Abif, 190–204. Lanham, MD: Scarecrow Press, 1996.

Policy and Standards Division. "Introduction to *Library of Congress Demographic Group Terms*." Library of Congress, April 27, 2017.

Prellwitz, Gwendolyn. "ALA awards 51 Spectrum Scholarships for 2013–2014." June 25 2013. http://www.ala.org/news/press-releases/2013/06/ala-awards-51-spectrum-scholarships-2013-2014.

Puente, Mark A. "ARL Diversity Scholars Selected for 2013–2015." August 21 2013. http://www.arl.org/news/arl-news/2877#.WXMyTfryu34.

———. "ARL/SAA Mosaic Program Fellows Selected for 2014-2016." September 17 2014. http://www.arl.org/news/arl-news/3374#.WXMzEfryu34.

Rankine, Claudia. *Citizen: An American Lyric*. Minneapolis, MN: Graywolf, 2014.

Roberts, Denton L. "Treatment of Cultural Scripts." *Transactional Analysis Journal* 5, no. 1 (1975): 29–35.

Robinson, Kathryn. "50 Obstacles to Leaving: 1–10." National Domestic Violence Hotline, June 2013. http://www.thehotline.org/2013/06/50-obstacles-to-leaving-1-10/.

RuPaul. *RuPaul's Drag Race*. February 2, 2009. Television Program. Los Angeles, CA: World of Wonder Productions.

Sagàs, Jimena, and R. Puig. "Libraries: The Forgotten Piece in the Diversity Puzzle." Presented at the Colorado State University Diversity Symposium, Denver, CO, September 2014.

Sampson, Zora J. "How Not to Be a Librarian." In *In Our Own Voices: The Changing Face of Librarianship*, edited by Teresa Y. Neely and Khafre K. Abif, 190–97. Lanham, MD: Scarecrow Press, 1996.

Sananes, Rebecca. "Effort by Dartmouth Students to Abolish Term 'Illegal Aliens' Gets Backlash in Congress." *VPR Vermont NPR News Source*, 2016. http://digital.vpr.net/post/effort-dartmouth-students-abolish-term-illegal-alien-gets-backlash-congress#stream/0.

Sanchez, Sonia. "Wounded in the House of a Friend." In *Wounded in the House of a Friend*, 3–15. Boston, MA: Beacon Press, 1997.

Schlesselman-Taranto, Gina. *Topographies of Whiteness: Mapping Whiteness in Library and Information Science*. Sacramento, CA: Library Juice Press, 2017.

Schonfeld, Roger, and Liam Sweeney. "Inclusion, Diversity, and Equity: Members of the Association of Research Libraries: Employee Demographics and Director Perspectives." Ithaka S+R , August 30, 2017. https://doi.org/10.18665/sr.304524.

Schott Foundation for Public Education. "Interactive Chart Dashboard for Maryland: 2013 Suspensions Rates Maryland vs. United States" and "2013 Grade 8 NAEP Reading: Maryland vs. United States." 2013. http://blackboysreport.org/states/?state=Maryland.

———. *Black Lives Matter: The Schott 50 State Report on Public Education and Black Males.* Revised Report. 2015. http://www.blackboysreport.org/2015-black-boys-report.pdf.

Schultz, Anne D., and Teresa Y. Neely. "UNM's Zimmerman Fire: A Case Study in Recovery and Return of Library Collections." In *Comprehensive Guide to Emergency Preparedness and Disaster Recovery,* edited by Frances C. Wilkinson, Linda K. Lewis, and Nancy K. Dennis, 160–82. Chicago: Association of Colleges and Research Libraries, 2010.

Sears, Suzanne. "Mentoring to Grow Library Leaders." *Journal of Library Administration* 54, no. 2 (2014): 127–34. doi:10.1080/01930826.2014.903368.

Shoptaugh, Terry. "The Next Generation." Review of *In Our Own Voices: The Changing Face of Librarianship,* edited by Teresa Y. Neely and Khafre K. Abif. *Library Journal* 121 (April 15, 1996): 7.

Solórzano, Daniel, Miguel Ceja, and Tara Yosso. "Critical Race Theory, Racial Microaggressions, and Campus Racial Climate: The Experiences of African American College Students." *Journal of Negro Education,* no. 1/2 (2000): 60.

Southern Poverty Law Center. "Post-Election Bias Incidents up to 1,372; New Collaboration with ProPublica." February 10, 2017. https://www.splcenter.org/hatewatch/2017/02/10/post-election-bias-incidents-1372-new-collaboration-propublica.

St. Lifer, Evan, and Corinne Nelson. "Unequal Opportunities: Race Does Matter." *Library Journal* 122, no. 18 (1997): 42–46.

Sue, Derald Wing, Christina M. Capodilupo, and Aisha M. B. Holder. "Racial Microaggressions in the Life Experience of Black Americans." *Professional Psychology: Research and Practice* 39, no. 3 (2008): 329–36.

Sweney, Mark. "Andy Murray Slaps Down John Inverdale's Claim He Was First with Two Tennis Golds." *Guardian,* August 15, 2016. https://www.theguardian.com/media/2016/aug/15/andy-murray-john-inverdale-olympic-tennis-bbc-williams.

Toomer, Jean. *Essentials.* Atlanta, GA: Hill Street Press, 1999.

Tooms, Autumn K., Catherine A. Lugg, and Ira Bogotch. "Rethinking the Politics of Fit and Educational Leadership." *Education Administration Quarterly* 46, no. 1 (2010): 96–131. doi: 10.1177/1094670509353044.

Townsend, Lori, Amy R. Hofer, Silvia Lin Hanick, and Korey Brunetti. "Identifying Threshold Concepts for Information Literacy: A Delphi Study." *Communications in Information Literacy* 10, no. 1 (2016): 23.

United States Department of Agriculture Economic Research Service. "Cash Receipts by Commodity State Ranking." 2017. https://data.ers.usda.gov/reports.aspx?ID=17844.

University Institutional Research and Reporting, Indiana University. "Proportion of Degree-Seeking Minorities among Known, Domestic Students (Diversity-Minority Proportions/Two or More Races)." 2016. https://uirr.iu.edu/doc/facts-figures/enrollment/diversity/ipeds-base-sets/bloomington-base.pdf.

University of New Mexico, Faculty Senate. "Faculty Handbook." https://handbook.unm.edu/.

University of New Mexico, Human Resources. "Career Ladder." 2015. https://hr.unm.edu/career-ladders.

U.S. Census Bureau. "Albuquerque, NM." 2010 U.S. Census, Quick Facts. Census.gov. Accessed May 28, 2017. https://www.census.gov/quickfacts/table/PST045216/3502000,56,48141,00.

———. "Bartholomew County, Indiana, 2016." Quick Facts. Census.gov. https://www.census.gov/quickfacts/fact/table/bartholomewcountyindiana/INC91021.

———. "Casa Grande, AZ." 2010 U.S. Census, Quick Facts. Census.gov. Accessed May 28, 2017. https://www.census.gov/quickfacts/table/PST045216/0410530,48141,4824000,00.

———. "Columbus City, Indiana." Census.gov. https://www.census.gov/quickfacts/table/PST045216/1814734,00.

———. "El Paso County, TX." 2015 U.S. Census, Quick Facts. Census.gov. Accessed May 28, 2017. https://www.census.gov/quickfacts/table/PST045216/48141,00.

————. "Laramie City, Wyoming." 2010 U.S. Census, Quick Facts. Census.gov. Accessed August 3, 2017. https://www.census.gov/quickfacts/fact/table/laramiecitywyoming/LND110210.

————. "Laramie City, Wyoming, July 1, 2016." Quick Facts. Census.gov. https://www.census.gov/quickfacts/fact/table/laramiecitywyoming,US/RHI725216#viewtop.

————. "West Virginia, 2017." QuickFacts. Census.gov. Accessed March 38, 2018. https://www.census.gov/quickfacts/WV.

————. "Wyoming." 2016 U.S. Census, Quick Facts. Census.gov. Accessed May 28, 2017. https://www.census.gov/quickfacts/table/PST045216/56,48141,00.

U.S. Census Bureau, American FactFinder. "Profile of General Population and Housing Characteristics: 2010." Census.gov. https://factfinder.census.gov/faces/tableservices/jsf/pages/productview.xhtml?pid=DEC_10_DP_DPDP1&src=pt.

————. "Median Household Income in 2015 Inflation-Adjusted Dollars—United States—States; and Puerto Rico Universe: Households." Census.gov. Accessed August 3, 2017. https://factfinder.census.gov/faces/tableservices/jsf/pages/productview.xhtml?src=bkmk.

————. "2016 American Community Survey 1-Year Estimates: Educational Attainment." Census.gov. https://factfinder.census.gov/faces/tableservices/jsf/pages/product-view.xhtml?pid=ACS_16_1YR_S1501&prodType=table.

U.S. Congress House of Representatives. *Legislative Branch Appropriations Bill 2017: Report 114-594.* 114th Congress, 2015–2016. https://www.congress.gov/congressional-report/114th-congress/house-report/594/1.

U.S. Department of Commerce. "1990 Census of Population: Social and Economic Characteristics—West Virginia." 1990. https://www2.census.gov/library/publications/decennial/1990/cp-2/cp-2-50.pdf.

U.S. Department of Education. "Definition of Hispanic-Serving Institutions." Developing Hispanic-Serving Institutions Program—Title V. 2016. https://www2.ed.gov/programs/idueshsi/definition.html.

————. "Tribal Colleges and Universities—White House Initiative on American Indian and Alaska Native Education." 2017. https://sites.ed.gov/whiaiane/tribes-tcus/tribal-colleges-and-universities/.

Voorhees, Rhondie L. "The Impact of a Peer Multicultural Dialogue Leader Training Program on Cognitive Development of College Students and Overall Learning: An Evaluative Case Study." PhD diss., University of Maryland, College Park, 2008.

Walch, Victoria Irons, Elizabeth Yakel, Jeannette Allis Bastian, Nancy Zimmelman, Brenda Banks, Susan E. Davis, and Anne P. Diffendal. "Special Section on A*CENSUS (Archival Census & Education Needs Survey in the United States)." *American Archivist* 69, no. 2 (2006): 291–527. http://www.jstor.org/stable/40294333.

Wang, Amy B. "'Final Act of Bravery': Men Who Were Fatally Stabbed Trying to Stop Anti-Muslim Rants Identified." *Washington Post*, May 27, 2017. https://www.washingtonpost.com/news/post-nation/wp/2017/05/27/man-fatally-stabs-2-on-portland-ore-train-after-they-interrupted-his-anti-muslim-rants-police-say/?utm_term=.f4e257f02c30.

We Here. "We Here." 2017. https://librarieswehere.wordpress.com/.

Wheeler, Ronald E. "About Microaggressions." *Law Library Journal* 108, no. 2 (2016): 321–29.

White, Sheree D. "In the Gate but Not the Door: Are We a Threat to the Status Quo?" In *In Our Own Voices: The Changing Face of Librarianship*, edited by Teresa Y. Neely and Khafre K. Abif, 330–44. Lanham, MD: Scarecrow Press, 1996.

The White House. "Executive Order: Protecting the Nation from Foreign Terrorist Entry into the United States." 2017. https://www.whitehouse.gov/the-press-office/2017/03/06/executive-order-protecting-nation-foreign-terrorist-entry-united-states.

Wikipedia. "1996 in the United States." Last modified May 10, 2017. https://en.wikipedia.org/wiki/1996_in_the_United_States.

————. "Barack Obama." https://en.wikipedia.org/wiki/Barack_Obama.

————. "Barbara Jordan." https://en.wikipedia.org/wiki/Barbara_Jordan.

————. "Blood Quantum Laws." https://en.wikipedia.org/wiki/Blood_quantum_laws.

———. "Carla Hayden." https://en.wikipedia.org/wiki/Carla_Hayden.

———. "E. J. Josey." https://en.wikipedia.org/wiki/E._J._Josey.

———. "I Was Here (song)." https://en.wikipedia.org/wiki/I_Was_Here. Video at https://youtu.be/i41qWJ6QjPI.

———. "List of Secretaries of State of the United States." https://en.wikipedia.org/wiki/List_of_Secretaries_of_State_of_the_United_States.

———. "Shirley Chisholm." https://en.wikipedia.org/wiki/Shirley_Chisholm.

———. "Sisyphus." https://en.wikipedia.org/wiki/Sisyphus.

———. "Unite the Right Rally." https://en.wikipedia.org/wiki/Unite_the_Right_rally.

———. "Weeble." https://en.wikipedia.org/wiki/Weeble.

Wilkinson, Lane. "The Problem with Threshold Concepts." *Sense & Reference*, June 19, 2014. https://senseandreference.wordpress.com/2014/06/19/the-problem-with-threshold-concepts/
.

Winston, Mark D. "The Minority Librarian: Why Your Role Is Different." In *In Our Own Voices: The Changing Face of Librarianship*, edited by Teresa Y. Neely and Khafre K. Abif, 360–71. Lanham, MD: Scarecrow Press, 1996.

———. "The Recruitment, Education and Careers of Academic Business Librarians." PhD diss., University of Pittsburgh, 1997.

WorkForce West Virginia LMI. "The 100 Largest Private Employers in West Virginia, 1999–2016." 2016. http://lmi.workforcewv.org/EandWAnnual/TopEmployers.html.

Yan, Holly, Devon M. Sayers, and Steve Almasy. "Charlottesville White Nationalist Rally: What We Know." CNN.com, August 14, 2017. http://www.cnn.com/2017/08/13/us/charlottesville-white-nationalist-rally-car-crash/index.html.

Yoder, Janice D. "Looking beyond Numbers: The Effects of Gender Status, Job Prestige, and Occupational Gender-Typing on Tokenism Processes." *Social Psychology Quarterly* 57, no. 2 (1994): 150–59.

Yoshino, Kenji. *Covering: The Hidden Assault on Our Civil Rights*. New York: Random House, 2006.

Yoshino, Kenji, and Christie Smith. *Uncovering Talent: A New Model of Inclusion*. Deloitte University Leadership Center, 2013. https://www2.deloitte.com/content/dam/Deloitte/us/Documents/about-deloitte/us-inclusion-uncovering-talent-paper.pdf.

Yosso, Tara J. "Whose Culture Has Capital? A Critical Race Theory Discussion of Community Cultural Wealth." *Race Ethnicity and Education* 8, no. 1 (2005): 69–91. doi:10.1080/1361332052000341006.

Zambrana, Ruth Enid, Rashawn Ray, Michelle M. Espino, Corinne Castro, Beth Douthirt Cohen, and Jennifer Eliason. "'Don't Leave Us Behind': The Importance of Mentoring for Underrepresented Minority Faculty." *American Educational Research Journal* 52, no. 1 (2015): 40–72. doi:10.3102/0002831214563063.

Zembylas, Michalinos. "'Pedagogy of Discomfort' and Its Ethical Implications: The Tensions of Ethical Violence in Social Justice Education." *Ethics and Education* 10, no. 2 (2015): 163–74.

Zong, Jie, and Jeanne Batalova. "Vietnamese Immigrants in the United States." *Migration Information Source: The Online Journal of the Migration Policy Institute*, (June 8, 2016). https://www.migrationpolicy.org/article/vietnamese-immigrants-united-states.

Zúñiga, Ximena. "Bridging Differences through Dialogue." *About Campus* 7, no. 6 (2003): 8–16.

Index

abuse, 78, 88, 154, 183, 184, 185, 186, 193, 195; emotional, 183, 185, 186; financial/economic, 183, 186; substance and alcohol, 127, 139, 146, 155

access to information, 96, 144

ACRL. *See* Association of College and Research Libraries (ACRL)

activism, xiv, xxvii, 202, 203, 219, 266

activist(s), xxix, 59, 113, 135, 140, 153, 158, 161, 202, 219

adoption, 219, 220, 225, 226

advice, xxiv, 16, 30, 31, 43, 45, 47, 48, 62, 63, 64, 66, 70, 71, 73, 102, 103, 106, 108, 121, 128, 156, 160, 161, 162, 165, 168, 169, 170, 171, 176, 212, 214, 243, 244, 253, 254, 257, 258, 260, 261

affirmative action, 4, 7, 10, 80, 154, 160, 242

aggressive, 10, 66, 67, 78, 139, 146, 245

Alire, Dr. Camila A., 65, 73

ALA. *See* American Library Association

alcohol, 24, 117; Indian, 193, 200, 247

alone, 61, 63, 64, 76, 84, 86, 92n1, 117, 195, 200, 207, 248, 261

ALS. *See* Amyotrophic Lateral Sclerosis

Amen, Samax, 163

the American dream, 183, 231, 232, 239

American Jewish Historical Society (AJHS), 220, 226, 227

American Library Association (ALA), xx; Spectrum Scholars, 167, 254

Amyotrophic Lateral Sclerosis, 45

Angelou, Maya, 200, 236

anger and angry, xxi, 63, 66, 78, 146, 160, 168, 193, 245; Black women, xiii, 66, 78, 80

archives, xxiv, 8, 44, 51, 52, 53, 54, 61

archivist(s), xxiii, 49, 53, 59, 61, 219, 220, 226, 227

Arizona, University of, 191; English 101 (Indian English), 191

ARL. *See* Association of Research Libraries

assimilate and assimilation, 84, 89, 90, 91, 202, 207. *See also* covering; passing

Association of College and Research Libraries (ACRL), 113; Information Literacy Immersion Program, 69, 71n2

Association of Research Libraries (ARL), 7, 8, 258

authentic and authenticity, 24, 25, 27, 88, 237, 241, 245; checklists, 27; inauthentic, 90

bias(es), 5, 6, 85, 96, 113, 154, 160, 179, 217, 222, 223, 226, 233, 234, 252; unbiased, 239

Blood Quantum (Indian blood laws), 3, 24, 28, 31n1, 247

About the Editors

Teresa Y. Neely (her, hers, she; black female, cisgender), MLS, PhD, is professor of librarianship and assessment librarian in the College of the University Libraries and Learning Sciences, University of New Mexico, Albuquerque.

Jorge R. López-McKnight (he, him, his; mixed-race, Mexican, Black, possibly White, male), MLS, was most recently the first-year experience librarian in the College of the University Libraries and Learning Sciences, University of New Mexico, Albuquerque.

About the Contributors

*José A. Aguiñaga (him, his, he; Mexican American, Chicano, male), MLS, MPA, EdD, is dean of library and instructional support at Rio Hondo College in Whittier, CA.

Camila A. Alire (her, hers, she; Latina, female), MLS, EdD, is dean emerita at the University of New Mexico and Colorado State University in Fort Collins, CO.

*Kimberly Black (African American, female), MLS, PhD, is chairperson of the Department of Information Studies at Chicago State University.

Jimena Bretón (her, hers, she; Mexican, female, cisgender), MLS, is college liaison librarian and assistant professor at Colorado State University (CSU) and a PhD student at CSU in education and human resource studies, with a specialization in organizational learning, performance, and change.

*Monica García Brooks (her, hers, she; Hispanic, Latinx, Tejana, female), MLS, EdD, is the associate vice president for libraries and online learning at Marshall University, Huntington, WV.

Jennifer Brown (her, hers, she; Black, African American, cisgender), MSI, is the emerging technologies coordinator at Columbia University Libraries, New York.

*Malore I. Brown (her, hers, she; Black, African American, female), MLIS, MA, PhD, is a regional public engagement specialist, formerly an information resource officer, for the U.S. Department of State.

*Lisa Burwell (her, hers, she; African American, female), MLS, retired, was the branch manager of the Chicago Public Library.

Joanna Chen Cham (her, hers, she; Taiwanese American, female), MLIS, is the lead for emerging literacies librarian at the University of California, Los Angeles.

Nicholae Cline (they, theirs, them; mixed-race, Brown, Coharie, Indigenous, nonbinary, gender fluid), MLS, is the scholarly services librarian and librarian for media studies and gender studies at Indiana University, Bloomington.

Monica Etsitty Dorame (her, hers, she; Diné, female, cisgender), MA, is a library operations manager in the College of the University Libraries and Learning Sciences, University of New Mexico, Albuquerque.

*Tanya Elder (her, hers, she; African American, female), MSLS, MA, is the senior archivist of the American Jewish Historical Society, New York.

*Dexter R. Evans (him, his, he; Black, male), MLS, is an academic regional sales manager for EBSCO Information Services based in Dallas, TX.

*Ngoc Mỹ Guidarelli (her, hers, she; Vietnamese American, female), MA, MA, MLS, is catalog librarian at the James Branch Cabell Library, Virginia Commonwealth University (VCU), Richmond.

Silvia Lin Hanick (her, hers, she; Taiwanese American, female, cisgender), MLIS, MA, is a first-year experience librarian and associate professor at LaGuardia Community College, a CUNY institution.

*Deborah R. Hollis (her, hers, she; Black, biracial, Afro-Asian, female), MLS, CA, is associate professor and head of special collections at the University of Colorado, Boulder.

*Mee-Len Hom (her, hers, she; Asian American female), MLS, MS, is assistant professor and reference/instruction librarian at Hunter College, a CUNY institution.

Irlanda Estelí Jacinto (Brown, Mexican American, female), MA, was most recently university archivist at the American Heritage Center, University of Wyoming, Laramie.

Sarah R. Kostelecky (her, hers, she; mixed-race, Native American, Zuni, female), MA, is assistant professor and education librarian for the College of the University Libraries and Learning Sciences, University of New Mexico, Albuquerque.

Sofia Leung (her, hers, she; Chinese American/Asian American, female, heterosexual), MS, MPA, is the teaching and learning program manager and liaison librarian to the Comparative Media Studies/Writing Department at the Massachusetts Institute of Technology.

Leni Matthews (Black/original, female), MS, is the user experience librarian at the University of Texas at Arlington.

Evangela Q. Oates, MLS, is the director of library services at SUNY Sullivan, a campus of the State University of New York system in Loch Sheldrake.

*Lisa Pillow (Black, female), MLS, is the collections strategy and development librarian at Carleton College in Northfield, MN.

*Zora J. Sampson (her, hers, she; American Indian, Choctaw/Chickasaw, female), MLIS, is the retired director of University of Wisconsin–Platteville's Elton S. Karmann Library.

Lori Townsend (her, hers, she; Shoshone-Paiute, female, cisgender), MLS, is associate professor and the learning services coordinator and engineering librarian in the College of the University Libraries and Learning Sciences, University of New Mexico, Albuquerque.

Madelyn Shackelford Washington (her, hers, she; Blackish, female, cisgender), MM, MLS, is the digital learning librarian at Berklee College of Music, Boston.

*Sheree D. White (African American, female), MA, MLS, is the library media specialist and Pen Or Pencil Program coordinator at Cheltenham Youth Facility, Cheltenham, MD.

*Mark D. Winston, MLS, PhD, is the executive director of the J. Lewis Crozer Library in Chester, PA.

Rachel E. Winston (her, hers, she; Black, female, cisgender), MSIS, CA, is the Black diaspora archivist at the LLILAS Benson Latin American Studies and Collections at the University of Texas at Austin.

Note: An asterisk (*) indicates OGs who are returning contributors from IOOV 1996. See the appendix.